Unequal Struggle

Interventions • Theory and Contemporary Politics

Stephen Eric Bronner, Series Editor

Unequal Struggle

Class, Gender, Race, and
Power in the U.S. Congress

John C. Berg

Westview Press

BOULDER • SAN FRANCISCO • OXFORD

Interventions: Theory and Contemporary Politics

Copyright © 1994 by Westview Press, Inc.

Published in 1994 in the United States of America by Westview Press, Inc., 5500 Central Avenue, Boulder, Colorado 80301-2877, and in the United Kingdom by Westview Press, 36 Lonsdale Road, Summertown, Oxford OX2 7EW

A CIP catalog record for this book is available from the Library of Congress.
ISBN 0-8133-1294-9 — ISBN 0-8133-1295-7 (pbk.)

Printed and bound in the United States of America

The paper used in this publication meets the requirements
of the American National Standard for Permanence of Paper
for Printed Library Materials Z39.48-1984.

10   9   8   7   6   5   4   3   2   1

To the memory of
Rick Dutka
and
Elizabeth Hallowell

Contents

Tables

Acknowledgments

A great many people have contributed to this book in some way; I can single out only a few for special thanks here. First of all, Suffolk University has been generous with two sabbatical leaves, extensive support by the research staff of the Mildred Sawyer Library, and funds to travel to conferences to test these ideas on my peers. A grant from the Dirksen Congressional Center funded several trips to Washington to interview members and staff of Congress.

My thinking has been clarified by exchanges over the years with a great many students and colleagues. Notable among the latter are Philip Brenner, who introduced me to the notion that Congress is inherently contradictory, and Melissa Collie, Eric Uslaner, and Alan Draper, each of whom discussed part of this book during a conference panel and in so doing made valuable suggestions.

Steve Bronner, Spencer Carr, and the staff of Westview Press have been stimulating, patient, and supportive throughout what turned out to be a very long writing process. My wife, Emily P. Berg, has not only clarified my thinking in many hours of discussion but has provided support in countless other ways.

Finally, I give thanks to two people who are no longer alive to receive them. One is Rick Dutka who, together with his wife, Irene Brodie, introduced me to many of the basic ideas about the capitalist state I have here applied to Congress. The other is Elizabeth Hallowell, an old family friend, whose hope to see my work in print drove me to write faster, but unfortunately not fast enough. This book is dedicated to their memory.

John C. Berg

Introduction:
Congress in the Public Mind

Americans are schizophrenic about Congress. It can provoke our contempt and dazzle us with its glamour. We see it as a pack of vultures and as an essential guardian of our liberty. Both perceptions are correct. Only by accepting this duality can we understand Congress's place in American politics.

Congress embodies our hopes. These can be broad and national, or particular and local. When national crises destroy public trust in the office and person of the president, as Watergate and the Vietnam War did in the 1970s, people turn to Congress for rescue. The reason, in part, is that there seems nowhere else to turn; but Congress does come through often enough to keep this sort of hope alive. When Congress fails to act, as it failed with Vietnam, this failure deepens the national despair and alienation.

Congress provides hope on more local matters as well. When a community faces the collapse of an important industry, the closing of a large federal installation, the threat of a disruptive new development, or even a natural disaster, it expects its local member of Congress to step in and lead the fight for community interests. Here, too, such efforts are successful often enough to keep people hoping.

If Congress bears our hopes, it also stifles them. During the civil rights movement the filibuster, the House Rules Committee, and the seniority system came to symbolize reaction and racist violence. Today the same emotions—the sense that Congress is out of control, that it is an enemy of ordinary people—fuel the movement for term limits and the craze to amend the Constitution so as to require a balanced budget. The politics are different, but today's conservatives share with yesterday's radicals the contempt and hatred for Congress as an arrogant, elitist institution.

As a professional student of Congress I have had both sides of this paradox brought home to me personally. One morning while I was sitting in a coffee shop, manuscript and pen before me, a woman at the next table leaned over and asked if I was writing poetry. When I told her that it was a book on Congress, she exclaimed, "Oh, how boring!" and left the restaurant. Another time I titled a paper "What Did Congress Learn from Vietnam?" Almost everyone who heard this title said, "Not much, I bet," usually with a cynical chuckle. Virtually any reference to the topic of "how Congress works" is sure to produce "You mean it does?" as a response.

But I have encountered fascination with Congress, too. Everyone wants inside information about what is going on—and is all too willing to treat even casual observations with great significance. Memories of a trip to Washington to observe Congress firsthand can keep students excited for up to a year. Even those who hate to enter the college library will put considerable time and energy into gathering biographical information about a representative or senator and, in doing so, will often accept the most shamelessly puffed-up press releases as gospel truth.

These are anecdotes and impressions, but there is hard evidence to support them. Opinion surveys have shown low respect for both Congress as an institution and its members as individuals over the last two decades at least. The Gallup Poll organization regularly asks people whether they approve or disapprove of the job that Congress has been doing; disapproval ratings are almost always in the majority. This disrespect, fueled by repeated corruption scandals, has been extended to elected officials of all sorts, but it applies most strongly to legislators. Even the Watergate crisis, hailed by many as proof of the strength of the checks and balances system, through which Congress saved the country from a dishonest president, increased public respect for Congress only for a few months before it fell once again to the same low level (Gallup 1978, 256-57, 346-57, 442, 531, 648, 1043, 1115-16; 1983, 226).

There is an even stronger contrast between opinions about Congress in general and opinions about the survey respondents' own representatives. The institution is seen as corrupt and remote. Its members are perceived as out of touch with most people's way of life and, hence, with their problems; instead, according to the respondents they seek to line their own pockets by catering to the special interests of the wealthy. The increasing importance of business-funded political action committees (PACs) in paying for campaigns is rightly seen as evidence that the corporations, not the voters, are calling the shots. Running against Congress is a time-tested campaign technique. It has worked so well for presidential candidates that many members of Congress now run against their own institution (Fenno 1978, 163-68; Parker and Davidson 1979).

Despite all this, individual representatives become ever more popular. The incumbent advantage—the additional proportion of the vote an incumbent receives simply because of his or her status as such—represents one of the major political changes of the last three decades; the safe seat, once the exclusive property of the Solid South and the Northern urban machine, now occurs everywhere. Often no one even bothers to run against a House incumbent. Senate elections have remained more competitive, but there are many safe seats there, too. Among the several reasons for this phenomenon is the popularity of individual members of Congress.

Incumbent popularity is not surprising. Members of Congress are, almost by definition, the most capable politicians of all those who want the job. They have large staffs, media resources, and free postage; the bureaucracy is usually glad to cooperate in fostering the illusion that any benefits received from the government by anyone in a representative's district are due to that representative's personal efforts (Fiorina 1977). The members use these resources competently to increase their political support. The only hard part of their task is to keep themselves from being tainted by the contempt in which the public holds the institution; almost unanimously, members achieve this end by portraying themselves as stalwart but outnumbered battlers against bureaucracy, arrogance, waste, and the federal deficit. Once we acknowledge the low level of political knowledge among the American public, and the media practices that perpetuate this deficiency, incumbent popularity follows as a matter of course.

We might learn something by asking why public awareness and media coverage of politics are what they are, and how they affect the nature of our political system; indeed, these questions will be explored more fully later on. But one point should be noted in the meantime. Early surveys of political participation in America discovered an unexpected category, more recently named "parochial participants" (Verba and Nie 1972, 67-69, 80). Although this group is not large—consisting of about 4 percent of eligible voters in the early 1970s—it is important as an extreme form of a broader phenomenon. Parochial participants do not take part in either political campaigns or community affairs, and they are not concerned about issues; but they still write or telephone their congressional representatives more often than most people do. The purpose of these communications is to get personal help, ranging from job or college recommendations to subsidized housing. The origins of this practice, and the question of whether it is effective, need not concern us at this point. But it reveals something about how people think of Congress. As demonstrated by the growing importance of constituent casework in every congressional office, personal help is becoming a larger part of what most people want from their representatives. Incumbents may complain about this state of affairs, but they also encourage it; they generally make a point of responding to such requests as quickly and positively as they can. Many now send mobile offices throughout their districts in active solicitation of requests for help. They do so because such efforts help them get reelected; but the public is also encouraged in its belief that doing favors of this sort is the proper role for an elected representative. More and more people now judge their senators and representatives not by their voting records or success in passing bills but by how well they answer their mail.

The combination of contempt for the institution and enthusiasm for its members gives us the worst of both worlds. The contempt produces a sense of powerlessness and apathy; with Congress full of crooks and bums, how can anyone expect it to respond to the people's problems or fight in behalf of the people's interest? To make such demands on such a body would be a waste of time and energy, so why bother? But the faith in one's own representative, the belief that at least one has a sympathetic ear, disarms and demobilizes the voter (or nonvoter) who might otherwise be angry enough to try to change things.

Organized groups, too, are schizophrenic about Congress. Social movements calling for environmental protection, nuclear disarmament, or an end to overseas military intervention hold Congress in as much scorn as everyone else does. Yet these groups need congressional action to gain their ends. So all too often they find themselves hat-in-hand, offering tacit support to members who oppose most of their goals in return for favorable votes on one or two modest measures. Even larger, more powerful movements, such as organized labor, find that there are few members who represent their full views; they, too, can get no more than support on particular votes, although in their case the number of such votes may be greater.

Representation of the African American movement by the Congressional Black Caucus, and of the women's movement by the few women in Congress, displays the other side of the coin. These movements do get multidimensional representation, but on most issues they have little hope of winning. One of the symbolic rituals of American politics (discussed more fully in Chapter 6) comes each spring when the Congressional Black Caucus offers its alternate budget resolution to the House of Representatives and garners fewer than 100 votes.

Whichever side of the coin we look at, what we see is incomplete representation. The result is organizational schizophrenia. To accomplish even the little that they do, organizations must mount all-out pressure campaigns, developing among their supporters a faith in congressional representation. At the same time, they have to realize that any small victory is probably more than they could realistically have expected—and so they are inhibited from demanding more.

These patterns are due to the weakness of the movements in question—and vice versa. Yet attitudes toward Congress are an equally important factor. A movement that believed Congress to be totally hopeless would not waste its time trying to win votes; rather, it would begin the hard task of building a popular movement to fight for power outside the conventional channels. Congress, however, is just slightly too responsive for most people to choose such a course. A movement that expected Congress to represent the aspirations of the American people would not settle for a few crumbs, instead it would fight for the transformation of the institution into what it ought to be. But the same schizophrenia that produces popular apathy leads too many organizations to confine themselves to lobbying semi-effectively on semi-important issues, with no strategy for going further.

The far left chooses the pole of total scorn for Congress. Critics of this persuasion point to popular apathy as evidence of the failure of democracy in America. There is some truth to this; but, unfortunately, apathy does not provide a force for change. Most political scientists have chosen the opposite pole. Professional students of Congress generally become enthusiastic about the richness and complexity of congressional politics, largely in a justificatory way; they tend to lose sight of Congress's shortcomings. We shall look more closely at political science's view in Chapter 1.

These contrasting attitudes toward Congress grow out of attitudes about the relative importance of politics and economics. On the one hand, leftists who dismiss Congress as irrelevant generally believe that the economic structure determines everything, and therefore that any efforts to win social reform by political means are doomed to failure. On the other hand, political scientists who study Congress are likely to view politics as an independent domain, and to lump economics with weather and geography as objective factors that define the outer limits of possibility but can be ignored in the normal course of everyday affairs.

The thesis of this book is that the truth lies somewhere in between. Congressional decisions do make a difference, and every significant social interest is represented in Congress and able to take part in the struggle over these decisions. But not all groups are represented in the same way, and the differences are not just a matter of numerical strength. Some interests are entrenched in the centers of congressional power, whereas others must approach Congress from the outside. The latter may come forward as militant demonstrators or as humble petitioners, but this important strategic choice makes little difference in their powerlessness. In Chapter 1, after a critical review of the state of contemporary congressional studies, I shall develop a framework for looking at these different kinds of representation. The concepts of economic and political *structure*, *class, hegemony,* and representation of the *dominated,* which are particularly important to this analysis, will be developed there.

These differences in group position and strength are more than just the result of past political success or failure. The structure of congressional power reflects the structure of society, which is largely economic in nature. The dominant economic powers of the United States, the leaders of the giant corporations, do devote time and effort to political matters; but on a day-to-day basis they hardly need to do so, for their concerns are so central to America's well-being that they must be catered to by anyone holding the levers of political power. In this sense, these interests can be called *hegemonic;* we shall look at how they are represented in Chapter 2.

Other corporate interests are less central to the economy but are still part of the dominant class coalition, the *power bloc.* These interests, too, work to support the status quo; but they also pursue very actively their particular interests as industries or businesses, by seeking favorable regulatory decisions, government subsidies, and individual contracts. Since they may be opposed by other, equally powerful, corporate interests victory is far from certain. A great deal of the day-to-day action in Congress deals with matters of this sort; such action often takes place in committees and subcommittees, hidden from public view. We shall examine the representation of smaller businesses in Chapter 3.

The hegemonic giant corporations and their allies in the power bloc are the *dominant* interests in Congress (and in American society); but the less powerful, the *dominated,* are represented as well. The category of the dominated includes the working class, but also applies to those groups oppressed because of *race* or *gender*—categories which may or may not be rooted in economics,[1] but that are certainly not included in the traditional concept of class. In Chapters 4, 5, and 6 we shall look at how some of the dominated—the working class, women, and African Americans—have been represented in Congress throughout American history. Much of this history has been the story of defeat; but enough victories have occurred to explain the American public's continuing fascination with Congress.

The structure of Congress reflects the economic structure of the United States, but it does not reflect it perfectly. At times of mass insurgency, Congress can respond to pressure from the dominated. For the most part, it acts as a swamp does in relation to a swollen river, soaking up the force of the flood by a combination of yielding and resistance. But members of Congress who side with the insurgents can help direct the flood to wash away the dikes of privilege and power, helping the movement grow rather than dissipating its strength. To do so, they must recognize the bias of the congressional power structure and ally themselves firmly with those excluded from it. In the last chapter we shall examine the careers of six members of Congress who attempted to follow such a strategy, and then consider the implications of their successes and failures.

1

Congress in Political Science

Political science literature on Congress is rich and detailed but ultimately unsatisfying because most of it stops short of placing Congress within a general theory of American politics. This literature can tell us a lot about such topics as the relative importance of different committees, the strengths and weaknesses of the congressional party organizations, and the magnitude of the incumbent advantage in seeking reelection; but (with a few exceptions) it has little to say about why committees or parties rise or fall in power, how the organization of Congress is related to the nature of American society, or how congressional action can advance or retard social change. My goal in this book is to present a Marxist theory of Congress that can answer such questions. But before I turn to this theory, it will be helpful to look at the state of congressional studies in more detail.

Up to about 1960, political scientists who studied Congress, like the general public, mainly asked evaluative questions. Should Congress be strong or weak? Was it doing a good job of representing the public? Was it obstructing the president needlessly? How could it be improved?

An early example of this approach was Woodrow Wilson's book, *Congressional Government* ([1885] 1956). In keeping with the fashion of his time, Wilson made little distinction between fact and value. He condemned Congress for its obstructive, parochial, and often corrupt role, but saw no need for a thorough explanation of how Congress had come to be like that. Congress's faults, he believed, were caused by bad rules and weak party discipline; therefore, the rules needed to be changed, and the parties strengthened. Wilson approached reform as if the nation had the capacity for conscious choice about what kind of Congress it wanted. *Congressional Government* was only partly a scientific study; more important, it was a manifesto for reform.

Similar manifestos, in the Wilsonian tradition, were produced in the 1960s and early 1970s by James MacGregor Burns (1963, 1972), whose approach was supported by many other studies, including two important books by members of Congress (Bolling 1965; Clark 1964). However, Burns did not merely criticize Congress for its faults; he also looked for the causes of those faults. He argued that Congress was inherently conservative because its members were elected by local rather than national majorities. This initial bias was then reinforced by various rules and practices of Congress, such as the seniority system, and by the lack of party competition in what at that time were the Democratic South and the Republican Midwest. The latter phenomenon made reelection nearly automatic, so that many incumbents effectively represented the political coalitions which had first brought them to office ten, twenty, or thirty years earlier, rather than the political forces of the time. Instead of a two-party system, the United States had a four-party system, with both the Democrats and Republicans divided into presidential and congressional branches, and both congressional parties far more conservative than either presidential one.

Burns's argument appealed to liberals in the 1960s. A few years earlier President Eisenhower, a Republican, had continued many of the Democratic New Deal programs, whereas conservative congressional Democrats had blocked passage of proposed civil rights laws and the implementation of such Keynesian economic policies as President Kennedy's tax cut. Burns's theory helped make sense out of all these contradictions and showed how they might be resolved. But then came the Vietnam War, the shift to the right of President Johnson, and his replacement by Nixon. Now Congress was called upon to restrict the imperial presidency, to block military interventions abroad and the gutting of popular social and environmental programs at home (Schlesinger 1974). It could now be argued plausibly—by Gary Orfield (1975), for example—that Congress was inherently more progressive than the president.

Burns had accurately portrayed the political realities of the time, and his analysis produced a clear agenda for reform: reapportionment of Congress, and of the state legislatures that drew the congressional district lines; easier cloture of filibusters; election of committee chairs by party caucuses not bound by seniority; more easily obtained recorded votes in the House of Representatives; and the subjugation of the House Rules Committee to the will of the majority and its leadership. This agenda occupied progressives in Congress for two decades—and its eventual achievement did transform national politics. Burns's work certainly helped to inspire this transformation, but it could not explain it. On the larger question of Congress's place in national politics, it seems clear enough that Burns and Orfield were simply discussing Congress at different times. The point is, though, that each spoke in more universal terms, and neither offered a theory that could explain how or when the executive and legislative branches switch from one role to another. We need such a theory.

More recent studies have sought to explain Congress, rather than just to praise or blame it. Scholars who make this attempt can roughly be sorted into two groups. *Pluralists* argue that Congress—along with other governmental institutions—is permeated and fragmented by group influence. Sometimes one group wins, and sometimes another. People's preference for a strong Congress or a dominant president then boils down to a judgment as to which branch is likely to provide a more favorable venue for whatever group they identify themselves with (Truman 1971, introduction; Griffith 1939, 182; Griffith and Valeo 1975, 55-56). Although not all pluralists would go this far, the purists among them see little point in studying Congress for itself. True, Congress is one channel for group influence; but so are executive bureaus, the media, political parties, and even the courts. Interaction among the groups determines policy; so Congress, its committees, and its members are important only when they embody or reflect group action. As Arthur Bentley put it, "Always and everywhere our study must be a study of the interests that work through government; otherwise we have not got down to facts" (1967, 271).

Institutionalists, by contrast, see Congress (along with other important political institutions) as an independent force in American politics. There are many kinds of institutionalism (as is the case with pluralism), but all share the premise that the beliefs, desires, and goals of the members of Congress are independent factors, not simply the result of outside forces.

Unfortunately, neither the pluralist nor the institutionalist approach gives us a satisfactory understanding of Congress. Recognizing this fact, members of both schools have developed more sophisticated versions of their theories. In each case the theory has become more complicated but not, I shall argue, more adequate as an explanation of congressional action. For the sake of clarity let us look at each theory in its simple form and then consider the later modifications.

The Pluralist Approach

There are many cases in which congressional action can be explained by group pressure; but there are also exceptions. Three recent examples are instructive: congressional control of foreign military intervention, the 1981 budget resolution, and reform of the seniority system.

From the end of the Korean War through 1965, Congress concurred, with scarcely a whimper of dissent, as a succession of presidents ordered the invasions Indochina, Lebanon, and the Dominican Republic and arranged the overthrow of democratic governments in Iran and Guatemala through covert operations. Popular opposition to U.S. intervention in Vietnam grew after the escalation of 1965, as did the expression of antiwar sentiment by members of Congress; but somehow this sentiment, even when expressed by a majority, never led Congress to cut off funds for the war, end the draft, or otherwise act on its declared beliefs. It was not until 1973, after the U.S. combat involvement had already ended, that congressional doves were able to pass measures effectively forbidding further troop involvement. All the measures passed had been nonbinding, and the executive branch had ignored them (Berg 1975).

However, in 1975, when the Central Intelligence Agency formed a bizarre alliance with Maoist China and racist South Africa to try to prevent the victory of the revolutionary Popular Movement for the Liberation of Angola (MPLA), Congress acted quickly to ban further U.S. involvement of any kind in Angola. Although the Ford administration did stretch out its intervention for some weeks in defiance of Congress (Stockwell 1978, 234-35), it was ultimately forced to comply, and the Angolan revolution triumphed. Whereas effective congressional action against the Vietnam War had trailed years behind public opinion, in this later instance Congress acted before most of the public even knew that Angola existed. Moreover, it did so without any significant support by organized interest groups.

By 1983 the circumstances had reverted to those of the early 1970s. President Reagan's congressional opponents took the lead in giving him almost a blank check to use troops in Lebanon, and opposition to the intervention in Central America was expressed not by a cutting off of funds for the intervention but, rather, by the attachment of feeble restrictions to their appropriation (Berg 1985; Central America Crisis Monitoring Team 1985).

A Congress whose actions are determined by public and interest group pressure should have acted strongly against the intervention in Vietnam, ignored the intervention in Angola, and acted strongly again in regard to Lebanon and Central America. Instead, it did just the opposite in all three cases.

Congressional action on Ronald Reagan's first budget provides another example. When Reagan was elected president in 1980, he carried twelve new Republican senators—giving the Republicans a majority—and thirty-three new Republican representatives into office along with him. This change was significant, but far from total; as the Democrats retained a House majority and enough Senate seats to sustain a filibuster, they had the potential power to block action. Yet drastic changes in legislation ensued. According to the conventional pluralist wisdom prior to 1981, one might have expected Congress to have hacked Reagan's program to pieces, with a multitude of interest groups each fighting successfully to get just a little bit more for its favorite program.

Here, as elsewhere in this chapter, I am speaking of pluralism in its pure form. Real pluralists tend to be less pure and more practical; few, if any, have gone so far as to rule out the possibility of drastic change completely. Still, the tenor of much pluralist analysis implies that such change would be very difficult. More important, although the possibility of greater change has usually been acknowledged, such a possibility is seldom accounted for theoretically.

For example, in his textbook on Congress, Randall Ripley concludes:

> Habits and patterns of personal interaction and thought about public policy develop and become firmly entrenched. Participants hesitate to stray very far from policies that are known to command widespread support, regardless of their true value, their shortcomings, or the nature of their impact on American society. Disruptive forces such as visionary or aggressive presidents or major party upheavals can and do alter this situation, but they are the exception and not the rule. Not all policy change is minute or slow-moving, but most of it is. (1975, 267)

Similarly, in the second (1976) edition of *Congress, the Bureaucracy, and Public Policy*, Ripley and Grace Franklin assert:

> In general, American public policy can be characterized as slow to change, as more responsive to special interests than to general interests, as more responsive to the privileged in society than to the underprivileged, and as tending to be defined as distributive and treated as such when possible. The reasons for this situation are rooted in the basic dominance by subgovernments of much of American policy-making, the great premium placed on cooperation between Congress and the bureaucracy, the lack of meaningful congressional oversight on a continuing basis for many policies, and the greater strength of forces pushing for no change or minimal change in policy as opposed to the forces pushing for greater change in policy.
>
> Yet, . . . our examination of the congressional-bureaucratic relationship has also found some exceptions to these generalizations. (1976, 165)

They later add, "powerful forces [are] working against change . . . yet some sizeable changes do occur, which suggests that there also may be individuals and forces working for it." These, Ripley and Franklin say, may include "the President and some of his appointees." However, no explanation is offered as to when "exceptions" might be expected to occur (1976, 178-79). In their fourth (1987) edition they add two pages on the "Reagan revolution" to this section, acknowledging the magnitude of his impact but still offering little explanation beyond Reagan's personal forcefulness and popularity (1987, 227-29).

To repeat, my point is not that pluralists predicted the failure of Reagan's agenda—whatever our theoretical leanings, we political scientists are too smart to do that! Rather, I am arguing that pluralist theory cannot account for Reagan's success but must resort to calling it an "exception." The theory in its nonexceptional form would suggest that Congress might have disaggregated Reagan's program into a multitude of bills to be parceled out to interest-dominated subgovernments. This did not happen. Instead, the House voted to tie its own hands, adopting a rule to limit itself to a single all-or-nothing vote on Reagan's budget cuts; then it passed the cuts. In retrospect, many pluralist explanations for these events can be and have been proposed (e.g., Penner and Abramson 1988, 41-58; Salamon and Abramson 1984, 31-68). However, there is nothing in the theory to have suggested these explanations as predictions before the fact.

The seniority reforms of 1970-1975 provide a final example. The House of Representatives was dominated for decades by a set of committee chairs who wielded nearly absolute power over matters within their committees' jealously guarded jurisdictions. Since chairs were chosen strictly by seniority, neither party leaders, presidents, nor the public were able to control them. Then, in a few short years, the balance of power was reversed. Chairs had to be nominated by party leaders and approved by the party caucus, and a number of once-powerful chairs were ousted. Seniority remained a consideration in the choice of chairs, but it was now less important than party discipline (Berg 1977, 1978a).

As Lawrence Dodd has observed, "Events of the 1970s caught students of Congress by surprise" (1986, 3). Reform of the seniority system had seemed unlikely, since both organized interest groups and the members of Congress themselves seemed to benefit from it. From the pluralist point of view, the system encouraged members to retain their early committee assignments, and let members and interest groups know, years in advance, who future committee leaders would be; and it removed effective power over many policy decisions from the floor of the House to the friendlier precincts of committees whose members largely shared the interest groups' point of view.[1] Aware of these features of the system, most congressional specialists in the early 1970s expected seniority to last forever; virtually no one predicted the drastic overturn of the system that actually took place (Hinckley 1971, 108-13). These three examples suggest that pluralist theory cannot explain congressional politics systematically.

There are problems with pluralism as a normative theory, as well. Pluralism's normative side originates in part from a desire to be realistic without being cynical. Faced on the one hand with the reality of interest group power, and on the other with studies showing that most voters have possessed remarkably little information about government, issues, or candidates (Stokes and Miller 1966, 194-211), pluralists seek to show that democratic government is still possible, through the medium of competing groups. If democracy means that all groups are able to influence policy, they argue, then the United States is more democratic than it seems (Bentley 1967, 447-59).

This argument has been attacked by those who believe that the United States is not very democratic at all because of the unequal propensity and capacity of groups to organize (Schattschneider 1960; Olson 1971). However, with some exceptions, both sides of this debate have agreed with the picture of government as a reflection of group interaction; the debate has been about how well the groups represent the people. This normative criticism of pluralism is cogent and telling; but a more valid empirical theory is needed if we want to understand American politics.

The Institutionalist Approach

Institutionalists avoid some of the problems of pluralism but replace them with problems of their own. The core tenet of contemporary institutionalism is that the members of Congress have been able to secure a high degree of autonomy, both for Congress as an institution and for themselves as individual members. Over the years, Congress has adopted rules and customs that serve to maximize the interests of its members by protecting them from the pressures of voters, interest groups, political parties, and the other branches of government. These rules and customs then shape the behavior of members of Congress in the future. There is considerable debate among institutionalists about how this system works, and especially about what the interests of the members really are. Some argue that Congress is designed almost entirely to help its members win easy reelection by garnering media attention, financial support, and opportunities to claim credit for helping constituents,[2] whereas others put more emphasis on members' desire to make what they consider good public policy (Krehbiel 1991). Richard Fenno (1973) has shown that these and other member goals can all be found within Congress, and that these differences in member goals help explain the differences among committees. But for our purposes, the important point is that Congress as an institution is autonomous.

The claim that Congress possesses institutional autonomy means that it is not only difficult but wrong to identify Congress with any particular group of social forces, since no outside force can have the power to influence congressional action to any great extent. Instead, scholars should look at the socialization mechanisms by which incumbent members try to pass on their culture to those who succeed them, and at the capacity of Congress to be effective in getting its policy decisions implemented. If Congress is autonomous, its actions are determined by the values of its members, with the only limitation on Congressional power coming from possible difficulty in imposing its decisions on others.

If we accept the principle that the members' own views are an independent cause of congressional action, we can avoid many of the problems of pluralism. For example, we can imagine plausible institution-alist explanations of our three cases (whether or not institutionalists have actually offered these particular explanations). We might argue that Congress banned intervention in Angola because many members had learned from the example of Vietnam that such intervention could be dangerous. Indeed, several senators and representatives made just this point during floor debate on the ban (Berg 1978b, 1979, 1985). Similarly, we could maintain that passage of the Reagan budget in 1981 was due to the belief of a sufficient number of members that a basic change in national priorities was desirable.

There is a particularly interesting institutionalist explanation for the House rules reforms of the 1970s. These changes can be seen as part of the development of professionalism and institutional autonomy in the House; from this perspective they are an extension of the principles behind seniority, rather than a reversal of them.

According to this argument, selection of House committee chairs by seniority was adopted in 1910 as a way to lessen the arbitrary power of the Speaker: if the Speaker could not control the choice of chairs, he would be less able to browbeat members into voting the way he wanted. This arrangement worked very well. In fact, by the early 1960s it seemed to Northern Democrats, at least, that it had worked too well; they had won a majority but found the passage of their program, particularly of civil rights bills, blocked by a handful of Southern Democrats who controlled crucial committees. Yet most of the time, for most representatives, seniority made life in the House easier. It continued to be useful as a way of avoiding bitter intraparty disputes. Moreover, seniority served the positive function of encouraging specialization, since a member had to remain on the same committee in order to move up the ladder toward a chairmanship. In those few cases where seniority produced an incompe-tent chair, that individual could be persuaded to resign, as was Theodore F. Green from the Senate Foreign Relations Committee in 1959 (*New York Times*, January 31, 1959, 1), or could be reduced to figurehead status by a change in the committee rules, as happened to Graham Barden (D-N.C.) of the House Education and Labor Committee in 1959, or to Thomas Murray (D-Tenn.) of the House Post Office Committee in 1965. In each case the immediate problem was solved without losing the advantages of the system (Goodwin 1970, 124; Fenno 1973, 68, 128, 135-37; Hinckley 1971, 111-13).

But there was a hitch. Members got better and better at satisfying the voters through constituent service, claiming credit for federal benefits, and generally entrenching themselves in their seats. As a result congressional careers grew longer, party competition decreased, and the number of members with ten or more years of tenure became considerably greater than the number of available positions as committee chair. Eventually the rules were changed; committee chairs, formerly chosen by seniority, would now be elected by the majority party caucus, whereas subcommittee chairs, formerly appointed by committee chairs, would now be chosen by seniority. As a result, there were now about one hundred powerful chairmanships for majority party members and a like number of ranking positions for the minority party, where before there had been about twenty of each. According to this application of the institutionalist approach, the reforms were adopted because they suited the personal interests of the members of the House, not because of interest group pressure, and not because they were inherently more democratic (Ornstein 1975, 89; Dodd 1977).[3]

This account is plausible and satisfying as far as it goes; but it raises as many questions as it answers. What factors lay behind the lengthening of congressional careers? Was this trend a mere coincidence? Was it the result of a maturation process that any legislature could be expected to undergo? Or was it caused by more basic changes in the structure of American society? The institutionalist approach gives us the conceptual tools to determine how much autonomy a legislature has obtained, but it does not explain why this degree of autonomy has come about.

The same thing may be said more generally about explanations of congressional action that are grounded in the beliefs and personal goals of the members. Arthur Maass (1983) has provided a clear summary of this approach, which he calls the "discussion model." In this model Congress is seen as discussing policies and programs in search of the national or public interest. Disagreement on bills comes from differing conceptions of the common good, not solely from differing private and group interests. Maass sees pursuit of the common good as the foundation of the congressional norm of responsibility; that is, the responsible legislator acts to accommodate his or her colleagues, but the result of this mutual accommodation is that all act together to serve the nation. Maass offers many examples of cases in which discussion of the common good, rather than the interplay of interests, has determined the outcome of congressional consideration. However, his work leaves two questions unanswered. First, what is meant by "common good"? Pluralists would deny its usefulness as a concept, whereas Marxists would argue that it veils the interest of the dominant class. Second, although Maass's examples are convincing, there are many counterexamples, too. Among the latter is the

1986 tax reform act, which began as a proposal to make the tax system simple but ended up making it more complicated. This outcome was due not to any conviction that a more complicated system represented the common good but, rather, to the intensive lobbying efforts of a multitude of particularistic interest groups. The "discussion model" applies, then, only some of the time; on other occasions, pluralism offers a better fit with the facts. But can we know in advance which model is appropriate? A more general theory is needed if we wish to answer this question.

Michael Mezey (1989) has recently analyzed the relations between Congress and the president using a framework similar to Maass's, but he has come to more negative conclusions. Like Maass, Mezey starts with the assumption that political institutions are designed, in this case by those who wrote the U.S. Constitution, to serve a purpose. This purpose is to make good public policy. Mezey realizes the problematic nature of the concept of *good* in this context, and he attempts to free the term of political and ideological bias by specifying both democratic criteria (Is policy reponsive to public wishes?) and managerial criteria (Is policy "informed, timely, coherent, effective, and responsible"?) for *goodness* (1989, 5-9 and *passim*). He concludes that the founders' fear of government and the subsequent "transformation" of the presidency and "evolution" of Congress have produced a situation in which policy stalemate can be avoided only by sacrificing either democratic or managerial criteria for good public policy, and frequently both (1989, 189-92).

Mezey believes that the poor design of America's government has allowed pluralist pressures to block the making of good public policy. In his view, "The single factor that most diminishes Congress's capacity to [make policy that meets democratic criteria] . . . is the intimate relationship between its members and moneyed interests" (1989, 202), and he proposes institutional reforms to counter these pressures. However, his most basic remedies rely on pure acts of political will on the part of both political leaders and the public:

> Many of the proposals that I have suggested require neither statutory nor constitutional changes. Reducing the degree to which power in the Congress is fragmented, as well as strengthening the structure and procedures for overseeing the executive, can be accomplished simply by changing the internal rules of the Congress. The major changes in the relative powers of the Congress and the presidency that I have advocated can take place if political leaders and the public are willing to alter their expectations about how these institutions should operate. No constitutional or statutory changes are required for the Congress to defer to the policy leadership of the president or for the Congress to alter the way in which its members view their responsibilities.

Mezey adds that change of expectations "certainly will not be easy" (1989, 218). This point is true enough; but it is difficult to understand theoretically. If politics consists at present of the interplay of economic interests, how can those interests be set aside while public-spirited politicians come up with a new interest free way of transacting business?

Most studies of Congress simply do not concern themselves with theoretical issues of this sort. Instead, they concentrate on understanding how Congress works today, focusing on such matters as the workings of the committee system, floor procedures, the changing role of staff, the extent of the incumbency advantage in elections, and the nature of congressional leadership. These efforts have greatly enriched our knowledge of Congress; but their success has brought us to the point where a larger theory has become both possible and necessary. Such a theory needs to explain why Congress sometimes responds to group pressures and at other times acts on its own initiative, and why its structure and role change over time (Peabody 1969).

One possible general theory is functionalism. Time and again we find expressions of the assumption that Congress works the way it does because that makes the political system stronger and more stable. Let us consider two such statements, one from a book on Congress:

> The history of politics could be written as an examination of the various methods of decision-making developed to reach binding decisions for the whole society. One method for reaching such decisions is a democracy, which theoretically maximizes the participation of all the citizens of society in the decision-making process. However, practical considerations prevent the continuous participation in every decision of all citizens in a large population or a large geographical locale; thus, as developed in many Western societies, the idea of representative democracy has been offered as the nearest approximation possible under contemporary circumstances. (Schwarz and Shaw 1976, 1)

The other comes from David Easton's formulation of political systems theory:

> The differences among diverse groups may be shielded from aggravation by building into the system additional expressive structural means that give the groups an opportunity to attempt to resolve their differences, if at all possible, under acceptable ground rules. A major device for this purpose is to be found in all kinds of representative structures, including those typical of but not exclusively confined to democratic regimes. It is a response that seeks less to mute the differences or blend groups than to provide avenues for negotiation and reconciliation. (1965, 251-52)

In both passages, the authors use the passive voice and so avoid the issue of *who* develops methods of decisionmaking, *who* offers representative democracy, or *who* seeks to improve decisionmaking and lessen aggravation. And in both cases the unwritten assumption is that society, as a historical subject, has designed its own institutions, either consciously or through evolutionary development, in such a way that the only interests built into them are the interests of the society—Maass's common good. However, what we find in every real historical case is that legislatures and other political institutions were designed by particular people with particular interests, who imposed them upon other people because they had the power to do so. These political engineers may have claimed to be working for "society"; indeed, they may have used language much like Easton's. The *Federalist Papers* contain many examples of such language. But we can always find examples of other people who rejected these claims, who resisted the new institutions as well as they could, but lost the struggle.

Marxism claims that this bias in what is advanced as "society's" interest is systematic. Some interests are always excluded from power; more accurately, the state is a mobilization of the power of some interests against others. In addition, Marxists hold that these interests are best understood in terms of social class rather than any other analytical concept, and that class is defined most fundamentally by the way a society's processes of production are organized. Let us examine the merits of these claims.

Marxism

First, it may be helpful to say something about Marxism itself. Marxism has never been very popular in the United States. Perhaps we should be surprised that it has survived at all: Marxists have been the target of legal and academic repression, sometimes more severe and sometimes less so, but always present, for at least the last forty-five years. But the weakness of American Marxism cannot be blamed entirely on its enemies. Until very recently, the Marxist political theory available in the United States was so unsophisticated that it had little appeal or usefulness to anyone with any detailed knowledge of politics. This theory began and ended with the statement that the United States was a dictatorship of the bourgeoisie. And Marxist political analysis consisted of showing how this statement held true in the case of any particular government action, either because the action in question added to the profits of the capitalist class or, alternatively, because it helped maintain that class in power by mollifying the workers.

Even in this crude form, Marxism provides a better explanation of reality than does the purest form of pluralism, since most government actions do add to capitalist profits, whereas pluralists would predict a more balanced equilibrium (Kariel 1961; Greenberg 1974). But pluralists have continually modified their theory to make it fit reality (Lowi 1979; Dahl 1982; Lindblom 1977),[4] whereas Marxism long remained stagnant.

However, Marxist theory has undergone changes—and these changes began long before the sweeping transformation of Eastern Europe in the 1980s. Mikhail Gorbachev's campaign for *glasnost* and *perestroika* was presaged by Nikita Khrushchev's attack on Stalin in 1956, followed by the Chinese Communists' attack on Khrushchev and the success in Cuba of a revolution that deviated widely from the official Marxist model. All of these changes undermined the myth of an omniscient central Marxist authority and helped open the way for the development of more sophisticated Marxist political theory. This development occurred most quickly in those European countries where the left was strong. The possibility that the left might win an election, and the potential necessity for making compromises in order to gain such a victory, inspired a rethinking of traditional Marxist beliefs on many questions. Could an electoral victory be meaningful? Or were elections a trap, distracting the working class from the task of smashing the state? What alliances could be made without endangering the goal of socialism? What could and should a left government do in a capitalist society? Was it possible to retain office without abandoning socialist principles? These questions were not new; they had all been raised in the 1930s, and earlier as well. But in the 1930s they were answered by party leaders and justified by theorists *ex post facto*. Inconsistencies were ignored, and embarrassing questions remained unasked; or they were pointed out and asked exclusively by the enemies of socialism, leading socialism's friends and supporters to close ranks and censor themselves out of misguided feelings of solidarity. By the 1960s party leaders no longer had the political or intellectual prestige to inspire similar circumspection. Instead, a theoretical explosion took place as both activists and academics (and some people who were both) took a fresh look at these old questions.

By the 1980s many had carried this new openness to the point of rejecting Marxism altogether, or at least rejecting its central concepts, while holding onto its political commitment to human liberation.[5] But those concepts—*mode of production, class exploitation*, and *economic determination in the last instance*—may yet prove to be better guides to understanding politics and society than the alternatives; certainly, that is one of the theses of this book.

Anyone setting out to apply Marxist theory to reality has to decide what Marxist theory is. Needless to say, there has been a great deal of debate about this. Summarizing and resolving this debate would be as fascinating as it is formidable, but doing so is far beyond my resources.[6] Nor is it my purpose here to argue for one particular viewpoint. Although

I feel closest to the approach taken by Nicos Poulantzas and will defend some of the elements of his approach, not all of the controversies that divide Marxists are relevant for explaining and interpreting Congress. My major purpose is not to choose among these alternatives but, rather, to demonstrate the utility of Marxist political explanations of Congress.

Marxism begins with the premise that although history is composed of a multitude of conscious actions by individuals, historical events are not the result of conscious choice by any individual or collective entity, whether that entity be society, the ruling class, the workers, or the spirit of progress (Poulantzas 1969). Historical events are the result of class struggle, but this struggle need not be a self-conscious one on the part of either class, or of its members, and it is misleading to discuss events as if this were the case.

To speak in these terms is not to deny the humanity of individuals or the reality of individual choices and actions. However, as classes and individuals exist on different levels of analysis, they cannot be directly related to each other. I find an analogy useful: Trying to explain classes in terms of individuals is like trying to explain the behavior of animals in terms of the molecules of which they are composed. Using the lower level of analysis is possible (at least in theory); in fact, it provides more detail. But it is also so cumbersome that we cannot get very far with it.[7]

Marxists believe that any society can be characterized by its *mode of production*—by the way in which it is organized to produce the necessities of life. In all existing societies this organization involves division into *classes*, with one class of people doing the actual labor of production while another class directs it and gets a disproportionately large share of the material benefits. In capitalist societies the class that works is characterized by *wage labor*, and is generally called the *working class* or *proletariat*. The class that directs is characterized by ownership of the means of production, or capital, and is called the *capitalist class* or *bourgeoisie*. Of course, matters are really a bit more complicated. Each class is further subdivided, a society may also contain traces of previous modes of production, and other divisions, such as gender and race, cut across the class divisions.[8]

The concept of *economic determinism* means that whatever class controls and reaps the benefits of the process of production—the *economy*—is likely also to control the levers of political power—the *state*—and to have its interests embodied in the dominant way of thinking—the *ideology*—of that society. Marxists sometimes call the economy the *structure* or *base* of society, and ideology and politics the *superstructure*. Absolute economic determinism would mean that the political and ideological levels of society were completely dependent on the economic base.

The major contributions made by Poulantzas (and Louis Althusser, although Poulantzas does much more to apply these theoretical ideas to politics) are, on the one hand, the idea that the ideological, political, and economic levels of society are *relatively autonomous* from each other;[9] and, on the other, that there is *determination in the last instance* by the economic level. One part of this theory—the notion of the relative autonomy of the state—has received the most attention. This notion allows us to think seriously about reform struggles and electoral politics in a capitalist society, and thus to escape the rigidity of the alternative theory that the state always serves, or is an instrument of, the dominant class.[10] At the same time, the stipulation of economic determination in the last instance permits us to take advantage of the explanatory and analytical power of the Marxist framework. Even more important, it helps us see the limits within which electoral and non-electoral reform struggles are confined.

However, these advantages can be reaped only if we are able to specify just what is meant by *relative* autonomy and by determination *in the last instance*. Otherwise, we have another meaningless formula, by which every state action which serves the capitalists is an example of economic determination in the last instance, and everything that does not is an example of relative autonomy. Alternatively, without a clearer definition we might end up with a restatement of pluralism in Marxist vocabulary, with the "last instance" deferred forever.[11] Misunderstanding of these concepts has produced widespread criticism of this version of Marxist theory, with emphasis on these two concepts.

Clear definitions of these concepts are also needed to distinguish this version of Marxism from what can be called *biased pluralism*.[12] Such leading pluralists as Robert Dahl and Charles Lindblom have modified their theory to take better account of the dominant position of big business in American politics. Lindblom, in particular, has argued that we must acknowledge both "the privileged position of business," meaning that the state cannot afford to interfere with profitability, and "circularity through indoctrination," meaning that business elites are generally able to control public opinion to produce "a historical and continuing narrowing of the range of political belief and attitude through favored class positions in instruments of communication: organized religion, government and face-to-face relations among others." These assertions lead him to conclude that there is "a real possibility . . . that we are imprisoned in our existing institutions with no way out." Lindblom also acknowledges the importance of "class hegemony" and estimates that (as of 1983) he is only 40 percent pluralist (1983; see also 1977).

All of this puts Lindblom, at least, very close to Marxism—and we may well ask why anything more needs to be said on the subject. This question will be answered more fully below; but in brief, I think that Marxism can offer a more precise understanding of how far the privileged position of business extends, and under what conditions that privilege can be undermined; of how far the indoctrination of public opinion can suceed, and how and when it can be resisted. By positing a linkage between the mode of production and the political structure, Marxism is both more pessimistic than biased pluralism about the possibility of stable incremental reform, and more optimistic about the chance of basic social change.

Marxists argue that the truly important historic events are changes in the mode of production; that today, for example, the question of capitalism or socialism is *the* basic political question. Events are thus more important when they are more closely related to this question. Marxists would expect legislative action on the minimum legal wage, public welfare, or factory closings to reflect the balance of class forces, but they would not necessarily expect to find as close a correspondence in legislation about the respective rights of snowmobile users and cross-country skiers who are competing for access to national forests.

However, a rule that economics determines politics on issues that are important for the mode of production but that politics is autonomous on other issues would be only a first approximation of the concept of relative autonomy. A more accurate formulation must distinguish also between single political events and the overall pattern of events. It is possible for workers to win passage of strong factory-closing laws despite the economic strength of the bourgeoisie. But it is *not* possible for a series of similar victories to gradually result in a change of the mode of production from capitalism to socialism, *unless* the bourgeoisie's economic, political, and military power is somehow broken. Such political victories by the dominated will tend to decrease the profitability of business—and therefore, given the nature of capitalism, to interfere with production. The resulting economic crisis would be resolved only if the state *either*—in accordance with the principle of economic determination in the last instance—restores profitability by serving the interests of capital more aggressively *or* mobilizes enough support to actually revolutionize the means of production (Poulantzas 1978a, 218-20).

This argument is somewhat circular, in that any given political reform can be explained either (a) as an event that is insufficiently threatening to capitalism to be ruled out, or (b) as a change that actually did (or would) transform the relations of production to socialist ones. Nevertheless, it does include features associated with specific consequences, which differentiate it from non-Marxist approaches, including biased pluralism.[13] In particular:

- Like acceleration near the speed of light, political gains for the working class should become more difficult as the tipping point between capitalism and socialism is approached.

- The change from capitalism to socialism is seen as qualitative and fundamental, and hence difficult to reverse. Therefore, we are unlikely to find any societies switching repeatedly back and forth between the two modes. (If they did exist, such societies would be beset by disruption and, probably, bloodshed.)[14]
- After the transition, the determination in the last instance of the superstructure by the structure should have a new effect. Reforms which previously met with much opposition and undercut economic prosperity should now be adopted easily and serve to increase prosperity.
- Therefore we should find an excluded middle—that is, an absence of stable social democratic societies in which power is balanced between capitalists and workers.

Looking specifically at the political level, I can add another element to Marxist theory. The structure of the political is limited by the economic; but it is also the result of past political struggles. Thus, on the one hand, the dominant class will normally enter any political struggle not only with more economic resources than the dominated but with more *political* resources as well. For example, present arrangements in the United States give finance capital not only considerable economic power over national investment choices (because investment decisions are regarded as a private affair) but also, through the Federal Reserve System, considerable political power over the size of the money supply.

However, the Federal Reserve is a political structure and could be changed through political struggle; it could be democratized by statute were there enough members of Congress who would vote for doing so. On the other hand, then, it is possible for the dominated to win favorable changes in the political structure, changes that increase their leverage in future struggles. For example, the late 1960s and early 1970s brought changes that gave African Americans greater access to elected office, provided channels through which women could fight employment discrimination, and made it easier for working class communities to block destructive development projects. In each of these cases, there was a change in the political structure that altered the probabilities of victory in future conflicts, but did not predetermine the outcome of any particular election campaign, anti-discrimination lawsuit, or struggle against an urban highway.

Poulantzas (1974) makes this point metaphorically by saying that the state is a terrain for class struggle. On this terrain a particular social force may occupy higher ground or a position that is otherwise advantageous. But the terrain itself may be altered by struggle, and the whole landscape may be collapsed by an earthquake—that is, by events on a deeper structural level.

In his later work, Poulantzas (1978a) rejects this metaphor in favor of another: The state is a condensation of the balance of forces in the class struggle at any particular time. His point is that to speak of classes engaged in struggle on the terrain of the state is to assume that those classes have their essential existence elsewhere—in other words, that a class first determines its goals, then enters into political struggle. This way of speaking brings us back to the instrumentalist view; but when we look at actual political struggles we see goals determined, coalitions formed, and classes and class fractions themselves constituted politically in the course of such struggles. They have no *a priori* existence on the political level, and their existence as economic categories need not lead to their political activity. The condensation metaphor is also meant to highlight the importance of ideology and its links with the political. Ideology is a major component of the political existence of a social force; conversely, it is often political action that constitutes individual political subjects as members of such a force (Poulantzas 1978a, 135-77).

The preceding discussion does not give us an account of Congress, only a theoretical vocabulary with which to construct such an account. A more detailed analysis is required if we are to pin down just how the economic, political, and ideological levels are connected to each other.

Philip Brenner has given us an excellent description of some of these connections. In his pioneering book *The Limits and Possibilities of Congress* (1983), he argues that the boundaries of congressional decision-making are set by the needs of the national economy and by the *hegemonic ideology* that sets the terms of debate; in other words, the members of Congress themselves tend to adopt the viewpoint of the nation's dominant economic interests. Brenner illustrates his argument with case studies of congressional action on relations with Cuba, aid to higher education, and reform of Congress's own rules. In each case, he shows that members of Congress were not compelled by outside pressure to do what they did but, rather, acted according to their own perceptions of the needs of American capitalism.

The concept of hegemonic ideology within Congress bears some resemblance to the more traditional concept of a responsible legislative style, with the advantage that it highlights the political content of such a style. However, an explanation is still needed for the differing outcomes of decisions made within that ideology, and for those occasions on which Congress acts against the needs of capitalism. Traditionally, as noted above, Marxists have explained the latter in terms of legitimation; that is, although Congress (or the state generally) usually acts to promote the accumulation of capital (and the profits of capitalists), it sometimes makes concessions to noncapitalists in order to maintain the legitimacy of the system. But the problem with this explanation is that it can explain absolutely anything, and therefore really explains nothing. A more specific explanation is needed. I believe that such an explanation requires adding a third dimension to economics and ideology—namely, politics.

Before proceeding along these lines, however, let us examine some solutions to the problems posed for other theories by the three examples raised earlier: Congress and foreign military intervention, the 1981 budget resolution, and seniority reform.

The pattern of congressional attempts to control foreign military intervention fits neither the hypothesis that state action is determined by interest groups, which would have produced exactly the opposite result; nor that which holds that the state is an instrument of the dominant class, since that class certainly would have wanted to keep fighting the Angolan revolutionaries; nor yet the simple majoritarian hypothesis that policy responds to public opinion. But the pattern can be explained if we assume two things. First, the central organs of state power—in this case, the command structures of the military and the intelligence apparatus—are occupied by people who identify politically and ideologically with the interests of large capital.[15]   Second, it is nevertheless possible for nonhegemonic forces, including the dominated classes, to undermine and limit the power of those central organs through struggle both outside and within the state structures. In this case, some of that struggle—although not the most important part by far—took place within Congress, and between Congress and the executive branch, during the Vietnam War. Although the struggle did not lead to congressional action to force an end to that war, it did result in a partial and limited restructuring of the political level. This left those who were ideologically opposed to such interventions as that in Angola in momentary control of enough levers of power to enable them to stop it. But by the early 1980s the continued hegemony of large capital on the economic level had generated a new ideological consensus in which its economic interests were more closely reflected, and this in turn—along with some political changes, which can also be traced to the continuing influence of the economic relations—rendered Congress no longer willing to use its newly won powers.

A great deal more could be said on this subject, particularly regarding the influence of the hegemonic ideology on the anti-war forces in Congress. But this brief sketch of an analysis is enough to suggest that a Marxist theory of Congress has something to offer as an explanation of events that are troublesome for pluralism.

Two features of the 1981 budget debate need to be explained: the sweeping Republican victory in the election, so different from the Nixon victories of 1968 and 1972 in that the party won not only the presidency but also the Senate, and made significant gains in the House; and the success of the new administration in getting its radical changes in the budget adopted without amendment (Ripley and Franklin 1976, 165, 178-79; 1987, 227-29). Pluralists in general, and pluralist students of Congress in particular, would have expected the presidential election to have little effect on Congress, and in any case would have predicted that the interest group-based "iron triangles" would have parceled Reagan's proposals out to a multitude of committees where they would have been hacked to pieces far from the public eye. Instead, the whole package was adopted in a single vote on the floor of the House, with no possibility of amendment, and the president prevailed.

After the fight was over, it all seemed to make perfect sense. President Reagan was a political mastermind; Carter was a dunderhead; Richard Viguerie, Terry Dolan, and other political strategists of the new right had invented a new campaign technology that caught the Democrats napping; and previously unrealized features of both the campaign finance laws and the Congressional Budget Act had provided an advantage to whoever first made use of them—in both cases, as it happened, conservative Republicans. Most of these points are valid enough, but they do not add up to much of a theoretical explanation. If we regard them as separate, unrelated factors which all happened at once, the coincidence of their working in the same direction becomes improbable. At the same time, pluralist theory can offer no underlying theoretical reason as to why this coincidence should have occurred.

From the Marxist point of view, the foregoing example is a simple case of structural limits on political struggle. Moreover, a closer look at this case can help us achieve a better understanding of how those structural limits exert their influence. We shall take that closer look in a later chapter. For now, another brief sketch will suggest some of what yet needs to be investigated.

First, early 1981 was a time not only of recession but of a deeper economic crisis, best symbolized by the neologism "stagflation." Economists who saw the situation from the standpoint of the capitalist were in agreement that this was a crisis of productivity and profitability; unprofitable corporations did not have the money to invest in new technology, and so became increasingly less competitive and less profitable. The crisis could be overcome only by increasing corporate profits or, in Marxist terms, by decreasing labor's share of the fruits of production and increasing the share of capital. Now, capitalists always want to do precisely this, just as workers always want to increase their own wages. And there are always some members of Congress who identify closely with business or with particular industries, who will support state action to lower wages. Similarly, there are always some members who depend heavily on the labor unions for political support, and who will represent the unions' interests. Neither group has a permanent majority, and the struggle between them can usually be described in pluralist terms of bargaining and coalition building. But in times of crisis, the labor representatives have a problem. In the case of most members, constituents are not likely to respond to, or even to be aware of, a vote on a particular bill or amendment; but they are much more likely to hold the president, Congress, and individual members of Congress responsible for the health of the economy. The graver the crisis, the less secure the members are in their seats. Unfortunately for the working class, the argument about profitability is correct within the context of capitalism; that is, as long as production is determined by the profit motive, a loss of profits will indeed lead to a loss of jobs. Of course, a revolutionary Marxist would reply, "Then so much the worse for capitalism!" and agitate for solutions that point the way toward a socialist transformation of the economy. But the number of revolutionary Marxists in Congress is very small. The vast majority of members, *and* of their constituents, think within the categories of the hegemonic ideology and arrive at the conclusion that the nation just cannot afford to spend any more on social benefits, environmental protection, or other luxuries that limit the accumulation of capital. Some reach this conclusion with glee, and others with regret; but it seems to everyone to be an acknowledgment of economic necessity, rather than an exertion of political power by capital.

This perception of reality magnified the impact of the 1980 election on the minds of the members of Congress. The House Democratic leadership attempted to use the usual maneuvers, but too many members believed that the economic crisis really did require exceptional measures, and that they would suffer at the polls if they were seen as resisting those measures in favor of politics as usual. This reckoning made the difference in the very close vote on the budget resolution, and in the even more important vote on the rules under which that resolution was to be considered.

My final example concerns the reforms made in the House seniority system, mostly between 1970 and 1975. Pluralists have not been very concerned with these reforms, believing as they do that structure is irrelevant. And most institutionalist scholars of Congress, having argued beforehand that seniority met the members' needs and was likely to last forever, pointed afterward to the influence of changing career patterns in the House.[16] As more and more members accumulated more and more seniority, they became less and less willing to defer to the small number of committee chairpersons. The reforms transferred power from the chairs of committees to those of subcommittees, thereby accommodating a much larger number of members. Significantly, seniority was made less important for committee positions but *more* important for subcommittee positions. This paradox is explained admirably by the career-needs theory, and not very well by anything else.

These observations about seniority are true enough, even if made only after the fact; but they say nothing about the wider implications of the reforms, thus trivializing them. From the Marxist point of view, the seniority reforms came as a result of the civil rights movement, the movement against the Vietnam War, and the more diffuse growth in the importance of urban interests and the labor movement. Whereas pluralists see these movements as just another part of the group struggle over policy, Marxists argue that they can be better understood as part of the class struggle—even if they are not conceptualized in that way by most of the participants.[17] The seniority reforms were part of a larger package that included the *Baker* v. *Carr* decision of the Supreme Court, the Civil Rights and Voting Rights Acts, and the War Powers Act. Spanning over a decade, these events amounted to a limited restructuring of the political level; in addition to changing policies, they changed the relative ability of various class forces to make or influence policy in the future, thereby defining the terrain on which the political struggles of today are being fought out. The oppressed social forces that had been attacking the system from outside were now partially incorporated within it, gaining strong positions on some of the newly empowered subcommittees. At the same time, more power was being centralized in the hands of party leaders, thus (as we shall see in the next chapter) helping to ensure that the hegemony of the giant corporations would be maintained (Brenner 1983, 152-59).

These three examples and others will be explored in more detail in the following chapters. They are united in that they show congressional action as being fundamentally rooted in the need of capitalism to maximize profits, whether through imperialist exploitation of other nations, racist exploitation of minority communities in the United States, or direct exploitation of the whole, multiracial U.S. working class at the point of production. At the same time, they demonstrate that there is some chance for the oppressed to fight back within Congress, and even sometimes to win. However, pending a basic change in the system, the possibility and scope of such victories are limited by the structure of the U.S. economy. In Chapter 2 we turn to an examination of that structure.

PART ONE

Congress and the Powerful

Money talks. Everyone knows that. It talks a lot to Congress. Well-heeled lobbyists, political action committees (PACs), expense-paid junkets, multimillion-dollar campaigns, and juicy honoraria are abiding elements of American political lore. Everyone knows, too, that the rich do better than other people at getting their opinions heard and their interests accommodated by legislators.[1] Average citizens, political scientists, and the members of Congress themselves join in bewailing the excessive importance of money in politics.

Although everyone may know these things, not everyone explains them in the same way. I believe that the most common explanations—those derived from the pluralist and institutionalist models of Congress—are superficial, and that the most commonly proposed solutions, such as banning PACs or providing public funds for congressional campaigns, would improve the character of Congress only slightly.

Pluralist theory, on the one hand, treats money as one weapon—albeit the major one—that interest groups deploy in the political battle. Some groups may enter the battlefield more heavily armed than others, but there are other weapons—votes, enthusiasm, publicity, moral righteousness, and information—that can be used by groups with less money; moreover, the battlefield itself is expected to be level. One implication of pluralism is that groups with less money but possessed of some other resource, such as a large membership or the perception that they stand for the public interest, may be able to hold their own in the conflict. A second implication is that if we can just eliminate money as a political resource, then interest group conflict will become fair and equal once again. Herbert Alexander describes this position as follows: ''The reform efforts of recent years, in addition to seeking to limit both real and perceived corruption, have attempted to smooth out the impact of political money—or, in current lingo, to 'level the playing field' '' (1992, 4).

The implication of biased pluralism would be that we may need to go further, eliminating the influence of wealth on public opinion as well; and that even then, the privileged position of business would force other groups to fight their way uphill. But to the extent that it stops short of economic determinism in the last instance, biased pluralism seems to imply that the power of money can be overcome "through tiresome sequences of increments" (Lindblom 1983, 385).[2]

Institutionalists, on the other hand, emphasize Congress's success in insulating its members from outside pressure. Institutionalists see the role of money in one of two ways. Some argue that it is largely irrelevant to the policy process, in that members of Congress can always get along without any particular contribution and often find that the vote that loses one contribution will gain another at the same time. Others believe that contributions are important, but that the direction of causality is reversed from that in common understanding. In other words, Congress is thought to have developed procedures that allow its members to extract the greatest possible amount of money from interest groups while doing more or less what they would have done anyway. Campaign finance limitations, then, would make members of Congress more honest, make the public less cynical about politics, and perhaps remove a burdensome cost from businesses; but they would not have much effect on policy output.[3]

The view of *Marxist* theory is that Congress looks out for the interests of wealth not only as a result of bribery and campaign spending but also because the economic structure of our society requires it. Bribes and campaign spending might be controlled by new regulations; changing our economic structure is a larger and much more difficult task.

Congressional politics is part of the fundamental social conflict in America. Congress is one arena in which this conflict takes place, but it is not an independent arena. Forces outside Congress influence what goes on inside it; in particular, if the Marxist theory is correct, Congress is influenced heavily by the economic structure of our society. Those who dominate the American economy dominate Congress as well. But Congress is also the most democratic part of our national government. Thus, oppressed social groups have found it the most permeable part of the state, often seeking to use congressional politics to advance their cause. The rest of this book is devoted to exploring these relations, beginning in Chapter 2 with the domination of Congress by big business.

We can see the effect of economic structure when we compare the way Congress handles different issues. In 1977, with the nation suffering from an energy shortage that restricted economic growth, hurt the balance of trade, inflated the cost of living, and forced many poor people to go without heat in winter, President Jimmy Carter presented a comprehensive national energy plan to Congress. After two years of hearings, backroom negotiations, and public debate, Congress managed to pass only one part of the plan: It removed price controls from natural gas, thus making energy even more expensive.

In 1989 the wreck of the oil tanker Exxon Valdez killed thousands of waterfowl, fish, marine mammals, and plants, threatened the ecological balance of Prince William Sound, and infuriated the public. Individual members of Congress responded with thousands of dramatic public speeches; but it was sixteen months before Congress as a legislative body managed to pass a bill raising the limits on liability of negligent oil shippers from $150 to $1,200 per ton of oil. Although the final bill was considered a victory by environmental lobbyists, several concessions had to be made to the oil industry before it could be passed. Double-hull requirements for oil tankers were deferred until 2010 (and to 2015 for most barges and for ships unloading offshore to lighters), oil companies shipping oil in tankers owned by others were exempted, and state governors lost any power to determine when a cleanup was complete (Congressional Quarterly 1991a, 283-87).

In the early 1980s a large number of savings and loan associations—known as thrift institutions, or simply "thrifts"—began to lose money; by 1987 many were in danger of failing. The Federal Savings and Loan Insurance Corporation (FSLIC), which insured thrift deposits of $100,000 or less, warned that it might not be able to pay all the claims. Congress gave the FSLIC another $10 billion in 1987, but otherwise did nothing until after the 1988 election. Then, in early 1989, Congress moved with remarkable speed to enact a complicated—and expensive—reorganization plan for the thrift industry. President George Bush proposed a plan on February 6 and signed a new law on August 9. The S&L Bailout—as it became known—would cost $50 billion by the end of 1991, and at least $110 billion by 1999;[4] some of the money would be paid to the holders of insured accounts, but much of it would be used to subsidize healthier, more profitable banks and thrifts in taking over unhealthy ones (Congressional Quarterly 1990, 14-15, 117-19).

In this case Congress acted not only quickly but ingeniously. Since the passage of the Gramm-Rudman-Hollings Deficit Reduction Act (GRH) in 1985, new spending programs had been difficult to create. The bill deftly evaded this problem. It simply labeled $30 billion "off-budget" and assigned the remaining $20 billion to a fiscal year that had already begun—and which therefore had already passed the GRH test.[5]

One could argue that Congress acted so quickly and smoothly in the savings and loan case because it simply had to. The nation faced a crisis, and failure to act would have had unthinkable consequences. However, this line of thought leads to further questions. What is a crisis? What sort of consequences are unthinkable? In 1991 a cholera epidemic broke out in

Peru, threatening to spread throughout South and Central America; it was expected to be hard to stop because the projected cost of the necessary sanitary improvements was prohibitive—$200 billion over twelve years, or about the same as the savings and loan bailout (Kong 1991, 46).

Closer to home, it has been argued that American public education is in crisis (U.S. National Commission on Excellence in Education 1983). Millions of young people fail to complete high school; millions more graduate unable to read, to multiply fractions, or to understand the basic nature of atoms and molecules. These consequences are unthinkably tragic, but they are happening, and Congress has not found the will to prevent them.

Marxists use the concept of *hegemony* to explain the differences between these two crises. Hegemony refers to the dominating power of a social class (or part of one) whose class interests have come to be widely accepted as equivalent to the interests of society as a whole. The United States today is dominated in this way by the giant multinational corporations. But before looking more closely at this domination, we need a clear understanding of the concept of class.

Unfortunately, the same word refers to two different concepts, superficially similar but fundamentally opposed. In America, *class* most commonly means "socio-economic status," a composite category with such components as wealth, income, education, occupation, and personal ethos, but most fundamentally defined by social prestige. In this sense the term refers to a position on a spectrum running from "low" to "high," with most people in the "middle." This is the sense in which sociologists generally use the word *class*, defined by Talcott Parsons as "an aggregate of kinship units of approximately equal status in the system of stratification" (Parsons 1951, 172).[6]

But for Marxists, *class* means something very different. The concept designates both a basic division of society and the relation between the two sides of that division, a relation that is essentially economic. Master and slave, lord and serf, capitalist and worker are not merely *different*, but *opposed*. Each class defines the other, and defines it through the relation whereby one produces a surplus and the other appropriates it.[7] Although *class* in the Marxist sense bears some relation to the components of socioeconomic status, the two concepts correspond inexactly. A worker may be highly paid but still belong to the working class because he or she is directly exploited by capital; a poor farmer or struggling shopkeeper may have less income and education than the worker but still be petty bourgeois. Classes are determined primarily by their relationship to the means of production, and secondarily by political and ideological class struggle. Moreover, *class* in the Marxist sense is not an infinite gradation.

A mode of production is divided into two fundamental classes: In the case of capitalism, these are the capitalists and the workers.

"Mode of production" is a theoretical abstraction; any actual society[8] is more complicated and has more classes than two. A given society may be in a state of transition from one mode of production to another, and therefore have both an aristocracy and a capitalist class, for example—as England did in the nineteenth century. And virtually every capitalist society will have a petty bourgeoisie, an intermediate class between labor and capital characterized by the dual sources of its income, some of which comes from control of capital and some from its own labor.[9] Finally, classes may be further divided vertically into fractions and horizontally into strata. These secondary divisions may be constituted by political and ideological characteristics as well as by strictly economic ones. Although such ramifications complicate the picture, the basic distinction between the Marxist and sociological senses of "class" must be kept in mind. Aristocrats may coexist with capitalists, but they cannot exist without serfs or peasants whose surplus they appropriate; the petty bourgeoisie is defined not by the level of its income but by the contradictory elements, labor and capital, of that income's source; and differences in the way these elements are combined are likewise at the root of the further divisions into fractions and strata.

The United States is clearly a capitalist society. Our economy is organized according to capitalist principles. Capitalists—whether individual capitalists or capitalist firms—control most of our national wealth. Capitalist values, such as property and contract, are widely upheld; indeed, Americans often equate capitalism with freedom and democracy (as when a hereditary monarchy in Saudi Arabia or a military dictatorship in Indonesia are considered part of the "Free World"). Accordingly, capitalists should dominate American government, including Congress. But some capitalists are more dominant than others. In Chapters 2 and 3 we will look at the differences between the very largest firms and their smaller class siblings, differences that are reflected in their differing relationships to Congress.

2

Congress and Big Business

The American economy is not just capitalist; it is dominated by a small number of gigantic capitalist corporations. In 1988, the 500 largest industrial corporations in the United States—the so-called Fortune 500—had total sales of over $2 trillion. One-fifth of this amount, $402,183,000,000, was produced by just five companies: General Motors (GM), Ford, Exxon, International Business Machines (IBM), and General Electric (GE) ("The Biggest Blowout Ever" 1989, 349-401). In the same year, there were about 3.5 million corporations, and 14 million nonfarm proprietorships and partnerships, in the United States (U.S. Department of Commerce 1989). The three major automobile makers alone employed 1,270,000 people, had assets of $356 billion, and earned profits of $11.2 billion ("The Biggest Blowout Ever" 1989, 349-401). The ten largest commercial banks—all but one of them located in New York City—had assets of $860 billion, with nearly one-quarter of that, $207 billion, held by one bank, New York's Citicorp ("At Last, Profits Worth Savoring" 1989, 364).

These giants are so big that the rest of the country needs them to be healthy. When Chrysler Corporation, only the third largest automobile maker, faced possible bankruptcy, the federal government stepped in to save it. It stepped in again to avert the failure of Chicago-based Continental Bank Corporation, the fourteenth largest commercial bank. As this practice has become more common, it has acquired a name, the "too big to fail" doctrine. It is one example of *hegemony*.

When Charles E. ("Engine Charlie") Wilson went from president of General Motors to secretary of defense in the Eisenhower administration, he told a Senate committee that he was not worried about any possible conflict of interest because he had always believed that "what was good for our country was good for General Motors, and vice versa. The difference did not exist. Our company is too big. It goes with the welfare of the country."[1]

In the largest sense, Wilson was dead wrong. GM has been a cumbersome, inefficient enterprise that has contributed greatly to a whole range of national problems, from low productivity to air pollution to worker alienation. But in the short run—that is, given that GM already existed—Wilson was right. GM's huge labor force, its annual sales, and its impact as a customer on other major industries were so great that a failure of GM—or of another giant corporation—might well have plunged the whole economy into recession.[2]

Corporate Hegemony

Until sometime in the early 1970s the giant financial and industrial corporations were able to dominate America and much of the rest of the world. This domination gave them a sense of security and led some to conclude that they were more interested in stability than in profits (Galbraith 1985). Since that time, however, their dominance has been threatened by growing international competition. The best-known example is the auto industry, in which the big three U.S. automakers have lost market share to Japanese and European competitors both at home and abroad; but the same thing has occurred in many other industries as well.

This new global competition has changed both the composition and the interests of the hegemonic bloc. By reviving the emphasis on profits it has reinforced the dominance of finance capital over industrial corporations. Such once-mighty giants as IBM have learned that Wall Street would rather shift its investments to other companies and industries than support them in fighting to preserve their corporate position. The willingness of many corporations to accept high wages and benefits and a certain amount of government regulation is likewise falling before international competitive pressure. These changes in the economic position of U.S. big business have had important political results, some of which we shall look at more closely in Chapters 3 and 4; but the basic division between hegemonic and nonhegemonic sectors of the capitalist class remains.

Politics and ideology tend to reflect economics. Thus, the state (including Congress) tends to further the interests of the giant corporations; and public debate tends to be carried on in terms that incorporate those interests—as in 1990, when President Bush referred to protection of Exxon's oil supplies in the Persian Gulf as a defense of "our way of life." This is not automatically so. The nonhegemonic classes can and do organize themselves to contend for political power, and to change the terms of public discourse. But they find it harder to win; and unless they succeed in changing the economic structure as well, such political and ideological reforms are likely to be only temporary. Let us look at some concrete examples.

The crisis in the savings and loan industry threatened to destabilize the whole financial system, endangering giant banks along with small thrift institutions. It thus struck at the heart of corporate hegemony. The nature of this hegemony is missed by much left rhetoric. For example, Manning Marable has written recently:

> Is it right for a government to spend billions and billions for bailing out fat cats who profited from the savings and loan scam while millions of jobless Americans stand in unemployment lines desperate for work? Is it fair that billions of our dollars are allocated for the Pentagon's permanent war economy to obliterate the lives of millions of poor people from Panama to Iraq to Grenada to Vietnam, while two million Americans sleep in the streets and 37 million Americans lack any form of medical coverage? (1993, 12)

The policies Marable decries are indeed neither right nor fair; but even those members of Congress who agree with this characterization fear that allowing the savings and loan industry to collapse, or (more debatably) cutting the military budget, would send even more millions to the unemployment lines or into the streets. For this reason, debate within Congress about the savings and loan crisis has centered on who should take the blame, not on whether to act.

By contrast, the crisis in education strikes at the U.S. working class, and cholera threatens workers and peasants in other countries. Millions of lives may be blighted, neighborhoods destabilized, and great human suffering caused, but most members of Congress still see a solution as optional—something we certainly ought to do if we can just find the money. Even the advocates of school reform find it useful to base their arguments on the need of capitalism for a more skilled labor force.

This is the theory of hegemony in its bare bones. Hegemonic interests are privileged in that Congress and the state act quickly and effectively to protect them; they find it more difficult to promote other interests that are equally vital in human terms. But students of politics must ask how this privilege is maintained. What is it about our political system—what is it about Congress—that makes it more responsive to hegemonic interests than to others?

In fact, the interests of the great corporations are well entrenched in the structure of American government. This structure is itself the product of past political struggles, dating back at least to the drafting of the Constitution. Some of these struggles have been won by the working class, farmers, and petty bourgeoisie; by women; by racial minorities; and by other democratizing forces. But on the whole, the trend has been toward the kind of state envisioned by Alexander Hamilton, a state dedicated to furthering business interests (Hamilton [1791] 1966).

Corporate hegemony is built into the structure of Congress on at least three levels. First, it has become part of our basic legal order. Second, it is built into the separation of powers, which places the most crucial decisions outside of Congress's reach. Finally, it is part of the internal structure of Congress itself. The end result of decades of conflict is that Congress finds it easy to act on behalf of corporate interests and difficult to act against them. These structural features are reinforced by the nature of the American electoral system, and by the weakness of anticapitalist ideology.

Americans think of our legal order as founded on individual rights. However, the meaning of these rights has been transformed since the U.S. Constitution was first written. On the one hand, rights have been broadened and extended in such a way that the universalistic language of the Declaration of Independence is now applied to the propertyless, to women, and to the descendants of slaves, none of whom had been included at first. On the other hand, the language of rights has been applied to big business, becoming a fundamental restraint on the power of Congress and other democratic institutions to regulate business in the public interest.

Perhaps the most important business victory was the extension of individual civil rights to corporations. Today this extension has become such a basic feature of our legal system that we tend not to notice it, but it came about only in the latter half of the nineteenth century. Through a combination of state and federal legislation and Supreme Court decisions, two legal doctrines became firmly established. First, corporations—which had been conceived of originally as quasi-state agencies chartered by the state in order to achieve an important public purpose, such as building a bridge or a canal, settling Massachusetts Bay, or conquering India—were transformed into a means of concentrating capital without exposing its individual owners to excessive risk, for the sole purpose of making money.

Second, these corporations gained the status of *persons* under the law, and as such won the legal rights granted to persons by the Fourteenth Amendment. This amendment had been designed to give federal protection to the freed slaves; but the Supreme Court ignored this purpose for seventy years, while using the amendment to protect corporations from government regulation. The Court has since backed away from some of its more extreme interpretations,[3] but the basic legal structure of corporate rights continues to place many possible policies beyond the bounds of congressional or state legislative action (Greenberg 1985, 62-64, 77-80; Robertson and Judd 1989, 45-46).

Most recently, the Supreme Court has extended freedom of expression to corporate persons. The Court ruled in 1975 that the First Amendment applied to commercial advertising and, in 1980, extended it to cover political advocacy by businesses. A constitutional provision intended to protect human democracy and individualism thereby became a barrier to attempts to protect democratic discourse from the domination of capital (Swidorski 1994).

The interests of giant corporations are also built into the operation of the constitutional separation of powers. Those who study the making of public policy know that the balance of power between Congress and the president varies with the issue at hand. The executive branch has the largest role in foreign policy, military action, and the regulation of the national economy. The president can order military action, recognize foreign governments, or sign Executive Agreements without congressional approval. Even when funds must be appropriated by Congress, he has considerable discretion to divert them to other purposes—and, as the Iran-*contra* case showed, he also has the *de facto* ability to exceed that discretion. He and his appointees also play the major role in attempts to regulate the national economy.

Congress, for its part, wields more detailed control over such issues as aid to education, environmental protection, housing, health, and welfare. In these areas, presidentially appointed officials must work with specific mandates and finite appropriations from Congress, and important issues are often decided by Congress, in committees or by floor amendments.

Some of these differences are rooted in the Constitution, whereas others have emerged since—as with the creation of the Federal Reserve System; but in general, those policy areas that are more vital to the interests of the great corporations are further removed from the influence of Congress.

Nonhegemonic classes and groups have better access to Congress than to the president and his inner cabinet, but this access does not give them proportional influence over those matters most important to the hegemonic fraction. The president can invade Grenada or Panama, go to war with Iraq, or sponsor terrorist attacks in Nicaragua, and Congress finds it hard to restrain him. The Federal Reserve system sets the nation's monetary policy, a key determinant of the fate of our economy, with little accountability to Congress or even to the president.[4] In the case of foreign affairs, Congress's power is limited by the Constitution, which makes the president commander in chief of the armed forces; but it has been unable to resist the erosion of its own power to declare war. The United States fought both the Korean and Vietnam wars without formal declarations of war by Congress, and in the case of Vietnam the fighting continued long after Congress had turned against it. Finding itself unable to stop a war that was under way, Congress passed the War Powers Act of 1974; but this act has proved ineffective, having often been ignored by the president.[5] However, the regulation of banking and currency are powers assigned to Congress; its loss of influence in these areas is the result of its own past decisions to create and maintain the Federal Reserve System. As a result, Congress must try to manage the economy—if it wishes to try at all—by raising or lowering federal taxes and spending, tools that are difficult to wield and uncertain in their effect. The powers to regulate interest rates and the money supply have proven more effective, but they have been removed from Congress and given to the Federal Reserve Board and the Federal Open Market Committee. In both cases, political struggles of the past have helped form structures that bias the political struggles of today.

The class basis of the separation of powers, and its changes over time, merit further study. As a simple approximation we could say that hegemonic interests dominate the presidency, whereas the influence of other social forces is confined to Congress.[6] But hegemony operates within Congress as well. Congress has been unable to stop presidents from encroaching on its traditional powers partly because the interests that dominate the presidency also control the main levers of power within Congress.

Decisionmaking in each house of Congress is formally democratic, usually by majority vote. Yet small groups of members have always possessed the greatest share of power over decisions. Such power can come from control over the flow of bills to the floor, as with the party leaderships and the House Rules Committee; or from control over important legislative subject matter, as with the appropriations, tax-writing, and budget committees. The Appropriations, Rules, and Ways and Means committees in the House are called "exclusive committees"— because they are so important that their members are not supposed to serve on other standing committees at the same time (a rule often broken, as it happens). The House Budget Committee is a special case; it is formed of selected representatives from other committees, and its chair, rather than being chosen by seniority, is elected by the House and considered a member of the House leadership. The Senate also recognizes certain committees as having extra importance: Appropriations, Budget, Finance (the Senate equivalent of House Ways and Means), and Foreign Relations (given special importance in the Senate because of that body's treaty ratification power). For ease of reference, all of these will be referred to from now on as *hegemonic committees.*

Both party leadership and hegemonic committee positions are almost always held by members who have incorporated the hegemonic ideology into their own outlooks. Several studies have shown that positions of power go to those members who have a "responsible legislative style," one of the essential elements of which is a willingness to put what is conceived of as the national interest ahead of narrow constituency interests (Fenno 1969, 130-32; Fenno 1973, 20-21; Masters 1969, 240-41; Clapp 1963).

For hegemonic committees, congressional leaders also prefer to pick members who come from seats that are relatively safe, so that they will be less subject to popular pressure on controversial decisions. There is also some self-selection of members. Richard Fenno, in a famous study of House committees, found that representatives were most likely to seek seats on the Ways and Means or Appropriations committees if they were more interested in achieving power as an end in itself than in promoting specific policies (1973, 2-5). Given the structure of American society, such power can best be pursued by choosing to side with big business.

These selection procedures do not work perfectly. However, potentially dissident committee members find themselves outnumbered and face strong pressure not to rock the boat. If they cooperate with hegemonic interests, they can use their committee positions to win significant benefits for their districts or for other interests they support; but if they come to be seen as troublemakers, such benefits are much harder to come by. Generally such pressures are enough to keep potential dissidents in line.

The hegemonic fraction does not dominate Congress through sheer force; its power is maintained only by the tacit, and sometimes open, support of a majority of the members, who could vote to change the structure at any time. One of the strengths of Congress is that its leaders understand this contingency and act consciously to maintain their support. "Responsibility" includes "reciprocity" and "accommodation"—the willingness of a member of Ways and Means, for example, to serve as a voice for interests in his or her region that want particular concessions in the tax code, and to cooperate with members from other regions with like interests. The willingness to grant such concessions from time to time provides the solid foundation for the Ways and Means Committee's ability at other times to gain acceptance of an omnibus tax bill under a closed rule.

As Fenno observes, the power of the hegemonic committees is reinforced by institutional pride. House members want the Ways and Means Committee to be strong, because its power is, to some extent, theirs as well (1973, 18).

In addition to a generalized willingness to be accommodating, hegemony within Congress can involve specific accommodations of particular groups. For example, the Rayburn-McCormack leadership of the House Democrats—whose successors, known as the Austin-Boston Axis, remained in control of the House Democratic leadership through the

1980s—won and maintained power on the basis both of a moderate New Deal ideology and of a very specific agreement that amendments to the tax code that were regarded unfavorably by Southwestern oil interests would not be allowed on the floor (Fenno 1973, 25n). The oil industry has since been forced to fight harder for its interests, but it continues to be well represented in the House and Senate tax-writing committees, and still receives tax treatment more favorable than that accorded to most other industries.[7] This arrangement is a reflection of the central position of the oil companies in the American economy—their inclusion in the hegemonic bloc—but it is not an automatic result of that economic importance. Rather, it is the consequence of a series of political victories by which the representatives of the oil companies have gained control of some of the levers of congressional power.

These three structural factors—the basic legal order, the division of powers among the branches of government, and the power of the hegemonic committees within Congress—provide the terrain on which pluralist conflict takes place. This conflict is fought out with the usual weapons of democratic politics—namely, votes and money; but the giant corporations enter the battle already in possession of the commanding heights and are therefore much more likely to win. We can see the difference this makes by looking more closely at one of the examples mentioned above.

The Savings and Loan Crisis

PAC spending and corrupt politics certainly played a part in the collapse of the thrift industry. Charles Keating's contributions to five senators and the shady role of President Bush's son Neal have entered the national consciousness. Keating and Bush are not atypical, either; the entire thrift industry has been a major player in the PAC game (Jackson 1988; Marcus 1989).

A common view is that the crisis was the result of pluralism run amok, distorted into what Theodore Lowi (1979) has called "interest group liberalism." The nation's savings and loan companies lobbied so well that they won control of the agencies charged with regulating them. They then used that control to remove important restraints on their activity and proceeded to swindle the taxpayer out of hundreds of billions of dollars. Their proceeds included such other plums as private jets, sports cars, vacation homes, and even Rubens's *Portrait of a Man as Mars*, which was purchased at auction for $13.2 million by Centrust, a Florida savings and loan, for its chief executive officer David Paul to keep at home and use while entertaining customers (Mayer 1990, 77).

Upon looking at the overall contours of the crisis, however, we find an interesting contrast between some of the details and the larger picture. In many particular cases, crooked thrift owners were able to buy political influence and use it to keep shaky institutions going while they milked them for a few more millions. But the net result of the crisis was that thrifts and their owners lost their niche in the American economy and were often swallowed up by large commercial banks.

Thrifts take their name from the virtue that they were designed to encourage. They were intended to pool the savings of local community residents to provide capital for housing and other consumer purchases. Two rules were necessary to bring about this objective. First, thrifts were not allowed to make certain kinds of investment, such as commercial loans, so that their funds would be available for long-term mortgages. And to make sure that such loans would be possible, savings account interest was limited by the Federal Reserve Board's Regulation Q, so that the thrifts would not have to pay their depositors more than they received from their borrowers. Other banks were held to a rate slightly below that allowed to the thrifts, so that thrift-based savings accounts would be attractive to small savers—those who did not have enough money to buy common stocks, U.S. Treasury notes, or other more profitable investment vehicles popular among the rich.

These regulations protected the thrift industry from the big banks, which otherwise could have undercut and ultimately acquired them. But they could not withstand the political and economic assaults of Wall Street in the 1960s and 1970s. Driven by their own competitive pressures, large financial institutions devised new ways to attract the money of small savers; most notable among the options they offered was the money market mutual fund. Anyone with $1,000—for some funds, only $250— could now get a better rate than the thrifts paid on passbook savings accounts.

The thrifts were left with two choices, neither viable in the long run. They could sit back and watch their deposits dwindle as depositors pursued the higher rates on Wall Street, although this option would leave them with no money for housing and other consumer loans, and no real reason to exist.[8] Alternatively, they could invent their own ways to pay higher rates—through daily compounding, certificates of deposit, and a bevy of special accounts. This latter course staved off disaster for the moment, but it also left the thrifts in danger of being whipsawed as the rates they were paying out on short-term deposits approached, and sometimes surpassed, those they were collecting on long-term mortgage loans.

That was precisely what happened, of course. The thrifts tried to save themselves through deregulation—that is, through changes in the rules that let them make ever more desperate attempts to pay higher rates and attract deposits, or to convert to joint stock corporations and attract equity capital from investors.

The Garn-St Germain Depository Institutions Act of 1982 was the biggest step in this deregulation. Immortalized by President Reagan's comment, "I think we hit a home run," as he signed it, Garn-St Germain is sometimes portrayed as the mistake that brought on the thrift crisis. As pluralists would have expected, the bill was the focus of heavy lobbying, particularly by the United States Savings and Loan League; but in reality Garn-St Germain was not so much the cause of the crisis as the beginning of the end—the last desperate attempt by the thrifts to beat back the assault from Wall Street. This attempt failed miserably.[9]

Every reform just dug the thrifts' hole a little deeper, while opening the door to abuses and fraud by the unscrupulous investors who are so abundant on the American financial scene. The sight of this open door inspired a stampede of embezzlement and theft; but this was the result, not the cause, of the thrift crisis.

As the dust from the collapse of the thrift industry begins to settle, we can begin to make out the outlines of the banking system of the twenty-first century. There will be fewer, larger banks, which will compete nationally and internationally; and regionally based banks will either expand, merge, or die. All banks, whether they began life as savings and loan associations, savings banks, or commercial banks, will compete on the same terms; consequently, homebuyers will have to compete with commercial borrowers for credit, and interest rates will rise accordingly. And, of course, the American taxpayer will pay the cost of salvaging the industry, a cost variously estimated at $200 to $500 billion over the next few decades.

If we applied the pluralist model, we might expect the thrifts to have benefited according to their PAC spending and political activity. However, this is only half the story. Both individual thrifts and their interest group, the United States Savings and Loan League, were indeed active lobbyists; but this lobbying must be seen in the larger context of the thrift industry's inability to defend itself from the giant national and international commercial banks. The thrifts won some political battles but lost the most important ones—not because they were outspent but because of the hegemonic structural position of their opponents.

The important points for our analysis are as follows.

1. The cause of the thrifts' decline was economic, not political; they were unable to resist the competition of larger financial institutions.

2. Intensive lobbying won them deregulation and the Garn-St Germain Act; but these political measures only delayed their economic defeat, while opening the door to and exacerbating their ultimate collapse.

3. Once the crisis appeared to threaten hegemonic financial interests, Congress moved quickly and almost effortlessly to solve the problem. The interest of the big banks, the investment houses, and big depositors (those with deposits above the insurance limit) were protected at the expense of the thrifts and the tax-paying public. In this stage of the crisis, lobbying and PAC contributions by the thrifts had little impact.

4. In confronting the crisis, Congress chose to limit its own future influence on the matter by creating the Resolution Trust Corporation (RTC), a quasi-governmental agency not directly answerable to Congress. Dissident members of Congress could then complain freely about the RTC's practices without interfering seriously with its operations.

In this case, business interests in the nonhegemonic sector (the thrifts) lost out despite their intensive political activity. If smaller business always lost out, the U.S. political system would be less stable than it is. However, most of the time smaller businesses are able to get much of what they need from Congress and, accordingly, continue to align themselves with the hegemonic interests as part of the power bloc. We shall look more closely at this aspect of Congress in Chapter 3.

3

Congress and Smaller Business

The giant corporations may rule America, but they do not rule alone. There are thousands of corporations that do not make the Fortune 500 list, many with owners who are rich and powerful in their own right. However, neither these companies nor their owners are as rich or as powerful as the great multinational corporations; and if the differences in wealth are perhaps only a matter of degree, the differences in power are more qualitative. The largest companies were once known collectively as the *monopoly sector* because of their ability to manipulate prices. Today, even the largest firms face international competition, which makes them far more susceptible to market forces than they were in the 1960s; but their size, their capacity to advertise, and the brand-name loyalty that such advertising creates still give them more room for maneuver than the firms in large but nonhegemonic companies—those in what may be called the *competitive sector* (Greenberg 1979, 103). Moreover, even as monopoly has declined, corporations have continued to grow through mergers and acquisitions, often producing conglomerates bound together by purely financial ties. This trend has not only reduced more and more business judgments to evaluations of quarterly earnings growth but has also increased the dominance of financial corporations within the hegemonic sector. Even today, executives of the fallen General Motors corporation know that if they raise the price of new Chevrolets, their sales will decline, but some cars will still be purchased. If they study the market carefully they may even succeed in predicting the magnitude of the decline and be able to plan their operations accordingly. But a wheat grower who decided to ask ten cents a bushel above the going price in the market would expect to sell no wheat at all.

To pluralists, businesses are businesses. They differ in size, of course, but this difference is a continuous variation along one of many dimensions. To Marxists, the distinction between the giant firms and their smaller brethren is more qualitative. Competitive-sector firms have political power but not the special power enjoyed by those concerns that are truly too big to be allowed to fail. Except on the local level, their individual demises would have little economic impact, so they cannot count on politicians' rallying to save them. Political concessions cannot be demanded as a matter of hegemonic right but must be won through positive effort.

Still, such firms have a lot going for them. They do have money, and they can spend it to influence both public officials and public opinion. They are well served by the overall probusiness ideology, the belief that business in general creates jobs and ought to be promoted by government, and that business works most efficiently when government keeps its hands off. Above all, they are seen by almost everyone—top government officials and managers of giant corporations included—as an essential part of American life.

The Power Bloc

Poulantzas used the term *power bloc* to describe the coalition of classes and fractions of classes that dominates a society politically (Poulantzas [1975] 1978b). As part of the power bloc, competitive capital shares some basic interests with the hegemonic fraction. These include their common interests as exploiters of labor power, such as low wages, weak trade unions, and unregulated working conditions; their interests as U.S.-based companies competing in the world market; and a general interest in economic conditions that are favorable to capitalist growth. But even here the bloc may be divided by differences of opinion and emphasis—and other issues divide it directly. The giants seek to expand their control; and the smaller companies, to retain some independence. Individual companies and industrial segments battle each other for market share and regulatory advantage. The structure of Congress today, which was shaped by past struggles, incorporates both the hegemony of the giant firms and the limited independent power of smaller corporations.

Issues that set the power bloc against the working class correspond loosely to what Theodore Lowi has called *redistributive* issues. In a famous book review years ago, Lowi classified policy issues into three categories: redistributive, regulatory, and distributive. Issues are redistributive when the two sides "are, crudely speaking, haves and have-nots, bigness and smallness, bourgeoisie and proletariat. The aim involved is not use of property but property itself, not equal treatment but equal possession, not behavior but being" (Lowi 1964, 691).[1] Lowi argues that such issues are generally marked by "the removal of decision-making from Congress" (1964, 715) to the upper level of the executive branch on the one hand, and on the other to peak (i.e., class-wide) interest groups where "in many respects the upper-class directors perform the functions in the re-distributive arena that are performed by congressional committees in the distributive arena and by committees and Congress in the regulatory arena" (1964, 711). He cites passage of the Social Security Act in 1935 as an example: "Except for a short fight over committee jurisdiction (won by the more conservative Finance and Ways and Means committees) the legislative process was extraordinarily quiet, despite the import of the issues" (1964, 705).

Lowi is too sweeping in his generalization—perhaps because he bases his conclusion on the institutionalist ground that Congress as a collective body lacks the technical capacity to balance rather than cumulate interests, not on an analysis of the social forces involved in various issues (1964, 715). Removal of a decision from Congress to the upper executive can protect the interests of the power bloc from possible challenges by the dominated;[2] and when a pattern of such removal develops, it becomes part of the structure of power. However, such removal may be opposed, and does not always succeed. Redistributive issues may arouse conflict in Congress in two cases: when the power bloc itself is not united, and when subordinate social forces mount a strong challenge to the status quo.

Even when the power bloc shares interests, there is often a difference in emphasis. At times, giant firms can pass along increased wage and regulatory costs to their customers, and may be willing to concede higher wages, fringe benefits, and even union recognition in return for greater stability. Competitive firms, though, have to live with the prices set by the market, and so must absorb higher costs out of profits. This constraint strengthens their opposition to progressive social legislation. Thus at the beginning of this century the National Association of Manufacturers (NAM), the organizational voice of competitive manufacturing capital, fought labor unions even while the larger companies represented in the National Civic Federation were promoting business-labor cooperation (Weinstein 1968, 15-17, 80-81) and continued to fight the social reforms of the New Deal long after those reforms had been accepted by what was then monopoly capital (Greenberg 1985, 95-112). Sometimes monopolies have even supported increased regulation for the purpose of squeezing smaller competitors out of the market by increasing their costs. Gabriel Kolko argues that this was the case with passage of the Meat Inspection Act of 1905. The act was opposed by small meat packing companies but supported by the large ones, which needed credible government certification of their meat in order to sell it in Europe—and got it, through the act, at public expense (Kolko 1967, 98-108; Greenberg 1979, 58-59).

Similarly, Robert M. Collins found that one source of business opposition to the National Recovery Administration (NRA) in 1934 was "small businessmen [who] complained bitterly that the competitive edge often enjoyed by smaller firms would be destroyed by NRA compulsion to accept unionization and pay higher wages while being barred from meaningful price competition" (Collins 1981, 32). The national Chamber of Commerce, which had supported the NRA and other New Deal programs at first, was almost totally in opposition by 1935 (Collins 1981, 34, 38-40). In response, the Roosevelt administration organized the more supportive Business Advisory Council, consisting of "several liberal executives from medium-sized firms and a disproportionate number of businessmen from truly giant corporations" (Collins 1981, 58).

In such cases, competitive-sector interests are likely to use whatever means they can to resist the pressure of the hegemonic fraction. And Congress, because it is more permeable, is likely to provide such means. In 1938 George Houston of the Baldwin Locomotive Works declared to the Chamber of Commerce convention, "In 1935 many of us said, 'Thank God for the Supreme Court.' In 1938, and again I hope in 1939, we are saying, 'Thank God for an independent Congress.' "[3] In the typical case the hegemonic fraction will prevail, but only after some concessions have been extracted from it. However, not all cases are typical.

Some redistributive struggles threaten only part of the power bloc. In rare instances, a popular movement may secure a voice of some sort—whether direct or indirect—in Congress.[4] Such struggles may lead to a restructuring of the power bloc, in the form of either a change in its composition or a change in the relative power of its components. The civil rights movement of the 1950s and 1960s is a good example. The class of Southern planters lost much of its regional power, along with its *de facto* veto over national racial policies, and the South became more open to penetration by the central economy. However, the structure of national economic power remained relatively unchanged; the major capitalist interests before the movement were still in place afterward. On the other side of the struggle, African Americans acquired basic political and economic rights, including the chance to compete for access to higher education and to professional white-collar work, but they nevertheless remained in an economically and politically subordinate position in American society.

Because of the triumph of capitalist ideology in the 1980s, threats to the basic interests of the power bloc are rare in contemporary American politics. Most of the political efforts of competitive capital, therefore, are devoted to what Lowi calls *regulatory* and *distributive* issues—efforts to change the rules of inter-industry competition or to win government subsidies, not to secure the preservation of capitalism. These are largely conflicts *within* the power bloc, rather than between classes; in fact, corporate participants in conflicts of this nature may well seek to ally themselves with sections of the working class from their own industry or firm.

Within this limited context, competitive-sector companies have used their resources to capture their own small (but important) corners of the state apparatus. It is here that the *subgovernment* phenomenon is found in its purest form. This term has been used to designate the use of state power to regulate and protect an industry in the interests of that industry, while insulating it from public political pressure. In its classic form, a subgovernment includes an executive bureau or independent regulatory commission, a congressional committee or subcommittee, and an organized interest group—all of which work out policy among themselves, then present a united front to the rest of the political world.[5] Such unity is necessary because this section of the capitalist class—unlike the hegemonic fraction—cannot assume that its interests will find general support.

Congressional committees and subcommittees constitute one corner of these subgovernments. Whereas such hegemonic committees as Appropriations, House Rules, and Senate Finance deal with matters that are central to the economy and polity, another group of committees is more narrowly focused. The House Interior Committee and the Senate Committee on Energy and National Resources, for example, are responsible for legislation affecting the operations of the Department of the Interior: national parks, Indian reservations, certain public lands, and the irrigation and dam-building activities of the Bureau of Reclamation. These matters are of some interest to citizens who visit (or might like to visit) national parks or are concerned about conservation. They are of intense interest to cattle raisers who lease grazing rights from the Bureau of Land Management, to Western farmers who need irrigation water to grow a crop, and to Western real estate interests that seek to develop federally held land with the promise of electric power from federally built dams.

Sometimes several interests share a committee. As of 1987, the House Committee on Energy and Commerce, one of the most complex in structure, had subcommittees on Commerce, Consumer Protection, and Competitiveness; Energy and Power; Health and the Environment; Telecommunications and Finance; and Transportation, Tourism, and Hazardous Material (as well as a subcommittee on Oversight and Investigations). The House Committee on Agriculture had subcommittees on Cotton, Rice, and Sugar; Livestock, Dairy, and Poultry; Tobacco and Peanuts; and Wheat, Soybeans, and Feed Grains (along with four others). The latter arrangement differed in detail but not in organizing principle from the situation studied by Charles O. Jones in 1958. In fact, Jones found a committee with eighteen subcommittees, ten of them based on one or more particular commodities, whereupon he made the following observation:

Committee organization has been strongly influenced by the commodity problems in agriculture. First, subcommittees are established to deal with currently critical commodity problems. Second, members are assigned to commodity subcommittees on the basis of their constituency interests. . . .

Party considerations dictate that some members must be on subcommittees of no concern to their constituencies. . . . For the most part, members who have little interest in the proceedings are expected either to remain silent during hearings or not to attend. (Jones 1969, 159-60)

Similarly, as Richard Fenno discovered:

Congressmen who ask for membership on the *Interior* and *Post Office* Committees have the primary goal of *helping their constituents and thereby insuring their re-election*. In place of talk about "power," "prestige," and "importance," one hears almost exclusively about "district interests" to be served, "projects" to be authorized, and "political help" to be gained. The close correspondence between the Interior Committee's jurisdiction and the most pressing constituency problems of Western congressmen make the Committee uniquely attractive to them. (Fenno 1973, 5; original emphasis)

The constituents being helped by members of the Post Office Committee are civil servants and union members; we shall examine this relationship in Chapter 4. But in the case of Interior they are the owners of competitive-sector businesses. As Fenno reports, "A northeastern Republican exclaimed, 'The biggest industry in my state is mining, so Interior is perfect' " (Fenno 1973, 6).

Competitive-sector firms are not the only players in the sub-government game. The giants are not above dealing themselves in when they see a chance to rake in a few chips. And the great banks concern themselves with the House and Senate Banking committees as well as with the Federal Reserve Board and the Treasury Department. The difference is that for competitive-sector industries, subgovernments are their *highest* level of political power.

The principle of member selection for these committees contrasts with that used for the hegemonic committees. In the latter case, as we have seen, the member's "responsible style," not his or her constituency interests, is most important. One component of such a style is a willingness to subordinate constituency interests to larger concerns, when necessary.[6] In contrast, members of nonhegemonic committees are expected to put constituency interests above everything else. A second difference grows out of this first one: The nonhegemonic committees are not as powerful. They rank lower on the scale of committee prestige, and they are less sure of the reception that their bills will find in the full House or Senate. Hegemonic committees present bills seen as responding to the national interest. And since there may be disagreement about what that interest is, their bills may face debate and (when permitted by the rules) floor amendment. Nonhegemonic committees, by contrast, present bills seen as serving the needs of a particular interest. If they are perceived as going too far, or if the sponsoring interest is itself in disagreement, they are more likely to be defeated outright. Regarding the House Interior Committee, Fenno observed that:

> the deeper problem involves allaying the suspicions of non-Western Members confronting the recommendations of a lopsidedly Western committee. Westerners are, after all, a tiny minority of the House; Committee Westerners do not sit there as the representatives of large state delegations on whom they can rely for floor support. Most important, the Committee's Westerners deal with the problem internally, by mollifying their non-Western Committee colleagues to the point where they will not foment an East-West controversy on the House floor. (Fenno 1973, 63)

Political Action Committees

Competitive-sector capital is, along with organized labor, at the heart of the activity of political action committees. Narrowly focused industry groups often form PACs to promote their ends. But because their narrow focus makes it harder for such groups to present themselves as the bearers of the public interest, they may rely more on contributions than do their more well-endowed cousins in the hegemonic fraction. Contributions from such PACs help to strengthen subgovernments.

Not all PACs are business oriented, of course. In fact, the PAC idea was invented by a labor union, the Congress of Industrial Organizations (CIO), which founded CIO-PAC in 1943 as a means of cumulating small contributions from its members, thus evading the Smith-Connally Act's prohibition of direct political contributions by labor organizations (Sabato 1984, 5-6). Business PACs began to grow in the 1960s, but that growth escalated in the 1970s after a series of federal campaign finance laws limited direct contributions by individuals to $1,000 per federal candidate per election and a total of $25,000 per contributor per year, while permitting unions, corporations, and other organizations to sponsor and pay the administrative expenses of PACs (Sabato 1984, 8). Barred from their old practices of channeling large individual contributions from their executives to candidates, businesses turned to PACs. Gary C. Jacobson (1992) found that in 1974, 89 corporate PACs contributed $2.5 million dollars to congressional candidates, while another 318 classifed by the Federal Election Commission as "trade/membership/health" (most of which are associations of profit or nonprofit corporations) contributed $2.3 million. The two together did not equal the contribution of the 201 labor PACs, which came to $6.3 million. But by 1988 there were 1,816 corporate

PACs, which contributed $50.5 million to congressional candidates, while 786 trade/membership/health PACs—financed by groups of businesses rather than by single corporations—contributed another $38.9 million. PACs from the financial industry alone gave $16.8 million to members of Congress for the 1990 election. Labor PACs also grew during this period, but they did not keep up with business; during the 1988 election cycle, 354 labor union PACs gave $33.9 million to candidates for Congress.[7]

There has been a great deal of discussion about whether PACs are undesirable, whether PAC contributions are really thinly disguised bribes, whether PAC activity changes the outcome of elections, and how much influence these contributions have on congressional policymaking. However, their greatest impact is simple and clear: They have lifted the cost of running for Congress beyond the reach of many candidates. The average House candidate in 1972 raised a little more than $50,000; Senate candidates that year averaged $350,000. Eighteen years later House candidates averaged almost $310,000, and Senate candidates more than $2,600,000 (Jacobson 1992, 65). The very availability of such sums generates a constant pressure on members of Congress and potential challengers to raise equivalent amounts, or risk being swamped by an opponent. For the members especially the easiest relief from this pressure is to develop strong relations with one or more well-heeled corporations or industries that can serve as a source of funds.

Debate over the legitimacy of PACs tends to focus on the issue of whether PAC contributions buy votes. This question was discussed extensively in 1984 at a conference organized by the Citizens' Research Foundation and attended by prominent politicians and lobbyists on both sides of the issue (Alexander and Haggerty 1984). Some see PAC money as a thinly disguised bribe, a contention that evidence suggests may often be the case. Mark Green relates some examples he has heard from members of Congress:

> Dan Glickman (Democratic congressman from Kansas) told me that when he lobbied a fellow Democrat to vote with him against the used car dealers—the Federal Trade Commission wanted to require [the dealers] to list known defects in cars and the National Automobile Dealers Association (NADA) didn't want to do that so they tried to get Congress to overrule the FTC—the Democrat said to Dan, "Sorry, I've gotten $5,000 from the NADA."
>
> Claudine Schneider, a Republican congresswoman from Rhode Island, said to a Republican colleague of hers, "I hope you'll join me in opposing the Clinch River breeder reactor. It's a waste of taxpayer dollars." . . . And her Republican colleague said to her, "Sorry, Claudine, I've gotten $5,000 from Westinghouse."
>
> What's amazing about this is not really that it occurs. How could it not? What's amazing is that these Members of Congress said it so routinely as not to be embarrassed. In other words they regarded it as part of the warp and woof of

the way politics is played out in the city of results. (Alexander and Haggerty 1984, 57)

Lester M. Salamon quotes a staff member of the House Banking, Finance, and Urban Affairs Committee who explains how PAC contributions can work more subtly:

> These guys come to Congress in their thirties as promising $20,000-$25,000-a-year attorneys and businesspeople, with high ideals and great enthusiasm. But after six or seven years they find themselves approaching middle age with decent incomes but no real security, while their former law partners back home are secure and prosperous. They need $50,000-$150,000 to cover campaign costs every two years, just to stay in office. Since bank funds are easy to get, since bank issues are complex and therefore easy to camouflage, and since these members are socially close to the middle-level business professional leadership of their communities in which local bankers play so crucial a role, support for banker positions on the committee comes to seem entirely natural. (Salamon 1975, 53; quoted in Domhoff 1983, 125)

These direct influences are important, but they do not tell the whole story. Consider the following statement made by Bernadette Budde, director of education for the Business-Industry Political Action Committee (founded in 1962 by the National Association of Manufacturers), at the 1984 conference. Budde was arguing for the benignity of PAC contributions, but her words have disturbing implications.

> PACs give to people because they like their voting record, or because they like the potential of what they think their voting record may be. I am always surprised when I see stories that "85 percent of the people who voted one way on an issue got 75 percent of the money." Well, it ought to be a hundred percent overlap if political action committees have done their research, which they do, and if candidates have been honest about what their stands are on the issues. . . . In my view you could eliminate all political action committees today and not have them exist until 1986, and those who got elected in 1984 would continue to vote pretty much the same way they have in 1982 and 1983, unless conditions changed and unless they were somehow changed in their attitudes toward the votes that they've cast. (Quoted in Alexander and Haggerty 1984, 63)

If Budde is correct (though Green's examples suggest that she is overstating her case), the honor of the individual members of Congress is restored; but in the larger sense it makes little difference whether business PACs get their way by buying votes or by buying elections for those they know will vote with them. Given the importance of money in elections, the impact on congressional policymaking is about the same either way.

Political science research on PACs has echoed the debate among activists, journalists, and the general public. Data on both PAC contributions and congressional voting are readily available in computerized form, providing the opportunity for ever more sophisticated mathematical models designed to test whether PAC contributions really do or do not influence the votes cast by members of Congress.[8] But however sophisticated the study, the results are never fully convincing; there is always another factor that might have changed them if it had been included. For example, Alan Neustadtl notes that labor PACs' contributions are more closely correlated with the recipients' voting record than are contributions from business PACs; but he points out that this finding does not mean that labor is more influential:

> If labor employs a strategy of identifying 'friends' of labor and rewarding them accordingly, the findings of this study reflect the 'built-in' influence of labor. . . . Labor, in other words, may follow a strategy of rewarding members rather than trying to influence their decisions.
>   Business, on the other hand, may be following a strategy of seeking "opportunity" to shift representatives at the margins of votes. (Neustadtl 1990, 558)

Neustadtl also argues that business may be better able than labor to shape the structure of votes before the fact. His study illustrates particularly well the futility of trying to measure PAC influence on voting by sophisticated mathematical means. It is not just that any results the researcher dislikes can be explained away, but also that so many of the rationalizations seem to be correct—roll call votes just aren't a very good reflection of the influence of social forces.

The mass of studies on this topic present a confused picture of PAC activity; but we can clear up some of the confusion by distinguishing among redistributive, regulatory, and distributive issues. For example, consider Lowi's prediction that business groups would line up together, against labor or other opposing groups, on redistributive issues. This prediction is borne out by the research of Alan Neustadtl, Dan Clawson, and Tie-ting Su, who used network analysis to identify a single large bloc of corporate PACs that made about half of the total corporate PAC contributions to congressional candidates in both 1980 and 1986. Bound together by conservative ideology, this bloc was less pragmatic—that is, less likely to give to members of Congress because of their powerful committee positions alone, and more likely to give to Republican candidates regardless of incumbency—than would be predicted by conventional wisdom (Neustadtl and Clawson 1988, 172-90; Clawson and Su 1990, 377-78).

Redistributive issues are defined in terms of class against class. On such issues, therefore, access is less important than loyalty, and there should be a strong connection between PAC contributions and the overall voting records of the recipients, as measured by broad ideological scales.

Since these issues are often settled by floor votes, committee membership is highly relevant.

However, given the political quiescence of the working class during the late 1980s and early 1990s,[9] much of Congress's time has been taken up by what Lowi calls regulatory issues—struggles among different components of the power bloc. As a result, corporate PACs have tended to line up against one another more often than not, and to frame issues on the basis of narrow interest rather than broad ideology. The hard-fought battle over cable television regulation in 1990 was a case in point; although it sometimes appeared to be an ideological conflict between partisans of the free market and of government regulation, much of Congress's attention was devoted to narrower questions.

Representative John Dingell (D-Mich.) opened the public debate with a ringing denunciation of the cable industry, telling the U.S. Conference of Mayors, "Since it was freed of regulatory constraints, the rapacious cable industry has ratcheted rates higher and higher. They are, in fact, a deregulated monopoly. Customer service is an oxymoron" (quoted in Mills 1990b, 2910). CablePAC, affiliated with the National Cable Television Association, responded by increasing its campaign contributions—mostly to incumbent members of Congress—to $491,426 for the 1990 election cycle, up from $338,992 during the 1988 cycle. Meanwhile, President George Bush was threatening to veto any bill that increased the amount of government regulation. A redistributive struggle for consumer protection seemed to be developing (Mills 1990b).

Bush's veto threat ultimately kept the bill from passing; but in the interim Congress paid little attention to the issue of regulation versus the free market.[10] If judged by the amount of interest that members of Congress showed in it, the real issue was a struggle for market share among three related industries: the established cable television companies; local telephone companies, which have the capacity to provide cable television service over their lines but are currently barred from doing so; and companies that offer television signals via newer technologies, such as direct satellite broadcast or "wireless cable," in competition with the cable companies. The bill could not go forward in the Senate until Senator Tim Wirth (D-Col.), "the cable industry's top congressional defender," reached a compromise with his colleague Al Gore (D-Tenn., as he was then), "an advocate of emerging communications industries, such as satellites and wireless cable, that compete with cable TV services" (Mills 1990a, 3506). Each industry segment veiled its economic interest behind a claim that it was defending fair competition in a free market, but in this case the veil was a very thin one.

The movement of the Clean Air Act Amendments through the House Committee on Energy and Commerce in 1989-1990 was another high point of PAC activity. A study by the staff of Congressional Quarterly found that committee members had received $611,945 in 1989—when the bill containing the amendments began to move through the committee—from PACs tied to industries with a stake in this issue. There were 110 of these PACs that gave at least $1,000 to a committee member (Alston 1990, 811-17).[11]

The biggest controversy involved a challenge to the oil and automobile industries—a requirement that auto companies make cars designed to use natural gas and other alternative fuels. In a display of hegemonic power, the natural gas companies themselves were persuaded to oppose this provision, which was removed by a 12 to 10 vote in the Subcommittee on Health and the Environment. Even so, contributions played a role; Congressional Quarterly found that the 12 subcommittee members who voted "yes" received an average of $6,021 from interested PACs, whereas those who voted "no" averaged only $2,755. In fact, 5 of those voting "no" received no contributions at all from these PACs (Alston 1990, 811-817). Incidentally, a requirement that some alternative fuel cars be built and sold was restored to the bill before final passage, but the final version applied only to cars sold in California (Congressional Quarterly 1991a, 243).

Some of the money was related to narrower interests. Of all committee members, Tom Tauke (R-Iowa) raised the most money from air pollution PACs—$50,800; but much of it came from a particular industry, namely construction and farm equipment manufacturers. Tauke had arranged to exclude off-road vehicles from the pollution controls in the bill (Alston 1990, 816).

PAC contributions help to cement relationships between business interests and members of Congress that may also involve lobbying activity (Humphries 1991, 364-68), electoral endorsement (Grenzke 1989, 14), and personal friendship (Alston 1991, 2317). Members come to identify with particular interests and to consider this identification to be legitimate; sometimes it is even a source of pride. The relationship of Senator Christopher J. Dodd (D-Conn.) to the insurance industry is a case in point. Many insurance companies' headquarters are in Hartford and other parts of Connecticut, and Dodd compares his support for the industry to "hogs in Iowa." More specifically, Dodd calls Paul A. Equale, lobbyist for the Independent Insurance Agents of America, the "head hog"; he had their picture taken together and autographed it as follows: "To my friend Paul—Warmest regards to the head 'hog.' They haven't butchered us yet and they never will. Best, Chris Dodd, U.S. Senate" (quoted in Alston 1991, 2314).

The Tax Reform Act of 1986

The appalling sums of money spent by corporate and other special-interest PACs in their attempts to influence legislation, and the equally appalling willingness of members of Congress to be influenced, make a mockery of American democracy. Nevertheless, we would be wrong to conclude that the country is simply run by PACs. No matter how much money they spend, corporate PACs sometimes lose. However, such losses are rarely if ever imposed by the democratic power of the general public; much more often they are brought about by the structural limits of the system—that is, by its built-in tendencies to protect the general interests of the capitalist class. Passage of the Tax Reform Act of 1986 provides an excellent example of how these limits work.

The basic idea of the Tax Reform Act was to cut the rates of personal and corporate income taxes without losing any revenue; this would be done by eliminating or reducing as many tax deductions and exemptions as possible. Put in this general way, the idea appealed to many. It would simplify the tax return, would make it harder for wealthy businesses and individuals to avoid taxes, and had an aura of fairness about it. However, that allure often evaporated when specific deductions came into question; few people wanted to eliminate those loopholes that they themselves used. Tax reform seemed almost an ideal example of an issue that pitted strong particularistic interests against a diffuse and weak public interest. For this reason, as Jeffrey Birnbaum and Alan Murray observed, "as appealing as the concept sounded . . . few in Washington thought it could be done" (Birnbaum and Murray 1987, 13). Many well-informed observers predicted at the time that the Tax Reform Act would fail (Witte 1985, 385-86; Davies 1986, chap. 14; King 1984, 29-30; Conable 1989, xii).

One reason for this pessimism was the amount and intensity of PAC and lobbying activity generated by the tax bill. The *Wall Street Journal* calculated that total PAC contributions to congressional candidates increased by 32 percent, from $50.7 million to $66.8 million, between the eighteen-month period ending in June 1984 and that ending in June 1986. Almost 1 million of these dollars went to one individual, Senator Robert Packwood (R-Ore.), chairman of the Senate Finance Committee. Other members of the tax-writing committees also did well. In the Senate, Robert Dole (R-Kan.) raised $839,319 from PACs; Steve Symms (R-Ida.), $870,560; and Charles Grassley (R-Iowa), $668,526. Dan Rostenkowski (D-Ill.), chairman of the House Ways and Means Committee, raised over $500,000, while among his colleagues Sam Gibbons (D-Fla.) received $317,096 from PACs; Henson Moore (R-La.), $333,620; James Jones (D-Okla.), $343,592; and Wyche Fowler (D-Ga.), $223,060 (Birnbaum and Murray 1987, 179-82).

So many lobbyists besieged the Senate Finance Committee during markup of the bill that they filled the hearing room and a large overflow auditorium, while the most powerful lobbyists of all stood for hours in the corridor outside the hearing room, their expensive tastes in clothing causing it to become known as "Gucci Gulch" (Birnbaum and Murray 1987, 4-5).

The vast majority of these lobbyists sought one goal: preservation of tax preferences for the corporation or industry they represented. Retention of these preferences would raise taxes for the general public; but the public had little conception of what was going on. Randall Strahan quotes one member of the House Ways and Means Committee whom he asked about the public interest in tax reform:

> You just didn't find any. There was no burning desire in this country for us to do this. It became an issue that took on a life of its own because of internal politics in Washington. . . . You got outside of Washington and nobody gave a tinker's damn [*sic*] about it. (Strahan 1990, 153)

Yet despite this seeming imbalance of forces, the Tax Reform Act passed. Over $500 billion in tax preferences (over a five-year period) were eliminated, and $120 billion shifted from individual taxpayers to corporations. Moreover, the individual cuts were progressive—for tax year 1988, individual cuts ranged from about 65 percent for those with annual incomes under $10,000, and 22 percent for those between $10,000 and $20,000, down to 1.2 percent for those earning between $75,000 and $100,000; the savings went up a bit for those earning more than $100,000 a year, but only to 2.4 percent (Strahan 1990, 141-42).

Why did special-interest PACs fail to block passage of the Tax Reform Act? Many reasons could be offered. My own view is that the act's passage was due to the existence of a broad consensus among policymakers that the major reforms would further the general interests of the American economy—that is, the interests of the capitalist class. Prominent tax experts, both conservative and liberal, had promoted the basic principle of *horizontal equity*—that equal incomes should be taxed equally, regardless of their source or what they were spent on—for decades; by the 1980s, this view had become accepted widely by members of the House Ways and Means Committee and Senate Finance Committee, and by the senior staff of the Treasury Department.[12] Donald Regan, the secretary of the Treasury, and Dan Rostenkowski, chair of the House Ways and Means Committee, each decided to pursue tax reform because each thought it would be politically advantageous to do so (Conlan, Wrightson, and Beam 1990, 49-52, 88-92); but once they had made their decisions, the content of the reform to be pursued was derived from the existing climate of expert opinion.

This view of the motivation for the Tax Reform Act is only conjecture at this point. What is clear is that, whatever the reformers' motivation may have been, the structure of congressional power served to help them fend off the PACs and lobbyists, however aggressive and well-financed they were. Chairman Rostenkowski of the House Ways and Means Committee, which had now come nearly full circle from its fragmented condition following the reforms of the 1970s (Strahan 1990, 143), wielded his extensive powers as chair to push the Tax Reform Act through the house. He used his personal control of the committee's staff as an intelligence network; excluded lobbyists, the press, and the public from meetings while the committee marked up the bill; and brought it to the floor of the House under an almost completely closed rule (Birnbaum and Murray 1987, 121-22, 162, 173). The outcome, as it happened, had been far from certain: The rule was defeated on the first try and passed on the second only after a personal visit by President Ronald Reagan to Capitol Hill (Birnbaum and Murray 1987, 169-70). In the end, however, the Ways and Means Committee worked just as it was meant to, overriding the strenuous efforts of individual industries and interest groups in order to promote the larger interests of the capitalist system—at least, as the committee saw them.

Matters were more complicated in the Senate, where the Finance Committee enjoys power and prestige similar to those of Ways and Means, but does not share the privileged positions given to the latter by the rules of procedure. Senate practice is for bills to be completely open to debate and amendment, with limits imposed only by unanimous consent; the floor debate on the Tax Reform Act lasted 106 hours, and sixty amendments were adopted before the Senate passed its version of the bill, 97 to 3, on June 24, 1986 (Conlan, Wrightson, and Beam 1990, 186). However, the decentralizing tendencies of the Senate proved to be relatively unimportant, as most of the changes were removed in the ensuing House-Senate conference. The single major exception serves to confirm the rule of hegemonic dominance: The oil and gas industry, always at the center of economic power in the United States, was able to retain many of its tax concessions (as did other mining industries and timber) even while most other industries were losing theirs (Conlan, Wrightson, and Beam 1990, 218).

This was not a triumph of democracy. There was a lot of public disgruntlement with taxes and the tax system, but little organized demand for tax reform. Moreover, although personal income taxes were cut for most people, and roughly $120 billion over five years shifted from individual to corporate taxpayers, this gain for the ordinary taxpayer was offset by increases in social security taxes.[13] Instead, what transpired here was a defeat of smaller industries, concerned with their parochial interests, by the large corporations, concerned with the health of American capitalism as a whole. This was hegemony at work.

Passage of the Tax Reform Act illustrates the limits on the power of the competitive business cycle, but that power is still considerable. The concern with PACs is well placed: Eliminating PACs would not be enough to make U.S. politics democratic, but leaving them in place is certainly enough to make that politics extremely corrupt. Such issues as the Tax Reform Act are rare; cable television regulation, an area in which corporate interests run amok, is far more typical. The spectacle of the lobbyists lining the halls of "Gucci Gulch" startled us because it was unusual; far more often, the same lobbyists are to be found in inner sancta and fashionable watering holes, wielding the instrument they use best—their clients' money.

In the pluralist schema, this last observation is not particularly alarming. Money does confer power on some interests, yet such power is counterbalanced by that of other interests with less money but more votes. The resultant of these opposing forces is considered by pluralists to be the best available approximation of the public interest. Unfortunately, the schema works only if the working class and other oppressed groups are able to mobilize real power. As we shall see in Part Two this is far from true.

PART TWO

Congress and the Rest of Us

Thus far we have looked at the rich and powerful elements of American society. Not surprisingly, we have seen that their power exerts itself in Congress; but this is only half the story. Pluralists might grant most of the points I have made so far but insist that I am missing the main point, for the pluralist claim is that the political power of monopoly and competitive corporations is counterbalanced by the power—also great—of other interests, such as labor unions, consumers, environmentalists, women, and minority racial and ethnic groups. Let us shift our gaze, then, from the corporate boardrooms to the workshops, the ghettos, the kitchens, and the laundries. In the remainder of this book, we shall look at three groups—the working class, African Americans, and women—that have not been part of the power bloc. These groups, too, are represented in Congress, but they are not represented in the same way.

As Marxists see it, those on the bottom of the social order do not just happen to have less of everything—money, power, health, education—than those on top. They *support* those on top through their labor (paid or unpaid) and are kept in a subordinated position by the social, political, and ideological institutions of society. I will not try to prove the economic side of this proposition here (that would require another book[1]) but I will try in the next three chapters to show how its political side is reflected in the operations of Congress.

These groups, though excluded from real power, are included in political life. However, they are included in a way that limits their goals while keeping their power to achieve even those limited goals to a minimum. In essence, they are asked to support the existing system in return for the right to participate ineffectively. Of course, such a bargain would not be made if it were put in those terms. One of my purposes here is to penetrate the illusions that so often weaken the political action of subordinate groups. Let us begin with a brief look at American constitutional history.

The framers of the U.S. Constitution expected Congress to help unite the new nation by giving peripheral interests representation in the political center. They voiced this expectation in *The Federalist*; and it has been reflected frequently in American legislative studies since that time (Hamilton, Madison, and Jay [1791] 1961).[2]

However, the framers seem to have been thinking mostly about interests based in the several states, and to have imagined that, once the smaller states had been protected by equal representation in the Senate, these interests would be united on a basis of approximate equality. Certain other interests were excluded from the Constitution and from the political community—women, African Americans, and Native Americans more or less explicitly so. The working class was excluded as well, by the property ownership requirements for voting found in each state.

These exclusions were not accidental. When Abigail Adams wrote to her husband, John, to ask that he "remember the ladies" in designing the new independent government, he replied, "I cannot but laugh."[3] Free black leaders such as Prince Hall pointed out the plain contradiction between the Declaration of Independence and the continuing existence of slavery, but found little positive response.[4] Freed slaves, and even African Americans who had been born free, were usually not accorded political rights. Paul and John Cuffe, free black property owners from Massachusetts, struggled unsuccessfully from 1778 to 1781 to win either the right to vote or exemption from poll and property taxes, giving up only after they were jailed for tax delinquency on December 19, 1780 (Harris 1972, 33-37; Thomas 1986, 7-12).[5] Most European American political thinkers shared Jefferson's view that the the white and black populations could never be combined into one people, for this reason:

> Deep rooted prejudices entertained by the whites; ten thousand recollections, by the blacks, of the injuries they have sustained; new provocations; the real distinctions which nature has made; and many other circumstances, will divide us into parties, and produce convulsions which will probably never end but in the extermination of the one or the other race. (Jefferson [1785] 1972, 138)[6]

Jefferson also believed that wage laborers would vote the interests of their employers, on whom they would depend economically; he thought that America ought to avoid the growth of manufacturing in order to avert this threat to democracy (Jefferson [1785] 1972, 165).

The struggle to apply the Declaration's principles universally is an ongoing theme in the subsequent political history of the United States. Prince Hall's allusion to that document was echoed by the campaigners for universal white male suffrage in the early nineteenth century, and by the Seneca Falls Declaration of the rights of women in 1848.[7] Eventually, most of the excluded groups were included, at first in the franchise and finally in Congress as well. But this was not necessarily inclusion as equals. As Poulantzas pointed out, the dominated can be brought into state structures *as* the dominated, present but still subordinate, participating in and reinforcing their subordination by their presence (Poulantzas [1975] 1978b, 190-91, 285-86).

But workers, African Americans, women, and other previously excluded groups have discovered repeatedly that their representatives are not just like all other members of Congress. Instead, they are on the losing end of all the structural biases described in Chapter 1. They have had to struggle, not always successfully, to gain *any* legislative attention for their concerns. When such struggle has netted them some influence within a committee, that committee has turned out to lack jurisdiction over the most crucial issues, and to have difficulty winning on the floor. When they have won majority support, they have found their way blocked by the filibuster and other obstructionist features of the rules—and have seldom been able to use such features themselves. When they have passed a law, they have found that passage was only the beginning of the struggle to make the bureaucracy implement it and the courts uphold it. Finally, they have discovered, usually too late, that whatever positions they have won within the structure of Congress have been built on a foundation of sand, subject to constant erosion by the steady waves of the capitalist economy.

These structural features constitute the terrain on which social struggles in Congress have been waged; but the outcome of such struggles has not been predetermined. Political leaders of subordinate groups have had to make important strategic choices. Should they seek to get their own members into Congress? Or should the groups use other methods to attain their goals? If they choose to use other methods, they might still seek to influence Congress through lobbying, campaign contributions, and mobilizing the votes of their members. A variety of less conventional methods has been available as well. These methods include militant direct action, peaceful demonstrations, and economic self-development. Groups that have gotten their members into Congress face further choices. In particular, they could seek to assimilate into the structures of power, using their positions to get concrete benefits for their constituents; or they could use their positions, and the visibility those gave them, to protest against the injustices of the system and rally their supporters for political confrontation. I refer to these henceforth as the strategies of *accommodation* and *protest*.

In her studies of the contemporary Congressional Black Caucus, Marguerite Ross Barnett describes two stages in the caucus's early political history, which she calls *ethnic* and *collective* (Barnett 1975, 1977). She observes that the caucus has oscillated between the two stages, arguing that this happens because neither strategy is adequate for dealing with the problems of African Americans. She concludes by describing a "double bind" faced by African American politicians. Efforts to win reforms piecemeal "cannot be effective in the long run without transformation of the underlying structural factors that differentiate and subordinate blacks. However, attempts to make structural change through legislation must win support from a whole panoply of groups with a vested interest in the status quo," and so may lead to excessive dilution of the original goals (Barnett 1977, 26).

Similarly, James Jennings speaks of the *traditional* and *progressive* "faces" of African American urban political leadership in the 1970s.

> Black electoral efforts under the traditional framework basically seeks [*sic*] access into the structures of wealth and power; these attempts, successful in some cases, historically allowed black officials to call upon white power brokers for favors, or concessions to the black community. Thus, some blacks were elected because they appealed to voters not as political leaders but rather as managers of patronage or as developers of cooperative partnerships with the corporate sector.
>
> Unlike traditional black politics, the new progressive electoral activism in the black community is not necessarily focusing on access, or patronage. Progressive electoral activism seeks to assault the city halls of America, not for the relatively few jobs that might be available by attracting downtown developers, but . . . to implement public policies which would have meaningful impacts on issues such as black unemployment, education, and the quality of life. (Jennings 1983-84, 36; 1984, 204)

Barnett and Jennings were thinking specifically of African Americans. But since the choices faced by African Americans are also faced by other subordinate groups in Congress, the two strategies can be considered more generally as the principal strategic choices available to oppressed social groups that find themselves formally present in the institutions of political power but effectively excluded from real power. Hence, I have given the two strategies the more general names of accommodation and protest.

Putting all this together, I think that Marxist theory recognizes four possible ways in which such groups can relate to Congress:

1. They can struggle to change a policy or law without changing the structure of the state. Gains won in this way are likely to be highly ephemeral at best, and at worst purely symbolic. Such a struggle is neither protest nor accommodation, but consists of humble petitioning.
2. They can engage in waves of protest leading to political change together with policy change. This struggle may involve the creation of new committees or bureaucratic agencies, or changes

in the rules under which they operate. These changes can bring real shifts in political power, as did the congressional reforms of 1910 or those of the 1970s. However, if the economic structure remains unchanged, it will exert increasing pressure either to destroy the new structures or to transform what once were tools for reform into props of the status quo.

3. After the waves of protest have subsided, subordinate groups can leave politicians who come from these groups, or who see themselves as representing their interests, in possession of strongholds within the state. The politicians can then use these positions to seek to promote and defend the interests of the groups they represent. However, in the absence of outside insurgency, such efforts are likely either to fail utterly or to turn into attempts to promote the narrow interests of a privileged stratum within the oppressed group—a "labor aristocracy," a "black bourgeoisie," or the patronage network of a political machine.

4. Occasionally, such strongholds may be used instead in efforts to arouse, energize, and focus broader struggles by the represented group, or by a broader coalition of have-nots, to transform the social, not merely the political, order.

Efforts of this last sort will face many obstacles, including control by the dominant social forces of the channels of communication and conflict with the established habits of popular thinking. Nevertheless, such efforts represent the most promising alternative, because they are the only ones that can lead to success. No subordinate social group can attain real integration into the political system unless that group also succeeds in changing the economic structure of society to overcome its economic powerlessness. Therefore, such change should be the long-term goal of the day-to-day political struggle. As insurgent groups near that goal, they can expect to find that they are fighting their way up an ever steeper slope; among other things, their partial victories start to interfere with capitalist profits. There are lulls in the fighting and ledges to rest on along the way, but these cannot be taken for granted. As long as the capitalist economy lasts, it will continue to undermine their positions until they find themselves sliding back downhill against their will.

The only hope of real change, then—if Marxist theory is correct—is a much bigger change in the economic and political structures together. This latter change, in turn, will have to be based on a change in people's *ideology*—their ideas about what is just and how things should work. Without a new understanding, people will not be prepared to press ahead in the face of the very real costs of dislocating the capitalist economy. The fundamental weakness of the accommodationist strategy is that it does not promote such ideological change. The protest strategy can do so—but only if those trying to use it have the strength and resources to overcome the bias of the major channels of communication. Change will not come easily.

Historically, most Marxists have held that such basic change could come only through a revolution—through a more-or-less violent struggle that would destroy the capitalist state from the outside and go on to restructure the economy and build a new socialist state. The record of such revolutions has been dismal. With few exceptions (and even those are debatable) they have led to repressive, authoritarian political systems that have proved incapable of building a real socialist economy. Moreover, the collapse of the USSR and its satellites suggests that such states cannot even be reformed into democratic socialist systems, but are fated to return to the misery of unfettered market relations. Aside from these negative examples, revolution of this type seems both unlikely and unnecessary in a country with democratic political institutions.

What I am suggesting instead is that political leaders of subordinate groups could build on the model of the civil rights movement, the women's movement, and the industrial union movement—with mass mobilization and struggle *linked* to action inside the political structure—to bring about systemic change. I shall return to this idea in the last chapter after first taking a closer look at the representation in Congress of the working class, women, and African Americans.

4

Congress and the Labor Movement

What is the working class? This concept plays a vital role in Marxist theory but has almost vanished from American political discourse. Today few Americans still accept the myth that America is a classless society, but a new myth has replaced it: the myth of the middle class. This class is often thought to include almost everyone, with the rest of society consisting of the rich (hardly anyone, and not very different from the middle class anyway), and the poor (numerous, invisible, exotic, and living on welfare).[1] As we have seen,[2] this way of thinking blurs the political picture and obscures the realities of capitalist power. It also hides the true situation of the working class, which is not just lower on the societal pyramid but actually supports the upper levels with its exploited labor.

For Marxists, again, a class is defined by its members' common relationship to the means of production. Workers are those who neither own nor control any productive resources except their own labor. Since labor cannot produce anything by itself, workers, in order to survive, must sell their labor power to capitalists—those who have land, tools, and/or raw materials, but need labor in order to make use of them. Since the capitalists control this process, workers do not always succeed in making a sale. Upon failing, they must scrape by on unemployment compensation, welfare, or whatever else they can find; and in the Marxist view, one purpose of such government aid is to maintain a pool of unemployed workers as a way of keeping wages down (Piven and Cloward 1971). Working class membership is determined not by the issue of whether an individual has a job at any particular moment, but by that individual's dependency on the sale of labor power as his or her sole economic resource. By this standard, then, many of those commonly thought of as "the poor" or "the underclass" are workers.

Many—but not all—belonging to what we call the "middle class" are also workers. Remember, it is the source of income, not its amount, that determines class membership. Relatively well-paid workers in construction, transportation, and manufacturing are often considered middle class, but they live by the sale of their labor power (which is exploited by their employers) just as migrant apple pickers or dishwashers do. Despite all the divisions and contradictions among workers, they share certain common interests that are fundamentally different from those of the owner of even the smallest business. Marxism's claim is that these common interests are ultimately more important than the divisions. As might be expected, this issue has generated huge arguments, particularly with regard to race and gender. Many theorists, including Marx and Engels themselves, have maintained that class is a more basic division than race or gender (Engels [1942] 1972), while others have claimed that either gender (Firestone 1970) or race (Robinson 1983) is more basic. Today, most theorists would agree that class, gender, and race are all important dimensions of oppression, and that none of these categories can be collapsed into the others. What the three categories have in common, I would argue, is that each is defined by a particular relation to the social division of labor. We have already seen how this is true of *class*. Its application to *gender* and *race* will be considered, respectively, in Chapters 5 and 6. In each case, I have chosen to call my approach "Marxist" because I see the ideological and political aspects of class, gender, and race as rooted in this material basis. This chapter will consider the congressional representation of the working class as a class, whereas Chapters 5 and 6 will take up the representation of women and—as the major example of an oppressed race in the United States—of African Americans.

The first problem we face in looking at working-class representation in Congress—and in American politics in general—is that such representation takes no organizational form. There is no working-class political party in the United States. The Democrats, who come closest to being one, nevertheless are dominated by the capitalist elements within the party coalition. In recent years Democratic leaders have labeled the working class a "special interest" and expressly sought to avoid close identification with its cause (Ferguson 1983; Ferguson and Rogers 1986). The absence of a working-class party is not a shortcoming of Marxist theory, but a facet of the political weakness of the American working class; still, it does make our job here harder.

Of course, there are the labor unions. Unions do represent workers as workers and on some occasions try to speak for the class as a whole. Unfortunately, their ranks do not include a large portion of the working class, however defined, and the portion that does belong is not representative of the rest—it is significantly better off, perhaps as a consequence of its union membership. Therefore, we need to widen our focus beyond the unions; but they are a good place to begin. Even if labor unions dominated American politics, there would be many unrepresented working people. In fact, as we shall soon see, even the more privileged and better organized members of the AFL-CIO are marginal to the political system.

Unions in Politics

Pluralist theory sees organized labor—*big labor*—as the necessary counterweight to *big business*. Labor unions' lobbying, endorsements, contributions, and campaigning—what Nicholas Masters has called their "sheer muscle" (Masters 1962, 258)—keep the pluralist balance from tilting too far to the other side, it is argued. Institutionalists, by contrast, are more likely to see the unions as a corrupting force, a "special interest" that—again, like business—pressures politicians to ignore the more diffuse interests of the general public (Mezey 1989, 128). Both schools of political theorists agree that organized labor is a major force in American politics.

Marxists see the issue of working-class power in a more complex way. On the one hand, the hope of socialism is rooted in the belief that the working class is strong—strong enough to prevail, by either revolutionary or democratic means, over the capitalists. On the other hand, such a victory would involve basic changes in the structure of society; without such a restructuring, the theory holds, the working class is weak. Working-class political actors must play a game in which their opponents always hold the best cards, and in which their possible winnings are strictly limited in any case.

The picture of politically powerful unions is plausible if we look only at the quantity of labor's political activity. As pointed out in Chapter 3, PACs were invented by the unions; 354 labor PACs gave $33 million to congressional candidates in the 1988 election cycle. This was only about half of the amount given by business-related PACs (including both corporate and trade/membership/health PACs), but labor's influence goes beyond money. Union members vote, and since workers necessarily outnumber management, this resource ought to tip the scales back toward labor. It might be reasonable, then, for us to expect labor to be one of the most powerful political forces in America, able to hold its own against corporate interests as it works to improve the lives of the working class.

However, a different picture emerges if we look at the concrete results of labor activity. Business—especially big business—influences policy across a broad range of issues, and, as we saw in Chapters 2 and 3, wins far more often than can be explained by its use of political resources. Labor, however, focuses its efforts narrowly on a few issues of particular interest to it; and even then it often loses. For although labor may sometimes field a strong political team, it plays the game in a stadium built by its opponents, the corporate capitalists, and according to rules which those opponents wrote. I refer here to the capitalist economy, and the economic law that high profits must be maintained.

Sometimes labor has managed to change the rules in its favor, to secure a little piece of the congressional or bureaucratic structure for itself. On those occasions its leaders have turned to accommodationism; in the belief that they have arrived as holders of power, they have felt that they could proceed to play the game of pluralist bargaining just like everyone else, expecting to win continued gradual improvements in workers' lives. But they have proved to be mistaken; even these small gains have been fiercely assaulted by organized capital, and have eventually succumbed to that assault. This is the difference between the positions of *hegemonic* and *dominated* social forces.

For example, consider the union record during the Carter administration, the last time before 1993 that the supposedly prolabor Democratic Party controlled all the branches of the federal government. The unions had campaigned hard for the Carter-Mondale ticket and planned to take advantage of its victory. Labor's main goal was to reform the National Labor Relations Act (NLRA). Employers had developed a variety of ways to delay and impede the process by which workers could seek recognition; often, by the time a union-recognition election was held at a company, many of the workers who had petitioned for it were no longer employed there. The AFL-CIO had a labor law reform bill prepared to deal with this problem; but first they took up what they thought would be an easier task, adoption of the Common Situs Picketing Act.

This horribly named proposal would have allowed striking workers on a construction project to picket the whole site, thereby closing it down. Under existing law, employees of a particular contractor could picket only their own employer, not the other companies working on the same site—even though all workers on the site had the same ultimate employer. The issue was arcane and confusing but of great interest to the building trades, the strongest force within the AFL-CIO. Besides, it looked like an easy victory; the bill had been passed in the previous Congress but was then vetoed by the Republican president, Gerald Ford, so it just had to be passed again and sent to the more supportive Carter for his signature.

However, much to their surprise, the union forces were routed during the first skirmish; the bill was defeated on the floor of the House of Representatives, 205 to 217, on March 23, 1977, and never saw the light of day again. Among those voting "nay" were thirteen freshmen who had been supported by the Committee on Political Education (COPE), the AFL-CIO's PAC. These thirteen—and others—had succumbed to an intensive lobbying campaign conducted by the National Action Committee on Secondary Boycotts, an umbrella group including the Associated General Contractors, the Business Roundtable, the National Federation of

Independent Business, the Chamber of Commerce, and other business groups, which had mobilized their members across the country to write, telephone, and pay personal visits to their newly elected members of Congress to ask them to vote against the bill (Congressional Quarterly 1981, 402-03).

There was much second-guessing after this defeat, and many circumstantial explanations were offered for it. Labor had been caught off guard, had been too optimistic in counting its votes, had not started soon enough or worked hard enough in its lobbying campaign, and had chosen an issue on which it was vulnerable to the charge that it was a special interest. Each of these explanations had some merit, but there was more to the total picture. As would be proven over time, labor's defeat on Common Situs Picketing was not an unfortunate accident but a portent of things to come. The extent of labor's weakness in Congress revealed itself more clearly the next year, when the AFL-CIO lost a battle it had counted on winning—namely, the proposed Labor Law Reform Act of 1978, intended to ease the process of winning recognition as a bargaining agent.

Prior to 1935, labor unions had little legal status, and were often treated by the state as semicriminal conspiracies. In response to the sit-down strikes and other struggles of the 1930s, Congress in that year passed the National Labor Relations Act, also known as the Wagner Act, after its sponsor, Senator Robert Wagner (D-N.Y.) (Aronowitz 1973, 237-40). This act created a procedure whereby workers at a company could ask for a federally administered certification election; a union that wins such an election is certified as the bargaining agent for those workers, and the company is then required to negotiate with it in good faith about wages and working conditions.[3] Once regarded as a federal endorsement of organized labor, the Wagner Act possessed several pro-union features, but these had been whittled away over the years. Concurrently, the Taft-Hartley Act of 1947 and the Landrum-Griffin Act of 1959 had put more limits on what unions could do and placed them more firmly under the oversight of federal regulators. The AFL-CIO had tried but failed to repeal these laws on several occasions.

Then, during the 1970s, a number of professional union-busting firms sprang up. These companies, which could be hired by employers who wanted to defeat unions in certification elections, found ways to exploit weaknesses in the Wagner Act. In particular, they learned how to delay certification elections far beyond the fifteen-to-thirty-day period (after the filing of petitions) called for by law. Often many of the workers who had signed petitions would have left the company by the time an election was held. A second tactic was simply to break the law, by firing pro-union workers, banning union literature from the workplace, and so on. Eventually, employers who did so would be fined, but the penalties were relatively light when compared with the perceived costs of granting better wages and working conditions to unionized workers (Knight 1979; Hook 1982).

The Labor Law Reform Act of 1978 was intended to prevent tactics of this sort. As drafted by the AFL-CIO, it would have sped up NLRB elections and greatly increased the penalties for employer violations of the Wagner Act; such penalties would have included awards of double back pay to any workers fired illegally for union activity. The Labor Law Reform Act would also have prohibited the awarding of government contracts to companies which were "flagrant labor law violators."

AFL-CIO leaders had entered the Carter period confident of winning this and other legislative victories. Shocked by the loss of Common Situs Picketing, they had concentrated much more seriously on the battle for Labor Law Reform; but the results were ultimately no better. Although the bill won easily in the House (passing 257 to 163 on October 6, 1977), that was as far as it got. Its sponsors were unable to overcome a five-week filibuster led by Republican senators Orrin G. Hatch of Utah and Richard G. Lugar of Indiana.

The bill had stimulated even stronger business opposition than its narrower predecessor. On the one hand, traditionally anti-union associations of competitive-sector capitalists, such as the National Association of Manufacturers, the Chamber of Commerce, and the National Federation of Independent Business, had improved their organization and increased their numbers throughout the 1970s. For example, the Chamber of Commerce had formed 2,300 "Congressional Action Committees" through its local affiliates and had developed an "Action Call" mailing list of 7 million names (Ferguson and Rogers 1979, 19). On the other hand, the multinational corporations, many of which had shown a willingness to live with unions since the days of the National Civic Federation but were feeling the pinch of heightened international competition,[4] decided to join the battle against the unions. After some internal debate the Policy Committee of the Business Roundtable, which during the 1970s had become the broadest lobbying grouping of the largest corporations, voted 19 to 11 to oppose the Labor Law Reform bill in August 1977. Even firms that had voted to stay neutral, such as General Electric, then joined the lobbying campaign against the bill (Ferguson and Rogers 1979, 19-20).

While big and small business was mobilizing, President Carter held back from the struggle. Carter revealed his own priorities when he asked the Senate to defer the Labor Law Reform bill until after it had debated the ratification of the controversial Panama Canal treaties. He insisted from the outset that the bill not include repeal of Section 14-B of the Taft-Hartley Act,[5] but otherwise left most lobbying for the bill to Vice President Walter

Mondale and Secretary of Labor Ray Marshall, neither of whom had Carter's ability (displayed strongly in the case of the Panama treaties) to sway Southern Democratic senators. Although Carter did join the effort at the last moment, it was not enough (Ferguson and Rogers 1979, 18-20). In six attempts the bill's sponsors were not able to get more than 58 of the 60 votes required for cloture; after the sixth failure, on June 14, 1978, the bill was taken off the floor for more negotiation.

The AFL-CIO leaders now found themselves in disagreement with their allies in the Senate: The AFL-CIO wanted to weaken the bill just enough to pick up the two additional votes needed for cloture, whereas the senators "argued that the only hope for the bill was a consensus proposal that would be acceptable to almost all senators"—and would therefore, of course, not meet labor's objectives. Faced with this impasse, AFL-CIO president George Meany declared the bill "dead for the 95th Congress" (Congressional Quarterly 1981, 419).

These two defeats demonstrate labor's general weakness, but a few features of that weakness deserve special mention. First, it is worth repeating that each of the defeats came during a Democratic presidency with Democratic majorities in both houses of Congress. Given the AFL-CIO's long-time support of the Democratic Party, its leaders expected to do much better than they did. The loss of the Common Situs Picketing and Labor Law Reform bills exposed what Thomas Ferguson and Joel Rogers call "the decay of [labor's] position inside the American party system," and specifically within the Democratic Party. As they put it, "The hegemonic element in President Carter's victorious coalition of 1976 was the free-trade oriented Trilateral Commission, not the ever more proctectionist A.F.L.-C.I.O"(Ferguson and Rogers 1979, 17-18). A decade later, almost all the national figures in the Democratic Party were anxious to show that they were not beholden to labor as a "special interest."

The role of the multinational corporations also deserves attention. Few if any corporations have ever been solidly in favor of unions; but over the years many scholars have argued that the giant firms had come to accept unionization as inevitable, and that their market power, carrying with it the ability to control prices, could even make the relatively higher labor costs brought by unions preferable to the disruption of a less regulated workforce (Galbraith[1956]1980, 1985; Gordon, Edwards, and Reich 1982). If this had been true at one time, it was becoming less true by the mid-1970s, when even the largest corporations found themselves forced to compete in the world market and therefore faced the same cost-cutting imperatives that their competitive-sector brethren had always experienced.

Labor did not give up after its defeats on these two bills. Before the Carter administration ended, the unions mounted yet another major lobbying campaign, and this time they won. This time, however, the issue was a bit different—it concerned a bill to provide federal loan guarantees to the Chrysler Corporation, which threatened otherwise to go bankrupt and close down, thus directly eliminating the jobs of 124,000 UAW members and indirectly threatening those of up to 200,000 more workers in the steel, rubber, and other related industries.[6]

After six months of debate, including unfriendly hearings before the Senate Banking Committee, the bill signed into law by President Carter on December 20, 1979, provided for a federal loan guarantee to Chrysler of $1.5 billion, on the condition that UAW members employed at Chrysler reduce their wages and benefits by $462.5 million.[7] In bargaining earlier that year, the UAW had already agreed to accept a less favorable contract from Chrysler (although one still providing for a pay increase) than from Ford and General Motors, providing a savings of $203 million to the company.[8]

Labor's greatest victory under Carter, then—one for which the unions waged a pitched battle—came in a fight to preserve the investment of a group of capitalists, the Chrysler shareholders, while lowering the income of union members, all in order to win the right for those workers to continue producing surplus value for Chrysler.[9] It would be hard to imagine a more graphic illustration of the strategic political weakness of labor in a capitalist economy.

There have been times when labor political victories were larger and more common. During the 1930s workers won government support for the right to organize unions and helped force the establishment of the basic social insurance programs incorporated in the Social Security Act. During the 1960s urban workers, most of whom were not unionized and many of them African American and Latino, won major increases in government anti-poverty programs and new tools to use against discrimination. Significantly, these victories came about during times of major social unrest, marked by sit-down strikes, massive demonstrations, and riots. Under these conditions the working class was able to win representation within the structures of *political* power, but never to overcome its *economic* oppression, since the latter is one of the defining characteristics of capitalism. As a result, even labor's political victories have rested on a foundation of sand, and have been undermined gradually during times of greater social stability—most recently during the conservative 1980s.

Working people in the United States are politically weaker today than they have been at any time in the last sixty years. Superficially, this weakness can be attributed to the decline in union membership, the abysmally low rates of voter turnout among workers, and the conservative ideological success of Ronald Reagan and his followers. The narrow-minded business unionism of many union leaders also bears some of the blame. But the basic cause of labor's weakness is the structure of the modern capitalist world economy and the failure of labor to challenge that structure.

Unions are not simply an interest group like the others. Their differentness is rooted in the structure of capitalism. I can illustrate with a simple comparison. When over-the-air broadcasters battle cable companies over television regulations (see Chapter 3), hundreds of millions of dollars are at stake; but there is no fundamental conflict between the two interests. If, for example, NBC were to decide that it could no longer survive as a broadcast network, it would have other choices. It could invest in cable technology itself, merge with a cable company, or even go into a completely different line of business. The essence of the corporation, its capital as an abstract exchange value, could be preserved. But whereas capital can exchange one concrete incarnation for another, capitalists as a class will never become workers; or rather, if they do the capitalist system will cease to exist. There are no conditions under which capitalist firms will not gain by lowering wages, cutting benefits, worsening working conditions, and generally undercutting the gains that unions win for their members. In addition, the more unions win, the more profits will suffer—and the more capitalists will feel the need to strike back. Just at the point when one side in an interindustry conflict might be ready to give up the fight, struggles between capital and labor are intensified.

Throughout the twentieth century the leaders of the American labor movement have striven to secure its proper place in the political establishment. Time and again they have thought they had arrived, only to learn from events that labor is not just an interest group like the others but, rather, that its position in the political structure continues to be undermined by its economic situation. In the early 1900s the AFL fought to change the letter of the laws that treated unions as illegal combinations in restraint of trade. The AFL succeeded when the Clayton Antitrust Act was passed, but it soon learned that the letter of the law made little difference as long as the judges remained hostile; the formal advantage in the laws depended on a position in the state apparatus that labor did not hold. Next, the massive strike waves of the 1930s led to passage of the Wagner Act; this act not only changed the law again but gave labor its own agency, the National Labor Relations Board (NLRB), to administer the new law. However, a decade later Congress passed the Taft-Hartley Act, seriously weakening the new law; and a few years after that, Dwight Eisenhower was elected president and began to appoint anti-union members of the NLRB. The unions now saw that their position in the state apparatus depended on their strength in electoral politics; the AFL and CIO merged, formed the Committee on Political Education (COPE), and became a mainstay of the Democratic Party (Draper 1989). In return, the unions won control of their own congressional committees and became so tied to the party's conservative establishment that they opposed the radical challenge posed by the McGovern movement in 1972. Unfortunately, their new structural strength has proved chimerical once again. Their attempt to reverse the erosion of the NLRA in the 1970s failed, and their strength has continued to decline to the present.

The leadership of organized labor has followed this accommodationist strategy throughout the century. From time to time dissenting voices have been raised within the ranks; but even while the conservatives were losing most of their battles within the political structure, they were always just successful enough to gain the upper hand over their rivals in the working class. In the early 1900s the Industrial Workers of the World competed with the AFL, while socialists bored from within; but the AFL's successes, however limited, in passing the labor provisions of the Clayton Act, electing labor representatives to Congress, and placing William B. Wilson of the United Mine Workers in President Woodrow Wilson's cabinet as the first secretary of labor helped it to win the ideological combat within the working class. Even more important, its participation in the state allowed it to support its own organizational interests while repressing its rivals. As David Montgomery has noted, "The consistent theme guiding [William B.] Wilson's work was that employers should be encouraged to negotiate with legitimate unions and to shun the IWW and other groups deemed 'outlaw' by the AFL." In the 1930s the Communist Party joined with John L. Lewis to organize the CIO in the hopes of building a broader revolutionary movement based in the industrial unions; but the very success of the movement in securing state recognition gave the conservatives a lever with which to pry the Communists out of the unions after the passage of the Taft-Hartley Act (which, among other things, provided that unions could not be certified as bargaining agents if they had Communists among their officers).

Moreover, whereas labor as a whole had trouble maintaining its position, its more privileged stratum was able to do better. The Davis-Bacon Act, which requires that union wages be paid on government-aided construction, made the AFL building trades directly dependent on state action for their continued ability to deliver high wages to their members. Accordingly, the construction unions had both a more immediate need for political influence and more resources with which to pursue it, with the result that they came to dominate the AFL-CIO's lobbying efforts (Greenstone [1969] 1977, 334-35; Draper 1989, 65, 101-02). The later spread of unionization among government employees created a similar situation, since these unions' wage gains could be won by direct political action. More recently it has become clearer that even this labor aristocracy does not have a secure political position; indeed it has become less able to defend its narrow interests precisely to the extent that it has isolated itself from the rest of the working class. Let us now give some of this history a closer look.

The Fight for Trade Union Legality

Trade unions have existed almost as long as the United States has but they have always had to struggle for acceptance of that existence. At the start of the twentieth century, unions were still in the condition that Michael Goldfield calls "trade union illegality":

> Through much of the nineteenth century, membership in trade unions and participation in strikes were often grounds for being charged with criminal conspiracy. Trade unions had only semilegal existence. Thus Chicago labor leaders were convicted and hanged after the Haymarket affair of 1886. Eugene Debs's American Railway Union was bloodily suppressed in 1894. Labor leaders were tried for conspiracy and sedition during World War I. And striking steelworkers at Republic Steel became victims of the Chicago police in the Memorial Day Massacre of 1937, almost two years after the passage of the National Labor Relations Act. (Goldfield 1987, 66-67)

With unions seen as criminal, employers could raise their own goon squads and security forces and attack them with impunity and could call on private mercenary police forces from such agencies as the Pinkertons for help in doing so (Boyer and Morais [1955] 1970; Goldstein 1978; McGovern and Guttridge 1972).

As corporations got bigger, the legal status of unions got worse. The Sherman Antitrust Act of 1890 did little to control trusts; but conservative federal courts interpreted the act to mean that unions were illegal combinations in restraint of trade. In the Danbury Hatters case of 1908, the courts found the United Hatters of North America liable for losses resulting from a union-called boycott of the Lowe Company and ordered the union to pay $240,000 in compensation—a sum that would have destroyed it (Foner 1980, 96).

There were several schools of thought within the labor movement of the early twentieth century. These might be called *syndicalists, socialists,* and *pure and simple trade unionists.* These corresponded—very roughly, with a great deal of overlap at the boundaries—to three organizations: the Industrial Workers of the World (IWW), the Socialist Party (SP), and the American Federation of Labor (AFL).

The *syndicalists* saw illegality and repression simply as further evidence of the unalterably capitalist character of the state and the need to overthrow it along with the capitalist economic order. The IWW was often attacked by the police, the National Guard, or the army; its members and supporters were arrested, tried, imprisoned, and sometimes, as with Joe Hill, executed. It led large, militant strikes—particularly in the Northwest, but also in places like McKees Rocks, Pennsylvania, and Lawrence, Massachusetts—that often shut down entire cities or regions. But the IWW believed it was impossible to reform the capitalist state, and therefore considered attempts to win legal reforms—such as state recognition of unions—to be misleading and dangerous; even union contracts with employers were seen as undesirable compromises of the class struggle. The IWW sought to destroy the capitalist state rather than to improve it (Zinn 1980, 322-31). In practice, it tended to oppose electoral politics or legislative lobbying of any kind, as suggested by the preamble of its constitution (adopted in 1905), which called for the working class to "take and hold that which they produce by their labor, through an economic organization of the working class without affiliation with any political party" (Zinn 1980, 323).

The *socialists* differed from the syndicalists not in that they sought the socialist organization of society as a long-term goal—so did the syndicalists —but in that they made electoral and legislative politics an important part of their strategy for reaching that goal. The four presidential campaigns of Socialist Party leader Eugene V. Debs (in 1904, 1908, 1912, and 1920) were central to these efforts, but socialists also sent Victor Berger of Milwaukee to the House of Representatives, elected several mayors, and were an important political force in many areas across the country. The socialists differed among themselves about strategy. Some hoped to achieve socialism through gradual reform of the state,[10] whereas others saw elections as only a means to mobilize and prepare the working class for the general strike or revolutionary insurrection that would finally destroy capitalism. But they were united in the belief that electoral politics mattered.

Just as the syndicalist position was typified by the IWW, socialism was typified by the Socialist Party; but the correspondence between strategy and organization was far from clear. Many people belonged to both organizations, including Debs himself, who was on the platform with Big Bill Haywood and Mother Jones at the IWW's founding convention in 1905 (Zinn 1980, 322). Activists from both organizations frequently worked together at the local level, with little regard for the strategic differences of their leaders.[11]

There was a similar overlap between the SP and the AFL. However, the latter organization was dominated by the strong antisocialist leadership of its founder and president, Samuel Gompers, and his associates. The SP hoped at one time to wrest control of the AFL from Gompers and transform it into a socialist union on the German pattern. In 1893 the SP faction within the AFL began a campaign for Plank 10, calling for "the collective ownership by the people of all means of production and distribution," as part of the AFL program. Plank 10 was referred to the affiliate organizations for debate, and then was defeated in the 1894 convention, but the socialists succeeded in replacing Samuel Gompers with John McBride of the United Mine Workers as president. However, Gompers won back the office the following year and gradually built up his support. Fights over socialist resolutions continued for a decade. The socialist high point came in 1902, when Max Hayes, a socialist trade unionist from Cleveland, introduced a resolution: "That the . . . A.F. of L. advise the working people to organize their economic and political power to secure for labor the full equivalent of their toil and the overthrow of the wage system and the establishment of an industrial co-operative democracy." A compromise version negotiated by Hayes with William B. Wilson (as noted, a leader of the United Mine Workers and a Democrat), which called only for giving "labor the full equivalent of its toil," was passed over Gompers's stiff opposition (Gompers [1925] 1984, 115-17; Foner 1964, 382-84). However, many of the votes for it were not votes for socialism. The socialists were never able to win such a resolution again and eventually gave up trying to do so.

The third strategy, *pure and simple trade unionism*, was centered on Gompers and, in fact, named for a catch phrase of his. Its essence was to improve workers' lives without any expectation, hope, or even desire that these improvements should eventuate in socialism. Gompers himself believed that improvement could come only from direct economic action by the workers, not from state politics, a philosophy that became known as *voluntarism*; but other AFL leaders favored laws regulating minimum wages, protecting child labor, and furthering similar progressive social policies. Since Gompers, too, supported some legislative goals, the difference within this camp was much less than that between it and even the most right-wing socialists. In fact, Gompers and Victor Berger, leader of the Socialist Party's right, were bitter enemies (Gompers [1925] 1984, 137-38; Foner 1964, 389n).

These three positions were debated in the labor and left-wing press, at election rallies and union meetings, and in camps and shops, prison cells and boxcars, across the country. But the issue was not settled by debate alone; differing reactions from the state also played a role in the outcome. The syndicalists believed in unremitting confrontation with the state and capitalism. Accordingly, they felt the full brunt of the state's repressive forces, and were ultimately destroyed by them. The socialists believed in using elections and elected office as part of a protest strategy. They too were repressed; Berger was expelled from Congress, and Debs imprisoned, for opposing World War I. But their meager toehold in the political structure helped them to survive and rally support–Debs got more votes than ever in 1920 when he ran for president from his cell in Woodstock Prison—until the worldwide debate over the Bolshevik revolution and the founding of the Communist International broke them apart.

In contrast, Gompers and his allies sought either to work with or neutralize the state, not to capture or destroy it, and so suffered less repression. With the IWW and the SP effectively removed from the scene, only the AFL remained, and it would have looked good if only by default. Since it also had some positive political accomplishments to its credit, its political strategy looked even better. From 1906 on, the AFL helped elect a growing number of unionists to Congress, and began to push its goals—most important of which was the attainment of trade union legality—as part of the broader Progressive legislative program. It soon became evident that the structure of Congress was preventing the enactment of this program, and the AFL then played a significant role in the revolt of 1910, which reformed that structure.

Adherents of pure and simple trade unionism were not in complete agreement about legislative goals. Gompers himself advocated "voluntarism," whereby unions should try to achieve their aims through economic action in the workplace, rather than seeking state intervention on their behalf; meanwhile, some of his allies looked more favorably on positive state action to improve working conditions. However, even Gompers saw a need for political action to keep the state from siding with employers through injunctions, prosecutions, and court judgments such as that in the Danbury hatters case. Since Gompers's program represented the least common denominator for a broad segment of the labor movement, it became the focus for legislative action. The most general goals sought were exemption of unions from the Sherman Antitrust Act, restrictions on the use of anti-union injunctions, and the right to a jury trial for those charged with contempt of court under such injunctions (Foner 1980, 122).

The rules of Congress placed high hurdles in the path of such legislation, as well as in that of other progressive causes. Two successive Speakers of the House, Thomas Reed (R-Me.) and Joseph Cannon (R-Ill.), had worked to increase the powers of their office. As of 1909, the Speaker had the power to appoint and remove members and chairs of House committees, and himself held the chair of the House Rules Committee, which then as now determined which bills would reach the floor and how they would be considered. Committee chairs, in turn, were able to control the agendas of their committees and to keep bills from being reported without their support (Foner 1980, 36, 91; Pitney 1991; Stewart 1991; Peters 1991; Atkinson 1911). Cannon was firmly opposed to the progressive agenda, including the union's goals, and used his powers to keep such bills from coming to the floor for a vote. This obstruction frustrated the small number of prolabor representatives and protected the other members of Congress from having to go on the record.

Speaker Cannon's power was overthrown in 1910 by a coalition of progressive members of the House. In March the House adopted a rules change, moved by George W. Norris (R-Neb.), which removed the Speaker from the Rules Committee and provided for the committee's members to be elected. Then on June 17 it passed House Resolution 808, the provisions of which had been drawn up at a meeting in Gompers's Washington office the previous year; it provided for the discharge of any bill from committee by majority vote and gave requests for such votes precedence in the House (Bolling 1968; Cheney and Cheney 1983; Jones 1968; Kennon 1986). However, Cannon and his committee chairs remained in office, and it was late in the session in any case. The hopes of labor therefore focused on the 1910 election.

Meanwhile, there was growing support within the AFL for the creation of a labor party, as the British Trade Union Congress had done in 1900. Six union members had been elected to Congress in 1906, and twelve in 1908, in some cases through independent union campaigns (Weinstein 1968, 23; Foner 1980, 92). In 1910 AFL bodies in New York, Chicago, and Philadelphia called for launching a labor party; local versions of such parties were actually created in New York and Philadelphia. Gompers and the AFL leadership continued to oppose this strategy in favor of the "reward-your-friend-and-punish-your-enemy" policy, but they predicted gains for labor in the election. The prediction proved true: Union campaign activity, together with the wider upsurge of the progressive movement, defeated many of the conservative Republican members of Congress. The Democrats won a majority of the House; Champ Clark (D.-Mo.), considered a friend of labor by Gompers, replaced Cannon as Speaker; and fifteen union members (including eleven Democrats, three Republicans, and one Socialist) were elected to the House (Foner 1980, 93-97). Gompers continued to oppose creation of a labor party but was not above using the threat of such a party for his own purposes. In 1911 he issued a pointed warning to the Democrats:

> Unless the Democratic Party shall take hold of the interests of the masses, as against the interests of the classes, wherever they clash, it is not going to be the party of the future for the mass of the people. I feel that the time has come when we shall have a constructive, progressive, radical labor party, unless the Democratic Party shall perform its duties.[12]

Four union members were appointed to the House Committee on Labor, with one of them, William B. Wilson, a member and former secretary-treasurer of the United Mine Workers, named its chair.[13] With the structural impediments removed, the 62d Congress passed twenty-seven bills from the AFL's agenda into law. A bill to exempt unions from the Sherman Act was passed by both houses, but it was vetoed successfully by President Taft (Foner 1980, 99).

The AFL won a limited victory on this issue with the passage of the Clayton Antitrust Act in 1914. Gompers had hoped to see Champ Clark nominated for president by the Democrats in 1912, and he had some sympathy for the Progressive Party campaign of Theodore Roosevelt; but Woodrow Wilson, who had condemned unions in the past, began to call for legislation to protect labor's "right to organize," and Gompers reluctantly endorsed him late in October. William Wilson was appointed secretary of the Department of Labor—itself newly created in 1913—with Louis F. Post, a prolabor journalist from Chicago, as Assistant Secretary. However, President Wilson continued to oppose exemption of labor from the Sherman Act. In early 1914 the administration agreed to include in the Clayton Act the statement:

> That nothing in the anti-trust laws shall be construed to forbid the existence and operation . . . [of unions] or to forbid or restrain individual members of such orders or associations from carrying out the legitimate objects of such association.

For a month the AFL fought to substitute first "shall not apply to" and, later, "shall not be construed to apply to" for "nothing . . . shall be construed to forbid the existence and operation of," but finally agreed to accept the original language with the addendum, "nor shall such organizations, or the members thereof, be held or construed to be illegal combinations or conspiracies in restraint of trade, under the anti-trust laws" (Foner 1980, 132-33). The Clayton Act was passed with this language and signed into law on October 2, 1914. Wilson sent Gompers the pen he had signed it with, and the latter hailed the act as "the industrial Magna Carta upon which the working people will rear the structure of industrial freedom." Wilson, however, continued to maintain that it was not an exemption from the Sherman Act. Unfortunately, Wilson and his attorneys general, James C. McReynolds and later A. Mitchell Palmer, were better able to enforce their interpretation. The Palmer raids of 1919 and 1920, during which over 4,000 suspected radicals were arrested and 840 deported, hit the left wing of the labor movement hard. Beyond this anticommunist repression, unions continued to face prosecution and conviction for conspiracy in restraint of trade, until Felix Frankfurter and Nathan Greene concluded in 1930 that "the position of labor before the law has been altered, if at all, imperceptibly" (Foner 1980, 132-41; Frankfurter and Greene 1930, 197-98).

Summing up this period, I should note that protest activity by the trade union movement won some positions in the structure of the state: the creation of the Department of Labor and the House Labor Committee, and changes in the content of antitrust law. But these changes did little or nothing to alter the balance of social power. Efforts to use the new positions for an accommodationist attempt to further the cause of the working class, or even to defend it from repression, were futile.[14] The unions arrived at the Great Depression almost as weak as they had been before passage of the Clayton Act.

The National Labor Relations Act

Trade union legality was finally established with the passage of the National Labor Relations (or Wagner) Act in 1935. In essence, the NLRA provided for government certification of unions based on workplace elections and required employers to negotiate in good faith with those unions that had been certified. A new federal agency, the National Labor Relations Board (NLRB), was created to implement the act.

The Wagner Act was the most important of a series of pro-union laws passed during the 1930s and part of the larger program of the New Deal. As with the Clayton Act two decades earlier, its passage was driven by outside forces. Congress and President Roosevelt were responding to widespread, often violent labor insurgency. The president had appointed Wagner head of the National Labor Board (NLB) in 1933. This agency, created by Roosevelt as "a temporary expedient . . . to deal with a sudden strike wave," tried to mediate labor disputes but "could play at best a symbolic role" because it lacked enforcement powers (Tomlins 1985, 109). Wagner sought to remedy this deficiency with the labor disputes bill (S 2926) that he introduced in February 1934, but he was not able to get the bill out of the Senate Education and Labor Committee.

However, that summer brought a massive outbreak of strikes. In Toledo, thousands of unemployed people, affiliated with A. J. Muste's American Workers Party, joined the picket lines at the struck Auto-Lite plant; the strike was won after a pitched battle with 900 National Guardsmen on May 24, in which two workers were killed and fifteen wounded. In Minneapolis, two successive Teamsters' strikes mobilized mass rallies of up to 100,000 people and shut down trucking in the city with flying squads of pickets. Despite the arrests of 68 union leaders and attacks by police, the Citizens' Alliance, and the National Guard, this strike, too, was won. In September a national textile strike featured flying squads of 200 to 600 pickets who moved from town to town to shut down unstruck plants. This strike involved over 400,000 workers who fought plant guards, police, and the National Guard before finally accepting a token settlement on September 22 (Brecher 1977, 158-77). All this led President Roosevelt to request an emergency resolution from Congress—Public Resolution (PR) 44, which was passed quickly. The National Labor Relations Board was created two weeks later by executive order (Tomlins 1985, 119-27). The following year, Wagner introduced the NLRA to make the board permanent, and it was signed into law on July 5, 1935.

The Wagner Act was passed in reaction to labor insurgency and became a major legal support for labor organization. However, the organized labor movement had a surprisingly small role in writing the bill. Wagner was guided much more by input from the staff of the embryonic NLRB; the AFL supported the bill but worried about giving a bureaucratic agency too much authority over its internal affairs. It sent its general counsel, Charles Ogburn, to the Senate Committee on Education and Labor to ask for a number of amendments, seeking particularly to limit the board's authority to specify industrial rather than craft-based bargaining units, but all of these amendments were rejected (Tomlins 1985, 132-41; Gross 1974, 131, 134). (Wagner did "reassure the executive council of the AFL that his bill would not destroy craft organizations" (Gross 1974, 146), but the board was left free to specify plant-wide or employer-wide units if it chose to do so.) The new agency was left with broad discretion to make its own policies and set its own direction.

This direction, too, was influenced heavily by the pressure of working-class insurgency. The next year saw the birth of the Congress of Industrial Organizations (CIO) in a massive wave of strikes. The high point came with a sit-down strike against General Motors in Flint, Michigan, that lasted from December 1936 to February 1937. Thousands of autoworkers occupied several of GM's Chevrolet and Fisher Body plants, barricaded the entrances, and prepared to defend them against company security forces, the state police, and the National Guard. After a month of mass pickets and pitched battles, with workers from all over the Midwest flocking to Flint to defend the seized plants, President Franklin Roosevelt intervened. GM accepted the United Auto Workers as bargaining agent at seventeen of its plants, and UAW membership went from 100,000 to 200,000 in a few weeks.[15]

In the ensuing years, however, both wings of the labor movement came to rely on the NLRA and other forms of state action, such as the Davis-Bacon Act, to maintain and increase their strength. This reliance led inexorably to the adoption of an accommodationist strategy by the unions. The unions offered themselves as a major component of the Democratic Party's campaign apparatus, trusting that this arrangement would give them the strength to defend their interests. CIO leaders launched the Non-Partisan League as a campaign organization in 1936, followed by the Political Action Committee in 1943. The AFL followed with Labor's League for Political Action in 1947, and, as noted earlier, the two were merged into the Committee on Political Education (COPE) after the two parent federations merged in 1955. These successive organizations provided both major financial support and grassroots campaign workers to the Democratic Party (Greenstone [1969] 1977, 49-57; Draper 1989, 20, 25-39). In return, the unions gained further control over certain pieces of the state apparatus. They won *de facto* veto power over Democratic appointments to the House Education and Labor Committee (Fenno 1973, 31-34) and were assured of favorable appointments to the NLRB—as long as a sympthetic president occupied the White House.

However, labor's new structural position had its disadvantages. For example, Alan Draper observes that:

> the Wagner Act did not prescribe any particular policy guidelines but branched off into several, sometimes conflicting, directions. It would be left to the NLRB which would reflect the prolabor or promanagement sympathies of the incumbent administration to interpret and administer the law. Like the shift in the site of policy making from the courts to Congress, the political character of the NLRB would bring labor policy in line with the relative political power held by labor and capital. (Draper 1989, 19)

The passage of the Taft-Hartley Act by a temporarily Republican Congress in 1947 and the appointment of an anti-union NLRB by President Eisenhower in the 1950s brought this lesson home.

As a result the AFL-CIO became more firmly tied to the Democratic Party and was pressured toward accommodationism. Democratic control of Congress was labor's only hope of blocking anti-union changes in the NLRA;[16] a Democratic president was the only protection against the appointment of an NLRB that would make it harder to win certification. Toward this end the AFL-CIO, through COPE, had to make itself part of the Democrats' campaign machinery. But beyond that, the unions now had a stake in keeping that party together. Rather than pushing its interests as hard as possible, labor had to temper its demands according to what national and congressional majorities would tolerate.

This point should not be overstated. COPE consistently supported civil rights, despite the reluctance of some member unions, for example (Draper 1989, 99). But it did limit unions' aggressiveness on both political and economic issues. This limitation had serious consequences. Michael Goldfield traces the beginning of the long-term decline in union density (the proportion of eligible workers who belong to unions) to the failure of the CIO's attempt to organize the South, "Operation Dixie," in the late 1940s, and argues that this failure was partly due to the "unwillingness of both the right and left CIO leaders to pull out all the stops in the South [which] was based on the disruptive effects . . . [this would have] on the Roosevelt coalition" (Goldfield 1989, 239-40).

Moreover, even after it had tied itself firmly to the Democratic Party, labor still was not an interest group like the others. For example, although unions, along with bankers, farmers, and other interest groups have secured dominant positions on various congressional committees and subcommittees, these positions have not given the unions a commensurate amount of influence. For the unions, these positions include the Democratic contingents of the House Education and Labor and Senate Labor and Human Resources committees. Writing in 1973, Richard Fenno quoted an anonymous AFL-CIO official's statement: "We have to control the labor committee. It's our lifeblood." Fenno also reported that new Democratic members of Education and Labor were routinely cleared through—and sometimes selected by—Andy Biemiller, director of the AFL-CIO's Legislative Affairs Department (Fenno 1973, 31-34). But the aforementioned committees are among the least successful in Congress when it comes to getting their bills passed. On this matter, Fenno quotes a Republican member of House Education and Labor: "Everything that comes out of this committee is changed, altered, or killed on the floor. It's not like other committees where the committee bill goes right through. That's because this is a stacked committee." And a Democratic member told him, "The Committee is suspect. That's because so many Southern members feel that it is a stacked committee on the Democratic side" (Fenno 1973, 234-42). Many committees are stacked, of course—but such stacked committees as Agriculture or Interior do not encounter the unrelenting partisan hostility that labor bills do. Accordingly, the unions cannot easily translate their positional strength into victories on their major goals; in consequence, as we have seen in the case of the Chrysler bailout, labor often finds itself involved in an all-out fight for legislation that will make the working class only marginally better off.

5

Congress and Women

The election of 1954 sent four new women to the House, raising the total to sixteen. When one of these representatives, Martha Griffiths (D-Mich.), first took her seat, the male at the next desk complained, "At this rate it won't be any time at all before you ladies have the majority here." Griffiths immediately exercised one of her new perquisites and asked the Legislative Reference Service of the Library of Congress how long it would take, at the existing rate, for women to become a majority of the House. The answer was 432 years (Lamson 1968, 87).

The years since that calculation was made have seen the growth of the second wave of the women's movement, whose impact on American life is well known. However, the growth of the women's contingent of the House sped up very little. The election of 1992, hailed as "the year of the woman" following surprise primary victories by women senatorial candidates in Pennsylvania and Illinois, brought the number of women in the House to forty-eight, or 11 percent of the House. This was an increase of forty-two in the thirty-eight years since Griffiths first won, yielding a rate of 1.105 new women each year; now the time needed for women to reach a majority was reduced to only 154 years.

The number of women in the Senate grew more dramatically in the 1992 election, from three to six, with a seventh elected in 1993, so that one senator in fifteen is now female. However, as the *total* number of women in the Senate had stood at or near two ever since the 1950s, we can see that the Senate's growth rate over a longer period has been very slow. Altogether, women now constitute 10 percent of the membership of Congress. The 10.8 percent of women in the lower house place the U.S. just below the top quarter of all countries with legislatures—still far below the 30 to 40 percent levels attained in most Scandinavian countries, but well above the 2.3 percent level in Japan (Teeters and Neathery 1992).

Even these limited gains have required tremendous struggle by the women's movement. A case in point is that of Rebecca Latimer Felton

(D-Ga.), the first woman senator, who served for two days in 1922. Felton was sworn in, answered "Present!" to a roll call, and made one speech, in which she promised:

> When the women of the country come in and sit with you, though there may be but a very few in the next few years, I pledge you that you will get ability, you will get integrity of purpose, you will get exalted patriotism, and you will get unstinted usefulness. (Quoted in Chamberlin 1973, 36)

Felton's successor, Walter George (D-Ga.), had already been elected and was present in the Senate chamber; Felton herself had sought to be sworn in only as a symbol. Yet this small gesture, which could have been granted as an empty courtesy, required a major struggle in which thousands of women wrote letters to demand a special session of Congress, and hundreds came to Washington to demand that she be allowed to take her seat, disrupting the Senate with tumultuous applause when she did so. As the *New York Times* reported at the time:

> As the applause continued in the galleries, one of the doorkeepers, a man weighing perhaps 250 pounds, rushed here and there waving his hands and shouting words which nobody heard. Finally, he took hold of a woman weighing about 95 pounds, saying, "If you don't stop this noise I'll arrest you."
> She whirled on him with fire in her eyes, while she kept on clapping her hands.
> "Why don't you pick on some one your own size," she yelled to the amusement of those close enough to hear. "Look at that row of Senators' wives down in front, any one of them would make two of me. Why don't you go and arrest them?"[1]

A similarly exceptional struggle was required for the installation of the second woman senator, Hattie Caraway (D-Ark.). Caraway was appointed in November 1931 to the seat of her deceased husband, Thad Caraway, partly in order to help her meet the heavy expenses of widowhood but largely because Governor Harvey Parnell thought (wrongly, as it happened) that she would not be a serious threat to his own bid for election to the next full term. Since such an appointment could not be made for longer than a year, and since one year and three days remained in the term, the law required a special election. The local election officials of Arkansas balked. Elections were normally financed by the filing fees of all candidates for all offices; but in a special election there was only one office at stake, leaving the local governments to pick up the difference, which they were neither willing nor, they claimed, able to do.

The resulting situation was declared "a challenge to Arkansas Womanhood." The Women's City Club of Little Rock organized a new Arkansas Women's Democratic Club, which proceeded to recruit women as volunteer election judges. By the time of the election they had organized seventy-two of the state's seventy-five counties. (Within a year they had gone on to demand an equal share in party offices and patronage as well, one source reports.)[2]

Governor Parnell was disappointed a few months later when Caraway filed for reelection to a full six-year term—an action she described in her journal as a chance "to try out my own theory of a woman running for office" (Kincaid 1979, 121). Given little hope at first, she won the support of her fellow senator Huey Long (D-La.), who joined her in August 1932 for a whirlwind campaign tour of her state. They personally addressed 200,000 voters at thirty-nine rallies in thirty-one counties. Caraway won the Democratic nomination with 127,702 votes (44.7 percent) and went on to win the general election easily. In 1938 she defeated John McClellan, who campaigned with the slogan "Arkansas needs another man in the Senate," but she finally lost to J. William Fulbright in 1944.[3]

Marxist and Feminist Theories

What can we learn from these stories? First of all, they tell us that women themselves have felt deeply about the symbolism of women in office. No one believed that Felton's senatorship would affect legislation; how could it, when she was never allowed to vote? Her swearing of the oath, her short speech, her answering "Present!" to a quorum call were themselves seen, for whatever reason, as meriting a letter campaign, a trip to Washington, an exuberant celebration in the Senate galleries—in short, a struggle. Second, struggle was necessary. Felton would not have sworn her oath, made her speech, or answered her roll call without it, nor would Caraway's first election have been held. Not only women but also the male holders of power appreciated the importance of these symbolic points.

But though the question of whether or not there are women in Congress is clearly important to everyone, it is not so clear how we should understand this issue theoretically. For pluralists, women are yet another player in the competition of interests (Sapiro 1981). Like other groups, women are divided by crosscutting interests and have a variety of ways of bringing their influence to bear. The membership of women in Congress is just one of those ways. For example, most feminist political organizations endorsed a Democratic man, Barney Frank, against a Republican woman, Margaret Heckler, when the redistricting of 1982 forced the two to run against each other in eastern Massachusetts, because Frank was seen as a more consistent voice for feminist concerns. And, indeed, the endorsements, contributions, and votes of these organizations helped him win.   Male members of Congress will need to respond to women constituents, just as women will need to represent other interests if they wish to keep their seats.   From this perspective, it is hard to see why the election or appointment of women has generated so much excitement.

From the institutionalist point of view, the importance of having women in office is easier to see.   If Congress and its members have substantial freedom to make policy, we can expect women to tackle problems and develop solutions different from those that would be undertaken by a Congress of men.[4]   What institutionalists need to explain is why the feminization of Congress—which increases that body's ability to deal with the nation's problems—has been so long in coming. Institutionalism has no obvious answer to the question as to what interests or other factors might be behind the resistance.

Marxist theory's record on this issue has not been good.   Marxist theorists and practitioners alike have often downplayed women's issues and women's political action as being less important than the unity of the proletariat.   The second wave of the women's movement began, in part, because women grew tired of being told that it would be divisive for them to raise feminist concerns at that particular time.   The time when it would be appropriate to raise them never seemed to arrive, and the experience of existing socialist societies was not such as to inspire confidence that all these problems would be solved easily once the proletariat came to power. Although some socialist societies did seem to be confronting women's oppression, progress in eliminating it was slow; and other socialist societies seemed not to take the problem seriously in the first place. Women activists grew disillusioned with the left; and the result, as everyone knows, was the explosive growth of the modern women's movement (Freeman 1975, 57-62).   At first a purely practical phenomenon, focused on the organization of women into autonomous groups and the raising of feminist demands in a wide variety of contexts, feminism soon gave rise to a rich development of theory.   Since Marxism was, and continues to be, the most fully developed existing theory of human liberation, the question of what to make of it has been one focus of this development.

In principle, Marxists have always stood for the emancipation and equality of women.   The Communist Manifesto declares that the communists' aim "is to do away with the status of women as mere instruments of production" (Marx and Engels [1848] 1978, 488), and Engels echoes enthusiastically Fourier's declaration that "the degree of women's emancipation is the natural measure of the general emancipation" (Engels [1848] 1978, 690).   Such pillars of Marxist orthodoxy as Engels [1942] (1972) and Bebel (1910) wrote treatises on this issue; the demand for women's equality has generally been included in the programs of socialist parties;

and socialist regimes in power have generally made some attempt to enact those demands, though with varying degrees of success. Nevertheless, there has been a practical reluctance on the part of many Marxists to take women's liberation seriously, a reluctance often linked to the theoretical belief that the oppression of women is somehow less important than that of the working class. This belief in turn stems from the view that women's oppression is caused by the needs of the capitalist system, and that it will vanish, or at least be easy to remove, when that system is destroyed. Following this approach, Marxists have often taken a strong stand for women's equality; but they have also argued that equality can best be gained by working for socialist revolution.

From this point of view, issues affecting women can be divided into three categories. First, there is the special oppression of women workers by the capitalists, characterized by lower wages, discrimination in hiring and promotion, sexual harassment of women by their employers, and so on. These are straightforward class issues, and virtually all Marxists would agree (at least in principle) that this sort of oppression should be fought against vigorously. Even if some male workers objected, Marxists would argue (again in principle) that they did so because of their ideological backwardness, which should not be catered to.

Second are the issues that divide working-class men and women. Examples include the division of household tasks and the double standard in sexual relations. Here the orthodox Marxist strategy is to resolve these secondary contradictions in order to increase the strength of the working class in its conflict with the capitalists. However, there has been little agreement as to how the contradictions should be resolved. One can begin with the assumption that proletarian unity is primary, and go on to make a case either for subordinating women's concerns to the needs of the larger struggle or for granting their demands for similar reasons. Unfortunately, since men have usually been in a stronger position, the argument has usually been for subordination. Moreover, the conservative social attitude of some Marxist leaders has sometimes kept them from seeing what their principles imply.

Finally, there are issues dividing women and men within the capitalist class, such as the right of women to hold management positions in capitalist firms or offices within the capitalist state apparatus. A whole series of Marxist leaders, including some of the more feminist ones, rejected these issues as fundamentally opposed to the interests of the proletariat. Alexandra Kollontai, writing in 1920, referred to "the poison of feminism" and declared, "The world of women is divided, just as is the world of men, into two camps: one is in its ideas, aims and interests close to the bourgeoisie, the other to the proletariat, whose aspirations for freedom incorporate the complete solution of the woman question"

(Kollontai 1977, 51). Kollontai's conclusion, often repeated in the Marxist movement, was that the struggles of bourgeois women were of little or no importance to the cause of the working class in general, or to working-class women in particular.

However, as Kollontai found in her own political career, Marxist parties and working-class organizations have seldom supported even the limited demands derived from this analysis. The general tendency of such organizations has been to ignore issues about women's participation in leadership; to give lip service, at best, to issues about power and the division of labor in the household; and to subordinate issues about women's pay, working conditions, and union membership to tactical considerations about what male workers were likely to support.[5]

There are also some theoretical difficulties with the reduction of gender to class. As many feminist theorists have pointed out, the Marxist analysis of capital does not require that either capitalists or proletarians must be men. In fact, Marx himself argued that capitalism broke down gender distinctions within the proletariat, along with the proletarian family itself, as women were forced into the labor market. But he did not seem to expect the same for the bourgeoisie. While he heaped scorn on the capitalist who regarded his wife and family as part of his property, he had no satisfactory explanation as to why this capitalist was not female. Essentially, this matter was left to be determined by historical coincidence.

Finally, if we reduce gender contradictions to class we have a hard time explaining why women's oppression persists across changing modes of production. Neither prior to capitalism, in the ancient world or in feudal society, nor after it, in existing socialist societies, have women achieved equality. Hence the explanation of their inequality must go beyond the requirements of the capitalist mode of production. This problem has produced a great deal of theory, with many alternative accounts proposed.[6]

One approach has been to ascribe women's oppression to non-economic causes, while at the same time insisting that noneconomic factors can be just as important and durable as economic ones. Ernesto Laclau and Chantal Mouffe (1985) have argued generally that ideology exists independent of the economic base, and that antagonisms rooted in ideology can be just as basic as contradictions rooted in the relations of production. Michele Barrett (1980) has made an essentially similar argument specifically about women's oppression.

Two related points can be raised about these arguments. First, as Poulantzas once remarked, once you have given up the idea of economic determination in the last instance, it is no longer useful to think of your approach as Marxist. Of course, as he immediately added, it cannot be taken for granted that a Marxist approach is the correct one. A more important objection to the rooting of women's oppression in ideology is that it leaves too much to coincidence. It is not at all clear why an ideology of feminine inferiority should have developed so universally everywhere in the world; and if we look for some other factor to explain this phenomenon, we are no longer taking ideology as basic.

The alternative is to see the oppression of women, like that of the proletariat, as rooted in economic exploitation. During the 1970s some Marxists tried to show that only capitalists benefited from this exploitation; but in the end the "domestic labor debate" forced the realization that, whereas women who are factory workers may be exploited by the capitalists, those who exploit women in the home are simply men.

This realization led Christine Delphy (1984, 57-77) and Heidi Hartman (1981), among others, to propose the existence of a domestic mode of production, sometimes called *patriarchy*, alongside of and intertwined with capitalism—an approach that has become known as "dual systems theory."

Proponents of dual systems theory, Delphy in particular, are sharply critical of Marxism and Marxists for trying to reduce women's oppression to exploitation by capital. At the same time, they point out that this interpretation is a perversion of Marx's own approach in that it treats capitalism, wage labor, and the appropriation of surplus value as the most fundamental concepts of Marxism. For Marx, these concepts were particular manifestations of the more general principles of class conflict, surplus, and exploitation, which take different forms in different circumstances. That is, Marx saw capitalism as a particular mode of production, one of several possibilities. Concerned with the emergence of capitalism out of earlier modes, he recognized the existence of long transitional periods in which two or more modes of production coexisted. *Capital* was meant very explicitly as an analysis of capitalism, not of society in general. Equally important, it was meant as an abstraction; Marx deliberately chose to portray the ideal type of pure capitalist production in order to highlight the essential capitalist relation, the exploitation of surplus value. He was perfectly aware that no existing society corresponded exactly with this pure form.

Hence, as Delphy points out, the argument that women's domestic labor cannot be exploited because it produces only use value but not exchange value is irrelevant.[7] The true implication of such an argument is not that women are not exploited in the home but that such exploitation is not capitalist.[8]

Conceptualizing women as one of the basic classes in the domestic mode of production also lets us make use of much of the theoretical framework of Marxism. The concepts of relations of production, surplus, exploitation, and superstructure are not specific to capitalism; rather, they take on particular forms in capitalism but can apply as well to different modes of production. Thinking of women as a class in this sense calls our attention to their exploitation and suggests that sexist ideology and sexist political structures alike are grounded in the domestic relations of production. However, since this use of the term *class* is unconventional and potentially confusing, I have generally used the term *gender* instead.

This approach can help us answer some of the perplexing questions about women in Congress. One of the most perplexing of these is why women are so badly underrepresented.

Causes of Women's Underrepresentation

There are few trade unionists in Congress because the AFL-CIO has chosen to lobby from the outside rather than seeking to elect its own members. There are few African American members of Congress because African Americans are a numerical minority in the United States, and because racism continues to prevent many white voters from voting for black candidates. However, women make up a numerical majority of the United States,[9] and the women's movement has consistently sought to elect women to public office. Why, then, has the number of women in Congress been so low and grown so slowly?

Voter bias does not seem to be the reason, at least not in the recent past. Survey data show that most voters are willing to vote for otherwise qualified candidates who are female; and when women do run they are as likely to win as men are, other things being equal (Darcy and Schramm 1977; Darcy and Choike 1986; Wilhite and Theilmann 1986). This is true both for general elections and for primaries, including primary contests for open seats, which offer the best chance of actually getting into Congress (Burrell 1992). Women running for Congress also seem to do as well as men in raising money. Studies have found no evidence of discrimination against women in the amounts raised from PACs (Wilhite and Theilmann 1986, 292-93) or from political parties (Wilhite 1988, 262);[10] nor is there evidence of discrimination in the total amount of money raised (Wilhite and Theilmann 1986, 287-88).

If voter bias does not keep women out of Congress, what does? Many people have studied this question, using statistical procedures to correlate several variables and detect underlying relationships. Three such relationships have been found.

First, the electoral system itself makes a difference. Women do best where legislatures are elected by proportional representation. But they do worst under the system used to elect members of Congress—namely, that involving single-member geographic districts (Rule 1987; Rule and Norris 1992; Matland and Brown 1992).[11] Some have suggested creating multimember House districts in order to improve women's chances of being elected. Unfortunately, the same change would hurt the chances of African American candidates, and probably of Latinos as well (Moncrief and Thompson 1992). Proportional representation would help both women and racially oppressed groups, but many consider it politically unfeasible because it would entail such a big change in our system of weak parties and strong ties between representative and constituency.

Whatever the prospects of such a reform might be, district structure is not very satisfying as a theoretical explanation of women's underrepresentation. It is clearly only a secondary cause. The usual logic is that voters who are reluctant to vote for women (and party leaders who are reluctant to slate them as candidates) will become more willing to do so when they can vote for (and slate) male candidates at the same time. But this logic presumes just what we are trying to explain, and what has been called into question by the studies discussed above—that voters (and party leaders) are biased against women.

A second explanation is based on the power of incumbency. Since incumbents have a strong electoral advantage,[12] studies of gender bias have attempted to control for this factor—in effect, comparing male incumbents with female incumbents and male challengers with female challengers. However, most incumbents are men, so in most elections there will be more women challenging male incumbents than there are men challenging female incumbents. To put it differently, even if voters do not discriminate against women candidates today, we shall continue to see the effects of past discrimination for some time to come.

The argument for a time lag due to incumbency is persuasive, but it is insufficient to explain either the degree or the persistence of women's underrepresentation. As a rather simplistic example, consider the situation in 1992, when there were eighty-six open seats in the House of Representatives. All other things being equal, and absent discrimination, forty-three of these seats should have been won by women. In fact, only twenty-two were (Congressional Quarterly 1993, 15A-43A).

Moreover, the power of incumbency itself has been called into question. Gary Jacobson argues that incumbents look as strong as they do mainly because strong challengers do not choose to run against them. Challengers do not do so, of course, partly because they do not think that they can win. To this extent, incumbent advantage is a self-fulfilling prophecy (Jacobson 1992, 171). To explain the underrepresentation of women in Congress, then, we must ask why few strong women candidates choose to challenge incumbents.

This question leads to a third explanation offered by the literature. Few women are elected to Congress because relatively few women, particularly those with the experience and credentials to be strong candidates, choose to run, either against incumbents or for open seats. For example, in 1992 only thirty-eight women ran as Democratic or Republican nominees for the eighty-six open seats; even if they had all been elected (and some were running against each other) they would not have won 50 percent of the open seats. About one-eighth of all Democratic and Republican general-election candidates for House seats in 1992 were women (Congressional Quarterly 1993, 35A-43A).

Why is this so? It might be argued that there are fewer qualified women than men; but there are certainly enough qualified women to provide strong candidates for every congressional seat (Rule 1981, 69).[13] Moreover, many women have won election by challenging and broadening the traditional occupational qualifications for office, as in the recent case of Patty Murray (D-Wash.), who was elected to the Senate in 1992 as a "housewife in tennis shoes."

Part of the answer, at least, lies in the structure of patriarchy. The unequal division of labor in the household makes it harder for women than for men to find the resources to run; and sexist ideology, which represents this division in popular consciousness, places an additional hurdle in the path of those women who do run. Virginia Sapiro accounts for both of these difficulties with the concept of *privatization*, which she defines in terms of:

> the domination of women's lives by private roles, concerns, and values. Even where women are involved in public life, as in the workforce and politics, their activities and concerns are expected to be imbued with the private significance of being a woman. This is what we mean by "privatization."
>
> There need not be a one-to-one correspondence of women's own ideology and the actual activities in which women are engaged. Many women are employed outside the home because there is no other way for their families to survive; they do not necessarily have a "liberated" understanding of women's roles and may, in fact, look forward to the day when they can "go home." Homemakers, on the other hand, may be intensely involved in public issues and activities. Many women in public office list their occupation as "housewife." It is also true that women can become involved in politics and remain privatized in a sense. These women become involved in issues that directly concern their families, often through organizations such as the PTA, and may continue to *interpret* their political activities as part of their roles as homemakers and mothers. (Sapiro 1984, 73-74)

As Sapiro also observes, "It is rarely noted that both sexes face conflicts between family and public life. The question is, how are these conflicts resolved?" (Sapiro 1984, 32). Women are more likely to resolve them by giving up or postponing involvement in private life: "Even among highly politically active women, political ambition and attempts to gain influence through obtaining political office are contingent upon whether one is married, a mother, a homemaker, or accepts the traditional existing ideology of privatization" (Sapiro 1984, 139). Moreover, as Ruth Mandel observes, "in the great majority of political families, children are affected by a mother's campaign far more than by a father's political activities," since to some extent these households' gender relations reflect the traditional pattern, in which "the children's daily way of life . . . has depended on the mother's presence, or on the way in which she has made arrangements for the minutes and hours during her absence" (Mandel 1981, 84).

In short, the structure of the patriarchal family limits women's ability to find both the money and the time to run. Mandel observes that many wealthy men have won elective office by spending large amounts of their own money, but wealthy women hesitate to spend what they see as family resources:

> In recent years many women who have decided to return to school after fifteen or twenty years of homemaking refuse to use the family's money to pay costs of their own education. They consider it selfish to spend the family's money for their personal improvement, and they suffer guilt at the thought of draining off resources. For similar and additional reasons, some female candidates for elective office refuse to fund their own campaigns. Some because of principle: "I don't believe in buying a seat," said one state legislator in Minnesota. Some because of personal consideration: "I promised my husband I wouldn't borrow," said a legislative candidate in Texas. (Mandel 1981, 199)

In the past, women have been more likely than men to refrain from running for office until after their children have grown (Kirkpatrick 1974, 38); and potential women candidates are likely to take the disruption of moving to Washington, if elected, more seriously than men do (Burrell 1992, 505). To call these obstacles *structural* is not to deny that they find part of their basis in the attitudes of women who are potential candidates but, rather, to emphasize that such attitudes grow out of and are continually reinforced by the socially constructed relations in which these women lead their lives, by the structure of the patriarchal nuclear family. Although these relations may be accurately called "psychological barriers" (Sapiro 1984, 183), and although it may be true that "women who challenge their designated role and actively seek public office will suffer psychological pain because they can no longer identify with nonpolitical women and are not accepted by their male colleagues" (Clark 1991, 71), it is also true that they will face considerable material difficulties if they try to break free of the traditional structure (Lynn and Flora 1977; Stoper 1977).

Women with children who overcome the psychological and material barriers to running may still find these barriers echoed in the attitudes of voters. Barbara Burrell reports that when Elizabeth Tamposi sought the Republican nomination for representative of the Second District in New

Hampshire in 1988, an open seat, "she was publicly scolded by Senator Gordon Humphrey of New Hampshire, who charged that a mother of a two-year-old could not adequately serve her constituents" (Burrell 1992, 505n).[14] And when Democrat Virginia Shapard challenged Representative Newt Gingrich (R-Ga.) in 1978, his campaign produced a comparison of the two candidates that included an item called "Family"; it read in part:

> The Gingrichs have two daughters, Jackie Sue, 11, and Kathy, 15. When elected, Newt will keep his family together. . . . The Shapards have four children, Virginia, 13, Robert, 11, Christy, 9, and Loyd, 7. If elected, Virginia will move to Washington, but her children and husband will remain in Georgia. (Quoted in Mandel 1981, 90)

We have already seen that such tactics do not result in a bias against women candidates on the part of voters; the finding that women who run do as well as otherwise similar men did not take account of age or the presence of children in the home. However, the possibility of encountering these tactics must surely add to the reluctance of some women to run.

To think of such barriers as entirely psychological suggests that they can be overcome if potential women candidates change the way they think. Such an analysis amounts to blaming the victim; moreover, it is not likely to work. It may be good advice for women about how to conquer an obstacle in their paths, but it does not remove the presence of the obstacle. What is really needed is to change the structure of the family so that women are as free as men of both material and psychological barriers to political activity.

Consequences of Women's Underrepresentation

Is the underrepresentation of women important? Does it make a difference? After all, many male members of Congress vote for feminist positions, and some female members do not. Feminist interest groups have even been known to endorse men running against women, as in the Frank-Heckler contest cited earlier. Why, then, should we care about the number of women in Congress at all? Is this issue purely symbolic?

The first part of the answer is that "purely symbolic" issues can be very important. Symbolic representation is often co-opting in nature, increasing the legitimacy of state action by giving the appearance of consent; but it can also serve to legitimize the group being represented. All other things being equal, women will be stronger in a society where they are included in a legislature than in one where they are not.[15]

Moreover, women do seem to make a difference. Jeannette Rankin (R-Mont.), the first woman to serve in Congress, voted against U.S. entry into World War I (and later, World War II), supported striking mine-workers in Butte, supported small farmers, and called for Irish independence. Though controversial, none of these positions distinguished her from male progressives; one newspaper even called her "the female LaFollette." But she also took several initiatives focused on women. At the request of Crystal Eastman, she sponsored a bill (passed after she had left office) to ensure that American women who married foreign men would not lose their citizenship. Another of her bills called for the government to educate women about venereal disease and birth control; although this bill was not passed during her term in office, it later grew into the Sheppard-Towner Maternity and Infancy Act of 1921, character-ized by Joseph Chepaitis as "the lone exception to the federal refusal to embrace responsibility for social welfare until the New Deal" (Chepaitis 1972, 214). Rankin worked closely on this and other bills with Julia Lathrop, head of the Children's Bureau, and its eventual passage was the focus of a concerted women's lobbying campaign, channeled through the Women's Joint Congressional Committee, an alliance of fourteen women's groups (Chepaitis 1972, 218). Her first speech in Congress (leaving aside the thirteen words she uttered, in violation of precedent, while voting against the declaration of war) was made in offering a successful amend-ment to the Lever Bill, which opened to women the jobs created by that bill (Josephson 1974, 85).[16]

Rankin also used the personal leverage of her office on behalf of women. When she heard of terrible conditions, including sexual harassment, among women workers at the Bureau of Printing and Engraving, she conducted her own secret investigation, ultimately forcing the Treasury Department to hold a public hearing that led to reform and to the resignation of the bureau's director, Joseph Ralph (Giles 1980, 109-16). When prosuffrage women picketing the White House, including Alice Paul, Dorothy Day, and Lucy Burns, were arrested on November 14, 1917, Rankin visited them in the Occaquan Workhouse to confirm the terrible conditions there; she was seeking a congressional investigation when they were released on December 3 (Josephson 1974, 95-96).

I am not arguing that no man could have introduced these measures. However, Rankin's position as a woman in Congress brought her to the public eye and gave her extra leverage, particularly when she could claim to be speaking for women. Sometimes this added visibility was to her disadvantage. She was one of fifty representatives to vote against World War I, but was pilloried for it far more than the others (Giles 1980, 100-01; Josephson 1974, 76-77); moreover, the *New York Times* and many other papers chose to describe her as weeping during the vote—a description flatly contradicted by several eyewitnesses—thereby adding to the criticism hurled against her (Giles 1980, 98). But Rankin received attention in more positive ways as well.   She got so many letters—about 300 a day—that she had to hire extra secretarial help (Giles 1980, 109); and it was her status as the first woman member of Congress that led Eastman, Lathrop, and the women printing workers to seek out her aid.

The presence of women in Congress was also essential to the inclusion of a ban on sex discrimination in the Civil Rights Act of 1964. As this fascinating story has been well told by Caroline Bird (1974, 1-18), it bears repeating here only briefly. The Civil Rights Act was intended to outlaw racial discrimination as broadly as possible. The battle for this act had been going on for decades, in the halls of Congress, in the streets, at lunch counters, in department stores, and on buses, as well as in voting booths and the halls of Congress. The mass civil rights movement was at its height, and President Lyndon Johnson, a Texas Democrat, was determined to prove that not all Southerners were racists. However, the vast majority of Southern members of Congress were, in fact, proclaimed advocates of racial segregation. Whereas their allies back home resisted civil rights by murder and terror, this group resisted the Civil Rights Act by constitutional argument and obstructive tactics. Their main constitutional argument was states' rights—the claim that the proposed bill went beyond the powers of the federal government; but by this time a majority of Congress was willing to accept broad interpretations of the commerce clause and the Fourteenth Amendment, so the argument was doomed to fail. Congressional racists were left with their structural power to obstruct action, a power they had developed carefully over the years.   The most important instances of this power were use of the House Rules Committee, then chaired by Howard W. Smith (D-Va.). to prevent House bills from reaching the floor, and use of the Senate filibuster to prevent bills from coming to a vote.

By early 1964, Smith's power had been broken; he was unable to keep the bill from the House floor. The major battle, invoking cloture in the Senate, still lay ahead.[17] Smith and his Southern Democratic allies in the House were reduced to petty delay and ridicule, and in this spirit Smith seized upon the suggestion of May Craig, a journalist described by Bird as "the official feminist of the White House Press Corps," that the bill's employment discrimination provisions should apply to sex as well as race. Smith introduced his amendment with a speech intended to be funny, but his serious purpose was to divide and embarrass the bill's liberal supporters. Floor manager Emmanuel Celler (D-N.Y.) and other liberal leaders responded to this purpose by opposing the amendment, which they would have succeeded in killing had it not been for the intervention of Martha Griffiths (D-Mich.), who declared, "I support the amendment because when this bill has passed, white women will be last at the hiring gate" (Bird 1974, 7).[18] Griffiths was then supported by all but one of the women in the House. The issue was now confused. A vote for the amendment might have been intended either as a vote against civil rights, or as a vote for women's rights. By opening up the latter possibility, Griffiths did what no profeminist man could have done: made liberal votes for the amendment legitimate. There were enough such votes, when combined with the 100 or so votes from the same number of segregationists, that the amendment passed, 168 to 133, and survived to become law later that year.

Six years later Griffiths won another triumph over Celler when she got two-thirds of the members of the House to sign a petition discharging the proposed Equal Rights Amendment (ERA) from Celler's Judiciary Committee (Bird 1974, 212-14). Here again, the fact of her being a woman and, by this time, a recognized voice for women in the House gave her the leverage to challenge the privileges of a committee chair and force other members to go on record as for or against women's equality. The ERA then passed the House 350 to 15; without Griffiths's petition, it might not have been voted on at all.[19]

As the numbers of women in Congress and state legislatures have increased, several studies have compared their voting records and ideological positions with those of men. Many but not all of these have found women to be slightly more liberal than men in voting.[20] However, this finding may be more related to the tendency of liberal constituencies to elect women than to any general characteristic of women politicians. A more important finding is that women are more likely to give priority to women's concerns, and to see themselves as "uniquely qualified . . . or responsible for representing women's concerns" (Reingold 1992, 509).[21] By electing a woman, then, women voters (and profeminist men) stand a better chance of getting a representative who will not only vote as they wish but also promote feminist concerns more actively. Conversely, a predominantly male Congress may be less likely to take up issues of particular concern to women, even if most of its members would vote for feminist positions on those issues it did take up.

Federal support for day care is a perfect example of such an issue. If we consider its impact on family budgets—at least in the case of families headed by heterosexual couples—such support lowers a family's out-of-pocket expenses and increases its potential earning power. These monetary benefits accrue to both parents, without regard to sex, and both sexes support day care by large margins.[22] However, if affordable day care is not available, the personal burden of additional work and restricted horizons is most likely to be borne by the mother; accordingly, members of Congress with the woman's point of view should be more likely to promote federal support.

Although female members of Congress are more likely than male members to put extra energy and effort into issues affecting women, the shortage of women in Congress can be compensated partially by outside pressure. Since women are found in large numbers in every state and every congressional district, they are well placed for effective grassroots lobbying—few if any members of Congress are so sure of reelection that they can afford to ignore women voters, whatever their personal view may be. To the extent that women voters both agree on what are seen as women's issues, *and* feel more intensely about such issues than men do, they should constitute a powerful pressure group.

Day care meets the opinion test. Indeed, public opinion has generally been growing more favorable to day care, but with a continuing gender difference. In 1980, 75 percent of women and 66 percent of men wanted day care to be increased, up from 63 percent of women and 47 percent of men in 1970.[23] As a result, members of Congress have certainly become more willing to vote for day care; but this voting support has not been enough to bring about the establishment of a comprehensive federal day-care policy.

The closest the United States has ever come to a strong day-care program was the congressional passage of the Comprehensive Child Development Act in 1971. The lobbying coalition behind this bill was led by a woman, Marion Wright Edelman, and included a self-consciously feminist contingent; but its prime sponsors inside Congress were men: Representative John Brademas (D-Ind.) and Senator Walter Mondale (D-Minn.). It passed Congress in 1971 with surprising ease. So far, at least, it might seem to contradict the claim that women are needed to represent women's interests.

However, the same act was then vetoed by President Richard Nixon on the grounds that it was "family weakening," "a long leap into the dark for the United States government and the American people," "the most radical piece of legislation to emerge from the Ninety-second Congress," and a commitment of "the vast moral authority of the National Government to the side of communal approaches to child rearing over against the family-centered approach" (Nixon 1971, 1636; Norgren 1982, 132n).[24] Various partial programs have since been enacted, including child-care tax credits (for those with enough income to benefit from them) and vouchers for women on welfare (if they manage to find a program with a vacancy). But the issue of a comprehensive, federal day-care program has never again made its way to the top of Congress's agenda. We are left with a shifting patchwork of tax credits and vouchers, inadequate programs that neither increase the supply of day care nor make it affordable to many of those who need it.

President George Bush's 1990 and 1992 vetoes of the Family and Medical Leave Act resembled Nixon's veto of the Child Development Act in blocking an action that Congress had taken in response to electoral pressure from women. But things had changed in one respect. Where Nixon chose to portray his act in language which can be seen, in part, as an open defense of the patriarchal family, Bush did not. Instead, Bush insisted that "I have always supported employer policies to give time off for a child's birth or adoption or for family illness and believe it is important that employers offer these benefits," and that his objections to the bill came only from his desire to "ensure that federal policies do not stifle the creation of new jobs or result in the elimination of existing jobs."[25]

The Family and Medical Leave Act was passed again early in 1993, and this time President Clinton signed the bill into law. This was a significant victory for the cause of women's equality—although the United States still falls far short of other industrialized capitalist countries, virtually all of which require employers to provide paid family leave.

Nevertheless, the history of the Family and Medical Leave Act illustrates that structural resistance to legislation for women still survives. The bill was first introduced in 1986, with somewhat broader coverage (employers of fifteen or more, not fifty) and higher mandated benefits (twenty-six weeks of unpaid leave, not twelve) than was called for in the version that finally cleared Congress in 1992. That year it was approved by the House Education and Labor Committee but never brought up on the floor. Reintroduced in 1987 by Patricia Schroeder (D-Colo.) and William Clay (D-Mo.), it became the focus of a lobbying battle between the National Organization for Women (which organized the sending of 25,000 Mothers Day cards to Congress) and the Chamber of Commerce; the House Education and Labor Committee approved it again, but only after limiting the coverage to employers of fifty or more—a provision which excluded 95 percent of employers and 40 percent of employees—and restricting mandated family leave to ten weeks over two years. Stalled by a Senate filibuster in the 100th Congress, the Family and Medical Leave Act—now calling for twelve weeks of leave—finally passed Congress in June 1990, only to be vetoed by President Bush on June 29. The House tried but failed to override the veto, 232 to 195, on July 25. Essentially the same scenario was repeated in the next Congress, with the House failing to override by a vote of 258 to 169 on September 30, 1992.[26] Finally, the bill was once again enacted—complete with the earlier weakening compromises—in 1993, and this time it was signed into law by the new Democratic president (Zuckman 1993).

These examples show the basically undemocratic nature of Congress. On the one hand, the women's movement and its allies have overcome the lack of women in Congress by demonstrating the existence of a women's vote and the electoral advantages of supporting women's equality.[27] To this extent women have been more successful than organized labor at influencing Congress. But on the other hand, resistance has simply been pushed back another step, to presidential vetoes (in these cases), bureaucratic inertia, or (in the case of the ERA) to the power of thirteen states to block a constitutional amendment.

The analogy between gender and class struggles is useful, but we should not apply it mechanically. Marxist theory's claim is that political power is rooted in the relations of production, not that all features of two different sets of productive relations, such as capitalism and patriarchy, must parallel each other. There are significant differences, and even more significant uncertainties. Most important, whereas it is clear that women's liberation requires a radical restructuring of family and household relations—perhaps to the point where it would be more accurate to speak of the destruction of the family and the household, and of their replacement with structures that are very different—it is not at all clear that men cannot be persuaded that such a restructuring is desirable. Many men and women are struggling in their own households to replace patriarchy with a variety of new arrangements. Such struggles are neither widespread nor always successful, but it would be difficult to maintain that they cannot succeed at some point in the future. Attempts to form voluntary small-scale socialist enterprises have generally failed when they collided with the logic of the capitalist market, but there is no analogous economic relation limiting changes in household relations.

It is equally unclear (although much debated) whether or not such a restructuring can be achieved in a capitalist economic environment. The resistance to day care and the Family and Medical Leave Act has involved, in varying proportions, both capitalists and defenders of patriarchy, but we can see from the experience of Western European countries that neither is inherently anticapitalist. Such feminist goals as the right to abortion and effective protection of women against rape and domestic violence seem even less anticapitalist. There would seem to be some hope, then, that the alliance of capitalism and patriarchy can be broken, opening the way to real change on at least some fronts; but all this is highly speculative.

More immediately, the increased number of women elected to Congress in 1992 suggests at least the possibility that even more women may run and win in the near future. Up to now, only countries (or American states) with some variety of proportional representation or multimember districts have managed to elect relatively high proportions of women (though they are still less than 50 percent).[28] Apparently, discrimination (whether by voters, nominators, or financial contributors) still comes into play in single-member districts. If women's gains in 1992 indicate a weakening of such discrimination, real equality of representation may become more possible in the future. If so, Congress may at last crack down on wife-battering and rape, mandate pay equity, provide an adequate child-care system, and otherwise lay the basis for true gender equality. But to say that this is possible is not to say that it will happen; and simply listing the necessary parts of such a program makes it clear how very far we have to go.

6

Congress and African Americans

The category of class is created by the division of labor in the production process; and that of gender, by the division of labor in the sexual act. Race is more problematic. We tend not to realize this because of the widespread false assumption that race is somehow biological; but a few moments' reflection should convince us that it is an entirely social construction. For example, there are people who would be considered black in the United States, colored in South Africa, and white in the Caribbean; there are people who are Native Americans while on a reservation but black when they leave it. Moreover, the supposedly biological rules of descent are different for different racial groups—one can be half Asian, but not half black.[1]

Recently, we have come to see race as a matter of cultural heritage, as the growing use of the term African American instead of black indicates. The new designation is more accurate, but we must then ask why Irish Americans were once but are no longer considered racially distinct from Americans of English or German extraction, while African Americans, Latinos, Native Americans, and Asian Americans still are so considered.

The traditional Marxist answer to this question is that cultural differences come to be seen in terms of *race* when they correspond to and reinforce differences between classes or class segments. In the course of American history, capitalists have used concepts of race to justify paying African American, Latino, and Asian American workers less than whites for the same work; white workers have used them to defend their privileged access to better-paid jobs; and African Americans, Latinos, and Asian Americans have used them to maintain solidarity in fighting to defend and improve their own position. This is not to say that the idea of *race* is created simply for the convenience of the capitalists but, rather, that differences may or may not come to be perceived as racial depending on the usefulness of that perception to all concerned. Nor does it mean that class is logically or historically prior to race as a social division. Cedric

Robinson, in his book entitled *Black Marxism*, has argued the opposite persuasively. In Robinson's view, class divisions were able to arise at all when dominant classes were able to perceive the dominated as a kind of people different from themselves, fitted by nature to serve them. Robinson traces this notion through the development of European feudalism as well as through that of American slavery. The implication of his argument is that race and class are inseparably intertwined, and that neither division can be overcome separately (Robinson 1983).

Nevertheless, race and class are never identical. The perception of *race* is no less real because it is rooted in class. For example, throughout nearly all of U.S. history African Americans have corresponded almost exactly with one or more classes or class segments—first slaves, then sharecroppers in the South, and finally unskilled workers, confined to certain occupations, in the North. The victories of the civil rights movement have made this correspondence less precise, but there is still a statistical correlation between race and the lower stratum of the working class. Yet there are always, and always have been, individuals who achieve different class positions but continue to suffer racial discrimination.

My intent here is not to arrive at a complete understanding of the role of race in American society but, rather, to understand Congress. For that purpose I have used the representation of African Americans as an example, to which I shall limit the rest of the chapter. The equally important but very different ways in which Native Americans, Latinos, and Asian Americans have sought to use Congress must be left for another time.

There have been two periods of African American membership in the U.S. Congress, from 1869 to 1901 and from 1929 to the present. The number of African American members has never been large; in all of the nineteenth century there were only twenty-two, twenty representatives and two senators, and today's delegation of thirty-nine (plus one delegate, who can vote in House committees, including the Committee of the Whole, but not on final passage of bills) is the largest ever. The two centuries show a reflective symmetry. African American membership in the House of Representatives ranged between five and seven during the years from 1871 to 1877, then fell off quickly to one, two, or none for most of the rest of the nineteenth century. That membership ended completely in 1901, not to reappear until the election of Oscar DePriest in 1928, after which it gradually increased up to the present. There have been only four African American senators in the history of the United States, never more than one at a time: Hiram Revels (R-Miss.) from 1870 to 1871, Blanche K. Bruce (R-Miss.) from 1875 to 1881, Edward W. Brooke (R-Mass.) from 1967 to 1979, and Carol Mosley Braun (D-Ill.), who entered the Senate in 1993.[2]

Reconstruction

During Reconstruction, African Americans fought their way into the halls of Congress behind the guns of the Union Army, a force in which many of them had served. Robert Smalls of South Carolina, for example, launched his political career while a slave working on the *Planter*, a steamer in Charleston harbor. On May 13, 1862, Smalls escaped with the *Planter* itself, sixteen fellow slaves, and a cargo of Confederate artillery and ammunition to join the blockading Union forces. General David Hunter sent Smalls to Washington, together with chaplain Mansfield French, to persuade President Lincoln and Secretary of War Edwin Stanton to authorize the enlistment of escaped slaves—known at the time as "contrabands"—into the Union armed forces. Smalls himself was commissioned as a second lieutenant in the United States Colored Troops and assigned to the *Planter* as pilot (under the regulations of the time he was ineligible for the Navy because he had not graduated from a naval school); by the end of the war he had fought in seventeen battles and risen to the rank of captain. After the war Smalls was elected to the South Carolina legislature and later to the U.S. House of Representatives (Taylor 1922, 130; Hine 1982, 342-43; Uya 1971). Not all African American members of Congress shared Smalls's personal involvement in the armed struggle; but all owed their ability to stand for election—and their very freedom as well—to the occupying Union Army.

If African Americans entered Congress at the point of a gun, they left it at the end of a rope, as hooded lynch mobs and racist local officials worked together to deprive African American voters of the franchise. After being driven from the congressional arena, the African American representatives suffered a second attack, this time against their reputations. Professor William Archibald Dunning of Columbia University launched a movement to carry over into the realm of ideas the victory that Southern segregationists had already won in the political sphere (Dunning 1898, 1907). Dunning and his students firmly established in the minds of most white Americans the view that "black leadership was either . . . venal and inexperienced . . . or under the total control of unprincipled whites" (Rabinowitz 1982, xi). No less a figure than Woodrow Wilson, while still a political scientist, wrote:

> Unscrupulous adventurers appeared, to act as the leaders of the inexperienced blacks in taking possession first of the conventions, and afterwards of the state governments; and in the States where the negroes were most numerous or their leaders most shrewd and unprincipled, an extraordinary carnival of public crime set in under the forms of law. (Wilson [1893] 1898)[3]

The attack of the Dunningites drew an immediate response, from W.E.B. DuBois ([1903] 1969, [1953] 1963) among others, thus beginning a long period in which debate focused on moral and political evaluation of the African American members of Congress; more recently, scholarly attention has begun to shift to the more detailed study of "how blacks gained, maintained, and finally lost power—in other words, how they *functioned* in Reconstruction politics and within the Republican party" (Rabinowitz 1982, xviii). We might also ask how their success or failure was related to the social position of the mass of African American freedmen.

In 1870 the former slaves constituted a group—in this case, one for which class and racial boundaries corresponded closely—that was oppressed economically but was now a subordinate member of the ruling political coalition, a coalition expressed in the form of the Republican Party. Like Marx's idealized proletariat, they were doubly free, free of the slave owner but also free of all means of keeping themselves alive unless they could sell their only commodity, their labor power; and the only buyers on hand were their former owners. However, they did have one other resource—their votes. Their best hope was to trade those votes for Republican help in reconstructing the South. If they could use the power of the state to break up the plantations and give the freedmen land, while creating schools to educate them and legal institutions to protect their rights, the Republican political alliance would acquire a permanent social foundation, opening the South to capitalist development and laying the basis for racial integration (Foner 1988, 158-64, 289-90).

That hope failed. Once the power of the slave owners had been broken, the now hegemonic Northern capitalists had no great need to reform the Southern economy. The freedmen's votes were not enough to make a difference. First, they were not needed. As James G. Blaine (R-Maine) told the African American John R. Lynch (R-Miss.) in 1875, the defeat of Reconstruction would produce "a solid North against a solid South; in which case Republicans would have nothing to fear."[4] More basically, the black franchise proved to be the effect, rather than the cause, of political power. Southern congressional elections—at least those in districts with substantial numbers of black voters—began with armed clashes at campaign rallies and frequently ended with a floor vote in the House of Representatives to decide which of two or more claimants to victory would be seated. Thus even the number of votes credited to a candidate depended on factors other than the number of votes actually cast for him. The freedmen organized into political clubs and armed militias to defend their position, but once they lost the support of Northern Republicans and the Union Army, they were no match for the white conservatives, the Confederate veterans, and the Ku Klux Klan.

For example, James Rapier (R-Ala.) was threatened with death during his 1874 reelection campaign. Rapier went to Washington to ask for federal troops to guard the polling places, but he did not get them. There was violence throughout the district on election day; freedmen seeking to vote in Eufaula were attacked and between ten and fourteen of them were killed. On this matter Loren Schweninger concludes: "In the three counties where racial violence was most prevalent, the Republican vote fell off sharply compared to previous elections. As a result, Rapier lost to former Confederate Jeremiah N. Williams by 1,056 votes" (Schweninger 1982, 86). In a related vein, Eric Foner describes Mississippi in 1875:

> On election eve, armed riders drove freedmen from their homes and warned that they would be killed if they appeared to cast ballots. "It was the most violent time that ever we have seen," said one black official. At Aberdeen, whites equipped with rifles and a six-pounder cannon "came armed to the polls and drove colored men away." (Foner 1988, 561)

The fading of hopes for radical reconstruction left the African American members of Congress with a choice between two more limited strategies. They could continue to demand equality and justice, but with little possibility of winning those demands. This protest strategy would serve the more limited goal of uniting their African American constituents, but it was difficult to sustain in the absence of tangible results. More and more they sought, instead, to help their constituents and themselves by seeking particularized benefits.

In the strategy of accommodation, the political leaders of oppressed groups seek to integrate themselves and their constituents into the existing system on the system's own terms (Barnett 1977, 17-18). For African American members of Congress in and immediately after Reconstruction, this meant working to get patronage jobs for their supporters and federally financed projects for their districts. In contrast, the strategy of protest entails using whatever political resources one has to call attention to injustice and to organize support and pressure from those outside the centers of decisionmaking (Barnett 1977, 20-22). African American members of Congress tried both of these strategies at one time or another. But Marguerite Barnett's observation (p. 68) about the Congressional Black Caucus in the twentieth century holds true for the nineteenth century as well. Given the imbalance of social and political power, neither strategy was very effective.

Patronage was central to the accommodationist strategy. As William C. Harris observed in a study of Senator Blanche K. Bruce (R-Miss.):

> To Bruce a wise federal patronage policy and security for Southern blacks were inseparable. Unless patronage could be extended to true Republicans, no

well-disciplined and viable party could exist in the South; and without a strong Republican party, able to challenge the Democrats for power, black rights could not be maintained short of military intervention, which, Bruce knew, northerners would no longer support. (Harris 1982, 3-38)

However, such concerns inevitably came to be seen by many as personal corruption, further undermining the reputation of the African American members of Congress.

Another part of the accommodationist strategy was the pursuit of particularized district benefits. If an African American member of Congress could deliver such benefits, then, like any other member, he (I say he because there were no women in Congress until the early twentieth century) could earn the gratitude and support of his constituents. From this perspective the job of the African American member of Congress could be seen as no different from that of any other member, and the successful delivery of district benefits could be taken as a measure of the extent to which the member had been able to integrate himself into the political system. Thus Smalls worked hard to convince the Navy of the advantages of the Port Royal harbor for a base, and Rapier sought $50,000 to dredge the Pea and Chochawatche rivers (Uya 1971, 92-93; Schweninger 1982, 82). Alrutheus Taylor reports similar district-oriented activity on the part of Benjamin S. Turner and his successor, James T. Rapier, of Alabama, who worked for the construction of buildings in their district, for river and harbor improvements, and for establishment of Montgomery as a port of entry; and on the part of Josiah T. Walls of Florida, "perhaps the most persistent [of the African American members of Congress] in the effort to secure improvements for his district and State," who proposed the building of customs houses, river and harbor improvements, a coastal lifesaving station, railroad and telegraph rights of way through public lands, and creation of a Navy yard at Pensacola (Taylor 1922, 159). But Taylor also noted the weak point of the accommodationist strategy:

two general types of legislation, the one proposing local improvements, the other seeking social justice for the Negro race, were preeminent in the measures proposed by the Negro Congressmen. . . . However, most of these measures, regardless of merit, met in general one of three fates: they were either sidetracked in committee, reported adversely, or defeated after debate in open session. . . .

There were two preeminent causes for the failure of some of these bills. The Negro membership in any Congress, in the first place always an exceedingly small minority, was never a determining factor in the passage of a measure proposed by one of this particular group. Secondly, the objects of the suspicion of their party colleagues, and regarded by them as an experiment in the legislative program of the nation, these men were not generally able to secure for their measures sufficient white Republican votes.[5]

The nineteenth-century African American members of Congress had turned to accommodation to adapt to the loss of power. But as the years went by they were less and less able to win even the particularized benefits they needed to serve their districts. Accommodation was a strategy without a future. Their numbers rapidly dwindled; from 1877 to 1901 there were never more than three African Americans in the House, and frequently there were none at all.

George H. White (R-N.C.) was the only African American in Congress from 1897 to 1901. White spoke out against speeches vilifying African Americans made on the floor of the House, introduced the first bill to make lynching a federal crime, and joined the efforts of Marlin E. Olmsted (R-Penn.) and Edgar D. Crumpacker (R-Ind.) to decrease the number of representatives allotted to states that had disenfranchised African American voters; but these efforts found little support. White chose not to run in 1900 (Logan 1954, 90-96). On January 29, 1901, he bid farewell to Congress:

> This, Mr. Chairman, is perhaps the Negroes' temporary farewell to the American Congress; but let me say, Phoenix-like he will rise up some day and come again. These parting words are in behalf of an outraged, heart-broken, bruised and bleeding, but God-fearing people, faithful, industrious, loyal, rising people—full of potential force.[6]

The era was over. The Phoenix would rise again, but slowly, and not until almost thirty years later.

The Twentieth Century

In some ways African American congressional representation in the twentieth century was very different from that in the nineteenth; in other ways it was not different at all. The earlier African American members of Congress had all come from the South, generally from rural areas. As state legal manipulations and Ku Klux Klan terror disenfranchised more and more African American voters, only those districts with the largest black majorities had any chance of continuing to elect a black representative; by the end of the century, black exclusion from the voting rolls had reached such an extent that even these districts could no longer do so.

Nowhere in the country were there enough white voters willing to vote for an otherwise qualified black candidate to make his or her election a real possibility anywhere but in a heavily black district. Eventually, such districts began to grow up in Northern cities. There is a long-running debate in the United States about the relative severity of racism in the

North and the South. Certainly it is strong in both places, but it takes different forms. In the North in the early and middle twentieth century, one form it took was that of rigid housing segregation. African Americans in Chicago, New York, and other large Northern cities found themselves confined to narrow ghettos almost exclusively. As these ghettos grew, fed by flight from the repression in the South, they began to be large enough to send their own representatives to Congress.

The cities in which the ghettos had grown tended to be those dominated by political machines. Since the machine bosses were generally fighting for control of their states, they wanted to maximize the number of voters in their jurisdictions; and they had well-developed mechanisms for keeping those voters under control. The combination of patronage and discipline that kept European immigrants in line would work just as well for African Americans, with the added advantage that the latter expected even less in return for their votes (Rakove 1975, 257).

The first twentieth-century African American member of Congress, Chicago Republican Oscar DePriest, was elected to the House in 1928. DePriest was allied with Chicago's flamboyant, corrupt Republican mayor, William Thompson; but Thompson and the Republicans were losing control of the city to the better-organized Democratic machine of Anton Cermak, and DePriest was defeated in 1934 by the African American Democrat Arthur Mitchell. Mitchell in turn was succeeded after 1942 by Democrat William Dawson, a former Republican DePriest supporter who had switched parties and become the Democratic ward leader in 1933.[7] Not until 1944 did a second Northern city send an African American representative to Washington—namely, Democrat Adam Clayton Powell, Jr., of New York. Powell and Dawson were joined by Charles C. Diggs, Jr., of Detroit in 1955, Robert N.C. Nix of Philadelphia in 1958, Augustus F. Hawkins of Los Angeles in 1963, and a second Detroit representative, John F. Conyers, in 1965. There was a brief setback in 1967 when Powell was suspended for legal improprieties, but the size of the African American delegation in the House then began to grow more rapidly, to nine in 1969, twelve in 1971, and fifteen in 1973, reaching its present total of thirty-eight representatives and one delegate in the 1992 election. The 1990 election had also brought the victory of Gary Franks of Connecticut, the first Republican African American member of the House since DePriest. There have also been two African American senators, Republican Edward Brooke of Massachusetts, who served from 1967 to 1978, and Democrat Carol Mosley Braun of Illinois, who took office in 1993.

Brooke, Braun, Franks, Ron Dellums (D-Cal.), Alan Wheat (D-Mo.), and a few other African American members of Congress have been able to win in districts with a majority of white voters, but this pattern has not been typical. It is almost as true today as it was in the 1890s that African

American representation in Congress depends on the existence of districts in which African American voters make up a majority or near-majority. For this reason African American political leaders have focused much of their energy on battles over the drawing of district lines. The Voting Rights Act of 1982, as subsequently interpreted by the federal courts, required that the redrawing of district lines after the 1990 census be done in such a way as to maximize African American and other non-white representation, a requirement that was almost entirely responsible for the increase from twenty-five to thirty-eight African American seats in the House. In the 1993 case of *Shaw v. Reno* the Supreme Court ruled that racial districting of this sort was unconstitutional, raising the possibility that African American representation has now reached its highest point (Kaplan 1993).

I remarked earlier that African American congressional representation in the twentieth century is a mirror image of that in the nineteenth. This is true of political activity as well as of numbers. The nineteenth-century African American members of Congress had turned to an accommodationist concern with particularized benefits and patronage as their hopes for major change had faded. Their counterparts in the mid-twentieth century never had much ground on which to expect real change, and some, like Dawson, concentrated on patronage and district concerns from the beginning; but others, like Powell and DePriest, though not averse to patronage, also chose to speak and act as the voice of African Americans for racial equality.[8] Early protest activities, such as DePriest's fight to integrate the House restaurant, were of primarily symbolic importance (Rudwick 1966); but even these helped stimulate the rise of the civil rights movement, which eventually made more African American legislative victories possible.

The growth of the civil rights movement in the 1950s and 1960s, and the black liberation movement after it, created new possibilities and new hope. Massive demonstrations, the moral strength of nonviolent protesters, the fury and bravery of ghetto residents who rose in disorganized and often bloody rebellion, and the need of Democratic Party leaders for African American votes (Piven and Cloward 1971, 248-84) combined to break the Southern segregationists' stranglehold on the congressional committee system and opened the way to passage of the Civil Rights Act of 1964, the Voting Rights Act of 1965, and the various parts of the War on Poverty. Powell, who had once been barred by his race from questioning witnesses before the House Education and Labor Committee, now found himself the committee's chairman (Barone and Ujifusa 1987, 885). Until he was driven from office in 1967, Powell used the leverage of his new position to force racial equality into the center of national policymaking. Perhaps his greatest contribution to the fight for racial equality was the

Powell Amendment, which provided that no funds authorized in a given bill could be spent for activities that were racially discriminatory. Powell had first offered this amendment in 1946. Now, as chair of the House committee with jurisdiction over all federal welfare, education, and health-care programs, Powell attached this amendment to a wide variety of bills. This tactic sometimes resulted in the loss of votes from Southern Democrats and the defeat or delay of such major initiatives as federal aid to education, and led to Powell's being attacked by white Northern liberals as a grandstanding obstructionist; but his use of the Powell Amendment made it clear that African Americans could no longer be counted on to accept discrimination in exchange for a lesser share of material benefits. The principles of the Powell Amendment eventually became Title Six of the Civil Rights Act of 1964 (E. Alexander 1983, 61-70; Christopher 1971, 200).[9]

Powell was also an early advocate of the worldwide unity of people who were oppressed by racism, colonialism, and imperialism. When leaders of Africa and Asia met in Bandung, Indonesia, in 1956 to protest the Cold War and declare that they represented a "Third World," committed to neither capitalism nor communism but to development, Powell urged the United States to send official observers. With the refusal of the Eisenhower administration—whose secretary of state, John Foster Dulles, was known for his view that neutralism in the Cold War was immoral—Powell attended as a private citizen, thereby highlighting the commonalities he perceived between African Americans and the developing world (Miller 1979, 248).

As had been the case with many of the nineteenth-century African American members of Congress, Powell's legislative and political successes were met with legal attacks. On March 6, 1960, he referred to a New York woman, Esther James, as a "bag woman"—that is, as someone who delivered bribes—during a television broadcast. When James sued him for libel, Powell (unsuccessfully) claimed Congressional immunity, and stayed out of the state of New York for eighteen months in order to avoid arrest. He was also accused of cashing the paycheck of his estranged wife, who was on his staff payroll but lived in Puerto Rico, and of traveling at public expense for private purposes. On March 1, 1967, the House voted not to seat him; he won a special election for the empty seat but did not actually return to the House until he had also won the regular election in 1968. In 1969 the Supreme Court ruled that his exclusion had been unconstitutional; but by this time Powell had lost interest in the job and was spending a great deal of time in the Bahamas. He lost the 1970 Democratic primary to another African American candidate, Charles Rangel (Christopher 1971, 203-08).

The Congressional Black Caucus

African American representation in Congress entered a new period with the organization of the Congressional Black Caucus (CBC) in 1971. This was a time of increasingly massive and militant protest by African Americans, with some degree of support for this protest in many parts of the white population. The caucus began with 13 members and 12 votes. (One member, Walter Fauntroy, was the nonvoting delegate from the District of Columbia.) As Senator Edward Brooke (R-Mass.) was not a member, the caucus has always been composed solely of members of the House and, until the election of Gary Franks (R-Conn.) in 1990, of Democrats.

The Congressional Black Caucus sought to give direction to the broader civil rights/black liberation movement. As Barnett put it, the caucus saw itself as "representative-at-large for 20 million black people." During its first year it traveled across the country to hold public hearings and develop a "Black Agenda," a platform for basic social change that, in turn, became the basis for the Black Political Convention held in Gary, Indiana, in March 1972 (Barnett 1977, 20-21). The convention marked a high point of the African American nationalist movement. More than 12,000 people took part as delegates or observers, and they spanned the political spectrum. The convention founded the National Black Political Assembly, with a revised Black Agenda calling for sweeping change:

> We come to Gary in an hour of great crisis and tremendous promise for Black America. While the white nation hovers on the brink of chaos, while its politicians offer no hope of real change, we stand on the edge of history and are faced with an amazing and frightening choice: We may choose in 1972 to slip back into the decadent white politics of American life, or we may press forward, moving relentlessly from Gary to the creation of our own black life. The choice is large, but the time is very short. . . . The crises we face as black people are the crises of the entire society. They go deep, to the very bones and marrow, to the essential nature of America's economic, political, and cultural systems. They are the natural end-product of a society built on the twin foundations of white racism and white capitalism.[10]

However, the Black Political Convention came under attack, particularly for its condemnation of Zionism, but more generally because of its militant nationalist tone and the hostility toward the Democratic Party expressed by many delegates. Although the convention had been called for by Caucus Chairman Charles Diggs (D-Mich.), it was never officially endorsed by the Congressional Black Caucus, and several caucus members felt the need to dissociate themselves from it. The caucus issued a declaration of support for Israel (Barnett 1977, 21) and later adopted its own "Black Bill of Rights" as a more moderate alternative to the Black Agenda. All but a few of the African American members of Congress stayed away from the follow-up convention in Little Rock in 1974, while the nationalist leaders attacked them as "misleaders" working in a "bankrupt electoral system" (Marable 1980, 80). With the breakdown of African American unity on the one hand, and the reelection of Richard Nixon in 1972 by an overwhelming margin on the other, hopes for continuing political change began to fade, and the African American members of Congress began to turn toward consolidation and accommodation.

Nixon's triumph, of course, was short-lived, and the Carter administration that eventually followed was more open to African American participation than any that had gone before. Thus the accommodationist trend was strengthened even further. Efforts by African American members of Congress to secure patronage from their fellow Democrat in the White House now were accompanied by some hope of success; and the president's positive rhetoric on racial justice also made it easier to believe that the lives of black people could be improved without more sweeping social change. All this changed with the Reagan Revolution. Far more than Nixon, Ronald Reagan articulated a radical and comprehensive rightward restructuring of public policy; also unlike Nixon, Reagan came to office with the political support he needed to put his program into action. Reagan's electoral margin in 1980 was large, but no greater than Nixon's had been in 1972. However, Nixon had made no inroads at all into the Democratic control of Congress, and Congress fought him to a standstill, or worse, across a broad range of issues. Reagan, by contrast, won control of the Senate and cut the Democratic majority in the House far enough that, at least in his early days, he was able to pass his programs virtually at will. The Reagan threat pushed the Congressional Black Caucus back toward the strategy of protest. The caucus developed a new tool, the Congressional Black Caucus Alternative Budget, as a way to unite and focus the many forces opposed to Reagan.[11]

The Alternative Budget

The Alternative Budget fits into the protest strategy. It requires unity among the black representatives and is a device for obtaining that unity. It has also served as a sweeping indictment of federal policy, intended as the basis for a potential multiracial progressive coalition. Therefore, such a coalition must begin to develop if the Alternative Budget is to retain its effectiveness as a unifying device. Although there were some promising early signs that such a coalition might develop (as will be discussed), the Alternative Budget has failed to gain in support over the years (see Table

6.1) and, perhaps in consequence, has also become less of a source of unity among the African American members of Congress.

The first Congressional Black Caucus Alternative Budget was presented in 1981. It was a reaction to the Reagan administration's program in general; but, more specifically, it responded to a challenge issued by President Reagan on February 18 for anyone who did not like his budget to come up with a better one.[12] It was also the result of frustration with the House Democratic leadership's strategy of seeking to moderate rather than to oppose the thrust of the Reagan program. The Congressional Black Caucus wanted to confront Reagan's budget directly. It proposed to balance the budget; to restore cuts in social service, welfare, and economic development programs; to increase the tax cut for low-income taxpayers; to cut military spending; and to raise taxes on the rich. The African American members of Congress hoped that their budget

TABLE 6.1 Votes For and Against Congressional Black Caucus Alternative Budget, with Number of Black Members Voting "Present" by Fiscal Year and Date

Fiscal year	Votes for	Votes against	Black members voting "P"	Date
1982	69	356	0	5/06/81
1983	86	322	0	5/24/82
1984[a]	—	—	—	—
1985	76	333	0	4/05/84
1986	54	361	1	5/23/85
1987	61	359	1	5/15/86
1988	56	362	2	4/09/87
1989[a]	—	—	—	—
1990	81	343	1	5/04/89
1991	90	334	0	5/01/90

[a] Alternative Budget not offered on floor.

Source: Calculated from roll call votes reported in *Congressional Record* and *Congressional Quarterly Weekly Report* for dates cited.

TABLE 6.2 Topics Assigned for Debate Presentation by Congressional Black Caucus Members: Alternative Budget Debate, May 5-6, 1981

Member (State)	Topic(s)
Chisholm (N.Y.)	Education
Clay (Mo.)	Economic impact of budget
Collins (Ill.)	Impact on local self-help efforts Welfare
Conyers (Mich.)	Military Taxes
Crockett (Mich.)	Urban assistance
Dellums (Cal.)	Military
Dixon (Cal.)	Foreign aid
Dymally (Cal.)	Positive role of federal government
Fauntroy (DC)	Sponsor and floor manager Housing
Ford (Tenn.)	Tax expenditures
Gray (Penn.)	Foreign aid
Hawkins (Cal.)	Employment programs
Leland (Tex.)	Energy
Mitchell (Md.)	Housing Small business Reconciliation procedure
Rangel (N.Y.) Savage (Ill.)	Taxes Transportation Economic development
Stokes (Ohio)	Health care and science
Washington (Ill.)	Justice and courts

Source: Tabulated from the Congressional Record, May 5 & 6, 1981.

would appeal to popular concerns for a balanced budget and lower taxes for most people while also taking on the Reagan administration squarely regarding issues important to liberals. However, the Democratic leadership favored another approach; in an unsuccessful attempt to hold on to the votes of the Southern conservative Democrats known colloquially as "boll weevils," it presented a budget that accepted most of the Reagan tax cuts and military increases, restored less of the domestic cuts than had been proposed by the caucus, and included a sizable deficit.

The presentation of the Alternative Budget on the floor of the House was a major event. Each of the eighteen black representatives was assigned an area of the budget to present in the debate (see Table 6.2); many spoke several times and engaged in floor colloquies with their colleagues. Representatives Gus Savage (D-Ill.) and George Crockett (D-Mich.) each made the presentation of the Alternative Budget the occasion for his maiden speech in the House. The debate consumed six hours over the course of two days and covered forty-seven pages of the *Congressional Record*, totals never approached again in the subsequent history of caucus budgets (see Table 6.3). The eighteen African American representatives made detailed presentations of the Alternative Budget; but the basic philosophy behind it may be summed up in three points. First, the caucus members argued that government has a positive role to play in

TABLE 6.3 Time and Space Taken by Congressional Black Caucus Alternative Budget Debate, by Year

Calendar year	Pages in Congressional Record	Duration of Debate
1981	May 5: 18 pp. May 6: 29 pp.	2 hrs. 4 hrs.
	47 pp.	6 hrs.
1982	May 24: 28 pp.	3½ hrs.
1983[a]	—	—
1984	April 5: 25 pp.	2 hrs. 50 min.
1985	May 22: 9 pp.	1 hr. 10 min.
1986	May 15: 12 pp.	2 hrs. 5 min.
1987	April 9: 9 pp.	1 hr. 30 min.

[a] Alternative Budget not offered on floor.

Source: Calculated from *Congressional Record*, 1981-1987, on the dates cited.

economic development and, therefore, that Reagan's proposed domestic cuts would hurt the economy rather than help it. Second, they argued that U.S. foreign policy was overly militaristic, that the nation stood to gain more from development aid than from military might, and that several major weapons systems under development were totally unneeded and therefore wasteful. Third, they proposed to raise sufficient revenue to balance the budget by eliminating loopholes in the tax system while actually lowering taxes for the majority of taxpayers.

The Congressional Black Caucus was directly opposed to the Democratic leadership on the link between domestic and military spending. Immediately before taking up the Alternative Budget the House, by voice vote, had adopted the Hefner amendment, which raised the defense-spending levels in the Budget Committee budget to the amount proposed by the Reagan administration. This was done, in the words of Budget Committee Chairman James Jones (D-Okla.), so "that we could put aside this issue of how much will be spent on defense and take that out of the partisan rhetoric" and to "get on with the more substantive economic decisions that have to be made." Caucus member John Conyers (D-Mich.) was not able to get enough hands even to have a recorded vote on Hefner's amendment. [13]

The caucus's strategy was exactly the opposite of the Democratic leadership's. Rather than accept Reagan's military requests in order to focus the debate on his economic program, Representatives Dellums and Conyers argued for the caucus that it was only Reagan's alarmist foreign and military policy statements that made it possible for him to get his conservative domestic agenda taken seriously. Conyers explained that:

> nobody on either side of the aisle, with either of the two major budgets before us, could have dared to come in with human resources cuts that they have offered in their budgets unless they could create the bugaboo of a military dilemma that required us to increase by roughly $40 billion in each budget to the highest peacetime increase in American history. The budget that they are now confronting us with at this point could not be done based on their palpably refutable economic notion of balancing the budget, getting Government off people's backs, reducing the deficit—none of which under their theories are going to work anyway—but never, on a straight economic approach, could they have come in with the inhumane cuts and the untold suffering that will be spread across our land for many, many years to come if what I am afraid happens in this Congress happens here today. [14]

Finally, these substantive points were tied together by a general theme: that the Congressional Black Caucus was performing a service of political leadership by providing a budget that—unlike the budget proposed successfully by Phil Gramm (D-Tex.) and Delbert Latta (R-Ohio)—would be good for all Americans, not just black people. As Caucus Chairman Fauntroy put it in his opening statement:

> The most serious problems confronting this Nation just happen to be reflected most acutely in the black experience. This is a program for all Americans. The elderly on limited income, most of whom are white; the struggling young couples all over the Nation who want but cannot find affordable housing anywhere, most of whom are white; the coal miners whose black lung benefits are being threatened, most of whom are white; young people from low- and middle-income families who would be denied guaranteed student loans and basic opportunity grants for higher education, most of whom are white; the sick, the cold, the hungry, the handicapped, most of whom are white and all of whose burdens will be made heavier by the Gramm-Latta budget proposal.[15]

The Alternative Budget offered comprehensive but controversial solutions to the nation's problems. Although its authors' utmost hope must surely have been that their budget would pass, their more realistic goal was to start a national debate in which the caucus and its budget would serve as a rallying point around which to begin to build a progressive coalition. However, they succeeded in making only very limited steps toward this goal. For example, Patricia Schroeder (D-Colo.) spoke in favor of the Alternative Budget, identifying herself as co-chair of the Congresswomen's Caucus and arguing that the Gramm-Latta budget would "just exacerbate and accelerate the movement of women into poverty." She urged members to vote for the Alternative Budget, and then to vote for the Jones budget as "an excellent compromise if this does not pass."[16] A majority (five) of Democratic congresswomen followed this strategy, a total that included the two black congresswomen, leaving white women Democrats evenly split. All of the Republican women, like the Republican men, opposed the Alternative Budget. Similarly, although Representative Robert Garcia (D-N.Y.) spoke in favor of the Alternative Budget as chairman of the Hispanic Caucus, he was not able to deliver the votes of the Hispanic members as a bloc (see Table 6.4).

Perhaps it is even more significant that very few nonblack representatives took part in the debate; other than the black members, only eleven people spoke in favor of the Alternative Budget, and only three spoke against it. The black representatives saw the Alternative Budget not only as a chance to take a political position but also as an accomplishment in which they took pride. They hoped to show the nation that black representatives could do at least as good a job as white ones in putting together a fairly technical document and in exercising political leadership. They felt that they deserved respect for having done so and were frustrated by the lack of attention their colleagues gave them. Representative Conyers pleaded, "Please begin to dialogue with us."[17] Savage

TABLE 6.4 Support for Congressional Black Caucus Alternative Budgets by Selected Groups, 1981-1987

Group	1981 #/% Y's	1982 #/% Y's	1984 #/% Y's	1985 #/% Y's	1986 #/% Y's	1987 #/% Y's
Democrats	69/28	86/35	76/28	54/21	61/24	56/22
White Democrats	52/23	71/31	56/22	35/15	41/18	33/13
Women Democrats	5/56	5/50	8/62	5/45	7/64	5/42
White women Democrats	3/43	3/38	6/55	4/40	6/60	4/36
Hispanic Democrats	3/60	3/60	4/44	4/40	5/50	na

Source: Calculated by author from roll call votes as reported in Congressional Quarterly 1982, 18H-19H; 1983, 28H-29H; 1985a, 22H-23H; 1986, 38H- 39H; 1987, 36H-37H; 1988, 18H-19H.

remarked, "I only wish that because of the present racial makeup of those in attendance, that they could call for a vote suddenly."[18] And Parren Mitchell (D-Md.) condemned "the Members [who] are not here because they are so racist they cannot accept a constructive alternative budget which emanates from a Congressional Black Caucus but which is designed to help all of the people of this Nation."[19]

Finally, after six hours of floor debate, the Alternative Budget was defeated by a vote of 69 to 356. Of the 69 votes in favor, 64 were from Northern Democrats (including 15 of the 17 voting caucus members) and none were from Republicans. Although 69 was a small number, it marked a beginning, the significance of which would depend on what happened in the ensuing years.

The caucus offered an Alternative Budget again in 1982 and increased its support to 86 votes, a promising sign for the future. The gain of 17 votes from 1981 to 1982 showed that it was possible for votes to be changed. The 1982 election increased the numbers both of liberals and of black members in the House, and increased the Democratic majority from 243-192 to 269-166. Five new black representatives were elected, all Democrats: Katie Hall (Indiana), Major R. Owens (New York), Edolphus Towns (New York), Alan Wheat (Missouri), and, following Harold Washington's resignation to become mayor of Chicago, Charles A. Hayes (Illinois). Shirley Chisholm had retired at the end of 1982, thus bringing the strength of the CBC to 21 members, including the nonvoting Fauntroy.

In addition, the House Budget Committee's budget proposal was defeated in 1982, putting pressure on the leadership to take more account of the caucus.

However, the caucus chose to pursue a more accommodationist strategy in 1983. In a move attributed to Julian Dixon (D-Cal.), then the chair of the CBC, and William Gray (D-Penn.), a member of the House Budget Committee, the CBC agreed not to offer its budget proposal as a floor amendment. In exchange, the budget as passed by the House included higher funding levels for social programs (Cohodas 1985). The House Democratic leadership, having gained enough seats in the 1982 election to outvote the Reaganite coalition of Republicans and Southern conservative Democrats, was anxious to prevent the offering of divisive amendments to its budget on the floor. The budget resolution was brought up under a rule that permitted only one amendment, to be offered by the minority party, thus limiting the potential for dissension among the Democrats. The caucus prepared and released its Alternative Budget as usual, but it was not voted on by the House.

Not all of the African American members of Congress had agreed with this strategy. Some had testified before the Rules Committee to ask for the chance to vote on their budget,[20] and Conyers spoke passionately against the rule in floor debate:

> Mr. Speaker, this is the saddest day in the history of the budget because the Congressional Black Caucus alternative budget for the first time in the years that we have been constructing one has been turned down for consideration and debate. It is an insult to the millions of Americans who have come to rely on it, to the labor, community, civil rights organizations, the churches, the nuclear freeze organizations, who have all been asking this Member, "Where is the Congressional Black Caucus alternative budget? Can we debate it? Can we get a vote on it? We got 86 votes last time. Unemployment is higher. The situation is worse than ever."

Conyers condemned "the leadership and some members of the Black Caucus" for not wanting to rock the boat, rejected as inadequate the opportunity to speak about the Alternative Budget for an hour during the annual Humphrey-Hawkins debate, and concluded: "Well, Mr. Speaker, and Mr. Leader, I consider that an insult to the black people, the working people and those who have looked for some inspiration from the alternative budget of the Congressional Black Caucus."[21] Conyers was able to persuade only two other black representatives, Dellums and Savage, to join him in voting against the rule; the other sixteen all joined the 230 to 187 majority by which the closed rule was adopted.[22]

In 1984 the Congressional Black Caucus once again offered its budget as a floor amendment, and it has continued to do so in most years since then; but the time for debate has been reduced considerably. Whereas the 1981 and 1982 Alternative Budgets were debated under the five-minute rule, which allows any Member to get at least five minutes by moving "to strike the requisite number of words," the rule under which it was considered in 1984 limited all debate to two hours. Similar limitations were imposed in 1985 (one hour), 1986 (two hours), and 1987 (one hour). Such limitations may well have been necessary to allow the House to deal with the increasingly complex budget debate; but they made it difficult for the caucus to give the kind of detailed, comprehensive presentation it had taken pride in during the first two years of its budget alternative. Members who had previously been able to get fifteen or twenty minutes for their presentations in 1981 and 1982 (extending their initial five-minute allotments by unanimous consent) now had to summarize what they wanted to say in two minutes, one minute, or thirty seconds. This arrangement interfered with two of the purposes of the Alternative Budget: to explain an alternative philosophy about such issues as military spending and its relation to the economy, and to give African American representatives a chance to demonstrate their technical competence to their colleagues and their constituents. For example, in 1984 the caucus once again assigned specific areas to its members for floor presentation, but only twelve such presentations were actually made, with two more inserted in the *Congressional Record*. The other supporting speeches were more general political statements.

Finally, the refusal of the Democratic leadership to respond to the challenge of the Alternative Budget was institutionalized by the change in procedure. House rules specify that the time for debate on an amendment is to be equally divided between the amendment's sponsor and an opponent. In the case of such a substitute amendment, the opponent would normally be the floor manager of the original bill, in this case the chair of the House Budget Committee. But in the case of the Alternative Budget, control of the opposing time was left to the Republicans: Delbert Latta (R-Ohio), ranking minority member of the Budget Committee, in 1984, 1985, and 1987, and Denny Smith (R-Ore.) in 1986. Budget Committee chair James Jones (D-Okla.) did speak in opposition in 1984 (he was the only Democrat to do so—and he used the caucus's time for that purpose); but even then he did not actually make any arguments against the Alternative Budget, instead merely pointing out the significant differences between it and the Budget Committee version, and arguing that "what you vote for today on a budget resolution is the way you should be prepared to vote in implementing the budget next week, next month, and over the rest of this year."[23]

One reason the caucus did not push its Alternative Budget harder during the years 1985-1988 was that one of its members, William Gray

(D-Penn.), had become chair of the House Budget Committee. The other African American members of Congress believed that Gray was having a favorable effect on the Congressional Budget Resolution, and they were unwilling to embarrass him with too much open criticism.[24] In 1988 Gray was a party to the "budget summit" negotiations between congressional leaders and President Reagan. The agreement reached by these negotiations kept the Alternative Budget off the floor entirely.

In 1989 Gray's term as House Budget chair had expired, and the caucus, now chaired by Dellums, did insist on a floor vote. But what was once a major political event had now become an empty routine, a symbol of the exact mixture of respect and disdain in which the Democratic Party holds its African American members.[25]

Why has the Alternative Budget never realized its potential as a progressive rallying point? I believe that there are two immediate reasons. Within Congress, a number of otherwise liberal white members have not been willing to vote for a budget proposal labeled "black"; and outside Congress, efforts to mobilize public support for the Alternative Budget have been hampered by strained relations between the Congressional Black Caucus and predominantly white liberal interest groups. Each of these immediate reasons is rooted in turn in the continuing racial oppression of African Americans.

The Alternative Budget presents a radically different alternative to the conservative policies of recent U.S. presidents. The strong opposition it faces is not surprising. However, many African American members of Congress believe that some of their colleagues have voted against it on purely racial grounds, even though they agree with its substance. Such racism might reside in a member's *intentions* (conscious hostility toward black colleagues), *perceptions* (belief that a budget proposal issuing from the Congressional Black Caucus does not merit serious consideration), or *political calculations* (fear that white constituents might resent a vote for a black-identified budget). In any case, the results are the same: a discouragingly low vote for the Alternative Budget each year.

At least one white member of Congress has shared this analysis. During the 1982 floor debate Mary Rose Oakar (D-Ohio), a strong supporter of the Alternative Budget, said that "lots of people have talked privately about agreeing with it, as they did in the last session, but they did not support it." Oakar added:

Unfortunately, I happen to believe it is because it is presented by the Black Caucus. I really feel very badly that I have to say that on the floor of the House of Representatives, but I personally feel that is why it is not getting more support.

It is about time that we openly acknowledged that there is that subtle form of prejudice that exists.[26]

We can get a rough estimate of the impact of racism by comparing members' liberalism with their vote on the Alternative Budget. Table 6.5 presents such a comparison, using ratings from the liberal interest group Americans for Democratic Action (ADA) as the measure of liberalism, for the votes in 1985 and 1986.[27]

Among members of Congress with ADA scores of 80 or higher (a cutting point chosen in order to include most of the Congressional Black Caucus members), support for the Alternative Budget is indeed significantly lower among white than among black members, suggesting that race does operate separately from ideology in determining the vote. But further analysis—including votes in other years and alternative measures of liberalism—would be needed to confirm this suggestion.

The caucus members, or at least some of them, also meant to use the Alternative Budget to help build an anti-Reagan coalition. They attempted to publicize the policies it embodied both to the national African American community and to others interested in education, health care, social services, and disarmament. However, these efforts had very limited impact, especially among the white population. There are many reasons for this, but I will mention only one here: differences regarding priorities and tactics between the African American members of Congress and the largely white staff members of progressive lobbying groups.

The caucus had its own network for mobilizing African American voters throughout the country. It had been developed by Walter Fauntroy, the nonvoting delegate from the District of Columbia, originally to support home rule for the city of Washington. Fauntroy maintained a huge mailing list of African Americans who would be asked to write or call their

TABLE 6.5 Support for Congressional Black Caucus Alternative Budgets by Representatives with 1985 ADA Ratings of 80 or more, 1985-1986

Racial group	1985		1986	
	# Y's	% Y's	# Y's	% Y's
White	26	34.2	32	42.1
Black	17	94.4	17	94.4
Hispanic	3	60.0	4	80.0
Asian	1	50.0	1	50.0

Source: Calculated by author from data in Congressional Quarterly 1986, 38H-39H; 1987, 36H-37H; see also *Congressional Quarterly Weekly Report*, April 20, 1983, pp. 748-49.

own representatives on caucus-supported legislation.[28] This network was used for the Alternative Budget with mixed success. Some individuals were clearly influenced by it. Lindy Boggs (D-La.), who represented a district with an African American majority, voted against the Alternative Budget in 1981 but switched thereafter (Berg 1987, 21-22); and Melvin Price (D-Ill.), a conservative, generally voted for the Alternative Budget solely in order to placate African American constituents.[29] As Table 6.6 shows, support for the Alternative Budget from 1985 to 1987 was higher for those districts with African American populations greater than 20 percent than it was for the House as a whole; but if we look only at those districts represented by white, non-Latino Democrats, support was lower than among all Democrats. A probable explanation for this negative relationship is that most of these districts are in the South. Historically, the presence of a relatively large black population in a Southern district has often been associated with racial conservatism on the part of the white population, such that the black voters are simply outvoted (Key 1964, 240-43). The figures in Table 6.6 suggest that this tendency may still be true in some cases; if so, use of the Fauntroy strategy may have prevented the support in these districts from dropping even lower.

Attempts to mobilize beyond the African American community had the potential to produce more support, but they were also more difficult. Jobs With Peace, a national membership organization that tries to link opposition to militarism with support for greater federal spending on such social needs as housing, health care, and education, has always supported the Alternative Budget. However, Jobs With Peace has usually not used the Alternative Budget for its educational campaigns but, instead, has developed its own budget, primarily because the caucus has not made the details of its Alternative Budget available early enough to meet Jobs With Peace's needs.[30] A broader effort was mounted in 1989, when a coalition of liberal Christian and Jewish groups, operating as "Budget Project 1989," took up the Congressional Black Caucus's budget—now renamed the Quality of Life Budget—as a focus. Over fifty religious organizations endorsed the campaign, urging their supporters to send postcards to their members. The groups assigned a total of about 25 lobbyists from their staffs to talk, first, to all House and Senate Budget Committee members before markup and, later, to 160 House members to ask them to vote for the Quality of Life Budget. The campaign—repeated in 1990 with more participation from nonreligious groups—was associated with an increase in the vote for the Quality of Life Budget to 81 in 1989 and 90 in 1990, and may have helped get some white liberal members of Congress to take the Congressional Black Caucus's budget more seriously.[31] However, it was not enough to keep the Quality of Life Budget alive in the face of a new budget summit and the generally conservative national mood.

TABLE 6.6   Support for Congressional Black Caucus Alternative Budgets by Racial Composition of Districts, 1985-1987

District type	Number of districts	Vote on/ Percent for CBC Budget 1985	Vote on/ Percent for CBC Budget 1986	Vote on/ Percent for CBC Budget 1987
All districts	435	54-361	61-359	56-362
		12.4%	14.0%	12.9%
All Democrats				
1985-86	252	54-189	61-183	
1987	258			56-190
		21.4%	24.2%	21.7%
Districts with more than 20% black voters	68	22-43	25-39	25-39
		32.4%	37.3%	36.8%
Represented by white, non-Hispanic representatives	50 (49 in 1986)	5-43	8-39	7-39
		10.0%	16.3%	14.0%
Represented by white, non-Hispanic Democrats	40 (39 in 1986)	5-33	8-30	7-30
		12.5%	20.5%	17.5%

Source: Calculated from data in Cavanagh 1984 and reports of roll call votes in Congressional Quarterly 1986, 38H-39H; 1987, 36H-37H; 1988, 18H-19H.

As with the earlier Jobs With Peace support for the Alternative Budget, the Budget Project's efforts were hampered by priority conflicts between itself and the Congressional Black Caucus. The caucus includes members with a variety of political views, and must undergo considerable internal discussion each year in order to decide whether to propose an Alternative Budget at all, and then to agree on what provisions that proposal should contain.[32] If it is to fill its chosen role as the political voice of all African Americans, the caucus needs to take the time needed for this process. Coalitions such as the Budget Project have more ideological unity and tend to be impatient with the time it takes the Congressional Black Caucus to come up with a proposal. For this reason among others, campaigning for the caucus's budget is likely to be a secondary activity for most coalition members.

In some ways the situation of African American members of Congress today parallels that of 1875. The civil rights movement of the 1960s won formal legal and political equality for African Americans and other groups defined as racial minorities. These victories brought much larger numbers of African American voters into the electorate and greatly increased the number of African American members of Congress. The movement also won some victories for its economic program: education, employment, urban redevelopment, and promotion of black-owned businesses. But these victories were never more than partial, and they are currently at risk of being reversed. The African American members of Congress have gained seniority, and several have moved into positions of committee and Democratic Party leadership. Although they have advanced much further than did the African American members of Congress of the nineteenth century, they have not been able to bring about an economic restructuring of the country, and many now seem to be turning back to the strategy of accommodation. Further progress toward racial equality is very much in doubt for the immediate future.

In sum, major changes in the position of the black population in the United States have been brought about by struggles outside of Congress. The Civil War, the subsequent occupation of the Southern states by the Union Army, the rise of the Ku Klux Klan in the nineteenth century, and the civil rights movement and urban rebellions in the twentieth did far more than congressional elections to bring about change, even though such change may then have been incorporated into law by congressional action. However, individual African American members of Congress have sometimes helped stimulate and lead such social struggles. This was the case, for example, with Adam Clayton Powell's repeated introduction of the Powell Amendments over the course of two decades. When members of Congress use the protest strategy in alliance with a powerful social movement, the two can reinforce each other and bring about significant change. But once that external social movement has dissipated or been defeated, continued protest and advocacy by those within Congress go virtually unheard and have little or no effect. George White fought many noble battles at the end of the nineteenth century, but his words were like seed cast on hard, dry ground, fated to sprout and take root only decades later.

When protest has been ineffective, African American members of Congress have sought alternative methods. The major alternative has been the strategy of accommodation, a search for particularized benefits for one's constituents, one's district, and perhaps oneself. In the twentieth century the protection of the seniority system in the House, which allows individual black members to rise to committee leadership, has made accommodation all the more attractive. African American representatives have become chairmen of several committees and subcommittees. Certainly there is power attached to such positions; however, as Powell and others have learned, this power is limited. It is easy to use this power in support of the status quo, and relatively easy to use it to advance narrow personal or district concerns; but a committee chair who seeks basic social change will soon learn that there are real limits on his or her power.

Members who turn to the accommodationist strategy also find themselves in a double bind. They may have chosen to concentrate their efforts on obtaining jobs and contracts for their constituents because the path to more basic change was blocked; but once they make this choice, they may be portrayed as petty, parochial, and corrupt. Indeed, once they begin to live and work in the world of patronage politics they may well slip into actual corruption. Hence the turn to accommodationism may contribute further to the negative political climate that brought it about in the first place.

If we ask which strategy is a better one for African American members of Congress to use during periods when there is no strong external movement for social change, the answer is that neither strategy is very satisfactory. Perhaps, then, that is the wrong question to ask. The correct answer may be that, in such times, little can be done within Congress, and the efforts of those of its members who represent oppressed groups might best be directed toward reviving such a movement.

7

Congress and Social Protest

The preceding chapters have returned again and again to one point: Congress has an internal structure, and positions in this structure give an advantage to those who hold them, but this advantage is biased; it is not equally available to the powerless and the powerful. Throughout America's brief history, when representatives of oppressed groups have used the accommodationist strategy, that strategy has failed. They have climbed patiently up the ladder of congressional seniority and committee position, only to find that they could not use their new power to effect the changes most needed by their constituents. Today's African American members of Congress, who have watched the African American community's economic status sink even while their own seniority positions rose, are only the latest actors to play out this ancient drama.

When financial institutions need to be saved or the tax system simplified to meet the needs of the big corporations, powerful members of Congress can use the leverage of their committee positions to push through a bill and fend off weakening or unrelated amendments. But on such issues as labor law reform, the Equal Rights Amendment, day care, or racial equality, each obstacle that is surmounted reveals another, greater hurdle lurking behind.

Thus stymied, some representatives of the oppressed have laid down the sword with which they once battled for basic change and picked up the tools of patronage. Some have used these tools to build a foundation for greater change in the future, reasoning as Blanche Bruce did that the resources of jobs and contracts to be gained by political power were necessary to the construction of a winning political coalition. Others have sought simply to build their own wealth, reasoning that everyone else was doing the same thing, and rejecting criticism as motivated by race, class, or gender bias. In either case, representatives who take this course find themselves only too likely to become the target of public scandal and criminal prosecution, forces that drive many of them from office. Cut off from the forces they once represented, they prove unable to defend themselves.

Six Who Spoke Out

Position within Congress is important, but it is not sufficient. The past labor, female, and African American members of Congress who *stand* out today are those who *spoke* out when they were in office, using their position to make their words carry further. Victor Berger, Jeannette Rankin, Vito Marcantonio, Adam Clayton Powell, Bella Abzug, and Ron Dellums each was able to use Congress to reach and mobilize a broad section of the American people. Each realized that power inside Congress could be effective as a force for change only if it was supported by such mobilization.

Victor Berger, the leader of the Socialist Party (SP) in Milwaukee, was the first Socialist candidate elected to Congress.[1] Berger was a leader of the SP's right wing and is viewed as a conservative among socialists because of his antirevolutionary views. Many in the SP left considered Berger's membership in Congress sufficient ground to condemn him (Miller 1973, 83-84). In the context of the House of Representatives, however, he was a flaming radical. He knew only too well that he could not enact the socialist program by political maneuver, so he used his position to articulate a sweeping vision of a socialist society, to proclaim workers' grievances and denounce oppression, and to help individual activists whenever he could.

Berger tried to find a way to use the leverage of his seat to reach a wide audience, but without the compromise of political principles that was so often justified as pragmatic. He reported to the SP convention in 1912, after his first term in office:

> There were two ways before me. I could make a free-speech fight all alone, try to break down all precedent and all barriers, speak about the co-operative common-wealth, as long as my lung power would hold out and wind up my short parliamentary career by being suspended from the House, and thus also make an end to political action by this 'direct action'. . . . Or I could pursue the other course, obey all rules and precedents of the House until they are changed—get the respect and attention of my fellow members, speak sparingly and only when measures directly concerning the working class are up for discussion, giving, however, close attention to all the business before the House of Representatives.[2]

Berger clearly favored the latter course, but this is not to say that he dissembled his views or compromised his principles. As he had declared upon learning that he had been elected:

> While I am not a visionary and do not expect to revolutionize the congress of the
> United States singlehanded, I know that I have been elected to represent the views
> of the working class—to give voice to the hopes, fears and aims of that class—to
> shed a new light on every question before the House—to consider every question
> from a new point of view—whether it be beneficial or harmful to the proletariat.[3]

When A. M. Simons, editor of *The Appeal to Reason*, asked Berger to
introduce a resolution calling for withdrawal of troops from the Mexican
border, he devised a procedure he was to use repeatedly. He asked SP
locals across the country to circulate petitions and presented the resolution
accompanied by 90,000 signatures (Miller 1973, 77-78). He arranged for
congressional hearings to investigate the illegal extradition from Kansas to
California of J. J. McNamara, a union activist accused of a bombing (to
which he later confessed), and to gain national sympathy for the "Bread
and Roses" strikers in Lawrence, Massachusetts. He worked with "Big
Bill" Haywood of the Industrial Workers of the World (IWW) on the latter
case; Haywood was a political opponent, but Berger considered himself the
voice of the working class in Congress. In the words of Sally Miller,
"Whether an issue involved conservative trade unions or the Wobblies, he
believed he was justified in aiding by any means open to him criticism of
the existing system" (Miller 1973, 81).[4]

Berger introduced bills to nationalize the railroads, to set up state
public-works funds to counteract unemployment, and to establish federal
pensions for workers. These were to be modeled after the pensions that
had been provided for Civil War veterans; Berger argued that "any toiler
who has faithfully labored for a meager wage for twenty years or more has
created more wealth than a pension in old age can repay. . . . The word
'pension' is a misnomer. The payment ought to be called 'Partial
restitution'" (quoted in Miller 1973, 82-83). He spoke on many other
occasions about the virtues of socialism as a cure for the ills of capitalism.
Miller describes his positive impact:

> In the House of Representatives Berger was cordially received by his colleagues.
> He was given opportunities to speak and a committee assignment, and he never
> had to complain about his treatment. The national press showed genuine curiosity
> about him and gave him far more coverage than any other freshman Congressman.
>
> His franking privileges enabled him to mail thousands of copies of his
> speeches throughout the country; the National Office of the Socialist party
> distributed more copies to the locals. The public seemed to respond and joined
> the party faithful in showering Berger with so much mail that his clerical staff
> required continual expansion. As evidence of public interest, Berger received an
> ever increasing number of speaking requests. Through a lyceum bureau hired to
> handle booking arrangements, he spoke in and around Washington, and, between
> sessions, he traveled as far west as North Dakota to fulfill engagements. The
> attention he received validated his original belief in the educational value of

elective office. The logical schoolhouse for mass enlightenment was the public
forum, Berger was convinced. (Miller 1973, 85)

Berger also exhibited severe weaknesses. Although he supported the
SP's positions calling for enfranchisement of African Americans and
women, he believed that women voters would be a conservative force, and
his own racial views led his biographer Miller to characterize him as a
"virulent bigot" (Miller 1990, 84). Internal divisions in the Socialist Party
limited its ability to take advantage of his position. He was defeated in
1912 but remained a power in Milwaukee and in SP politics. Berger spoke
out strongly against World War I—an easy position, of course, in German
Milwaukee—and was elected to the House once again in 1918 while under
indictment for having written antiwar articles. When the House refused to
seat him, he won again in a 1919 special election and, once again, was
refused a seat. Finally seated in 1923, after still another electoral victory,
he served until 1928, one year before his death (Walsh 1991).

Berger's successes did not come from his own efforts alone; indeed,
he was part of a broad socialist movement. But his activity in Congress,
along with the presidential campaigns of Eugene V. Debs and the work of
Socialists in many local governments, helped that movement develop by
bringing socialist ideas to a far broader public than the party could have
reached otherwise.

Berger's service in the House coincided with that of William B. Wilson
of Pennsylvania, an ally of Samuel Gompers and an officer of the United
Mine Workers Association. Wilson was elected to the House of Representatives as a Democrat, rose to be chair of the Committee on Labor (as it
was called at the time), and then was appointed by Woodrow Wilson to
be first secretary of the new Labor Department in 1913.[5] The two careers
provide an interesting comparison of the strategies of protest and
accommodation, but the test is not conclusive because each failed in the
long run. Wilson's great achievement was the creation of the Federal
Conciliation Service, which he hoped would improve the lot of working
people without the need for strikes or violence. The service helped
maintain stable production during World War I but was unable to defend
the labor movement during the postwar reaction, as Wilson found himself
almost powerless to restrain his colleague, Attorney General A. Mitchell
Palmer.

William B. Wilson's accommodationist strategy failed to secure
long-term gains; but Berger's politics of protest fared no better. The point
of such a strategy is to build a social movement, and then to focus that
movement's efforts to bring about change. However, the American
socialist movement fell apart early in the 1920s. Its collapse was due in
part to repression (including William B. Wilson's use of his office to

support more conservative unionists over socialists whenever possible,[6] along with the more severe repression embodied in the Palmer raids), but in even larger part to sectarian infighting in the SP over the Bolshevik revolution and the formation of the Communist International. Berger was able to keep his seat in the House, and to hold together his electoral organization in Milwaukee (which survived Berger and continued to elect Socialist mayors until the late 1950s), but he no longer had a national movement to call upon or inspire.

Jeannette Rankin's career in Congress was discussed in Chapter 5. Like Berger, Rankin thought it more important to speak the truth and educate the public than to make political deals and hold onto her seat in Congress. From her declaration that "I cannot vote for war," which broke the House rules, to her personal investigation of the grievances of the women at the Bureau of Printing and Engraving, from her visit to the Occaquan Workhouse to her intercession for the mineworkers of Butte, Rankin used her seat to speak beyond Congress to the people and thereby attained a degree of influence far beyond what her two widely separated terms would suggest.

Vito Marcantonio represented East Harlem in the House for fourteen years, from 1935 to 1936, and again from 1939 to 1950; he was about to run again in 1954 when he fell dead in the street of a heart attack. A Republican for his first term, he served the other six as the sole member of the American Labor Party (ALP) delegation in Congress[7]—although, under New York's cross-filing law, he sometimes won the nominations of the Democratic and/or Republican parties as well (Schaffer 1966; Berg 1991b). Like Berger, Marcantonio considered it his job to educate the public by introducing and speaking out for programs that were ambitious enough to be real solutions to pressing social problems. In this endeavor he was completely outspoken, and unmoved by considerations of political expediency. Thus in 1940, with over 4 million young people out of work but with the New Deal in retreat before a conservative coalition that had gained in the 1938 elections, Marcantonio introduced the comprehensive American Youth Act, a $500 million program that would have provided a new Works Progress Administration (WPA) for unemployed young people, a work program for college students, free vocational and psychological counseling for young people, a national apprenticeship program linked to the unions, and federal scholarships for undergraduate and graduate education (Schaffer 1966, 71). He explained the philosophy of the bill in a radio address:

> The American Youth Act is not only an augmenting of the present National Youth Administration but it is fundamentally different. The present set-up is grossly inadequate and temporary, dealing with the problem of the American

youth on a year-to-year basis. The American Youth Act authorizes an adequate appropriation and sets forth a permanent program for a permanent problem. It is not stopgap legislation; it is directed toward a solution. (Marcantonio 1956, 115)

This bill presaged policies (financial aid to higher education and college work-study) that were not adopted until thirty years later, along with others (a national apprenticeship program) that are still needed today. In addition, it demonstrated how a member of Congress could work with a mass organization to mobilize its constituency around a policy program. The American Youth Act had been drawn up by the American Youth Congress (AYC) and was introduced by Marcantonio at the request of this organization. The bill never had a chance in the House; such debate as there was consisted of red-baiting of the AYC for Communist Party influence, followed by Marcantonio's spirited response:

These boys and girls came here with a problem: 4,700,000 young men and young women out of work, without educational opportunities; they came here and said to the Members of Congress, to the fathers of this country, to the elder statesmen of America: "What are you going to do for us?"

And what do you say? "Save America from communism!" (Marcantonio 1956, 116)[8]

The lines were thus drawn for a battle of public debate, organization, and mobilization, rather than closed-door compromise and negotiation. Marcantonio took a similar approach to a broad range of issues, including unemployment relief, extension of social security, and full sovereignty for Puerto Rico.

Marcantonio combined his outspoken politics with an extraordinary level of constituent casework. Such casework—which provides help to constituents with their individual problems—has grown considerably in the last few decades, as members of Congress have come to see it as the best road to electoral security (Cain, Ferejohn, and Fiorina 1987, 3); but Marcantonio pursued it to a level that would have been unusual even today, and he did so without today's enlarged staffs. He maintained two district offices that were open seven days a week, from ten in the morning to at least six at night, and spent much of his own time there from Saturday through Monday; Richard Rovere estimated that he saw 30,000 constituents a year personally.[9]

Close relations with his constituents gave Marcantonio the electoral strength to take controversial stands and serve as a voice for the left nationally, but it never gave him the kind of security enjoyed by many of today's incumbents. Every election was a battle. For most of his career Marcantonio took advantage of his popular support to compete in and often win the Democratic and Republican primaries as well as his own; but in 1947 New York passed the Wilson-Pakula Act, which, as Alan Schaffer observed, was "broad in scope but aimed directly at the radical from East Harlem and at the party he controlled." Under this law, a candidate had to belong to a party in order to enter its primary, unless he had permission to cross-file from the other party's county committee (Schaffer 1966, 186). Marcantonio fought and won a tough three-way race that year, confronting a charge that he was "Moscow's mouthpiece" with the forthright statement that "however much these views and action of mine may resemble the 'Communist line' in the opinion of the *New York Times*, I nevertheless stand by them. I am confident that history and the final judgment of the people will support me in the future as they have so consistently in the past."[10] But in 1950 the opposition united to defeat him. To begin with, the onset of the Cold War and the passage of the Taft-Hartley Act had weakened labor support for the ALP; only those left-wing unions that had been expelled from the AFL and CIO still supported the party, while most unions had gone over to the new Liberal Party. In addition, the Republicans, Democrats, and Liberals now put the "defeat of red Vito Marcantonio" ahead of everything else. The three parties united to nominate James Donovan, who won with 49,000 votes to Marcantonio's 36,000 (Schaffer 1966, 206-07).[11]

During the next few years the American Labor Party, under tremendous pressure from the Cold War and McCarthyism, fell apart. Marcantonio thought the party should act as an independent radical voice in American politics; but the Communist Party (CP), always an important force within the ALP, disagreed. Perhaps because it bore the brunt of legal repression in this period, the CP saw defeat of the slightly more conservative Republicans as an overwhelmingly important goal and wanted the ALP to work with the Democrats as a junior partner. Marcantonio won majority support for preserving the ALP's independence, but he was unable to unite the party behind this view. The ALP ran Clifford McAvoy for mayor of New York in 1953, but he did very poorly; Marcantonio resigned from the party the day after the mayoral election, declaring that because of internal dissension the ALP "has ceased any longer to be the effective instrument for independent political action in the State of New York." He then formed the Vito Marcantonio Political Association and was preparing to run for his old seat when he died suddenly on August 9, 1954 (Schaffer 1966, 209-10).

Unlike Berger, Rankin, or Marcantonio, Adam Clayton Powell, Jr.—whose career was discussed more fully in Chapter 6—found a secure electoral base that allowed him to climb the seniority ladder of the House. Driven from office by legal persecution after a long career, Powell yielded to the temptation to thumb his nose at the nation and left us with the image of himself on a beach in Bimini, taking the sun while he dodged process servers. But during his many years of previous service in the House, Powell was a strong voice for protest and an effective wielder of such levers of power as came within his grasp. Powell's long tenure was due in part to the ghettoization of African Americans; since black voters were geographically concentrated by housing segregation, it was difficult to prevent them from electing members of Congress who looked like them. However, it is to Powell's credit that for most of his career he was not content to sit back and reap the benefits of his office—unlike William Dawson—but continued to speak out and act in protest, from Harlem to Capitol Hill to Bandung. The Powell Amendment to cut off federal aid for racially discriminatory programs brought him criticism for years from those who considered it nothing but a rhetorical flourish,[12] but today it is the cornerstone of federal civil rights enforcement. Moreover, Powell's attendance at the Bandung Conference, widely portrayed as a gathering of America's enemies, helped create the political space for opposition to the Cold War.

Like Berger, Rankin, and Marcantonio before him, Powell aroused the ire of the political establishment, which raised his removal from office to the level of a crusade. When he proved invulnerable electorally, removal was sought by other means. Unfortunately, his personal weaknesses provided an opening for legal action, and he was eventually, after a long struggle, stripped of his seat.[13] This stain on his record suppressed understanding of Powell's real contributions, which have only recently begun to be appreciated again (Haygood 1993); but for twenty years he demonstrated the leverage that a determined individual member of Congress could have in the cause of racial justice.[14]

Bella S. Abzug (D-N.Y.) served only three terms in the House of Representatives and has been out of office since 1977; yet she is probably better known to the public than most of the current members. Abzug, who had been legislative director of Women Strike for Peace, decided to challenge an incumbent liberal Democrat in the 1970 primary. She explained her reasons in a published memoir of her first year in office:

> It's very interesting that the man I defeated in the Democratic primary, Leonard Farbstein, who had been in Congress for twelve years, had many of the same views on the issues that I did. His only problem was that—unlike me—he was not part of the constituency. You never knew him or felt him. He was not an activist. "He's like a piece of furniture," somebody said to me in the campaign. "It's time he should be moved."
>
> I am an activist. I'm the kind of person who *does things* at the same time that I'm working to create a feeling that *something can be done*. And I don't intend to disappear in Congress as many of my predecessors have. My role, as I see it, is among the people, and I am going to be *outside* organizing them at the same time that I'm *inside* fighting for them. That is the kind of leadership that I believe will build a new majority in this country, and it was primarily in the hope of being able

> to exemplify that kind of leadership that I ran for Congress. (Abzug 1972, 5-6; original emphasis)

Abzug lived up to her intentions. On her first day in office, January 21, 1971, she followed the official swearing in with her own ceremony, staged before a thousand women on the Capitol steps, in which she took an oath "to work for new priorities to heal the domestic wounds of war and to use our country's wealth for life, not death." She then returned to the House to introduce a resolution, with twenty-eight co-sponsors, calling for complete U.S. withdrawal from Vietnam by July (Abzug 1972, 13-14).

Meanwhile, Abzug was waging a vigorous public campaign for appointment to the House Armed Services Committee, maintaining that the

> admirals and generals and munitions-makers should have to answer for themselves, every step of the way. If I get on the committee, I'm going to raise tremendous objections to their requests for appropriations, to their cost overruns, to their never-ending need for this new weapon and that new weapon, and I'm going to get the hearings opened up so people can see what's going on. (Abzug 1972, 16)

She also argued that there should be a woman on the committee; there had not been since Margaret Chase Smith had left the House twenty-two years earlier. Abzug noted that of the twelve women then in the House, five were assigned to Education and Labor, and none to Rules, Judiciary, or Armed Services. Abzug fought for the assignment with two simultaneous tactics. In accordance with House tradition she got the support of her state delegation and lobbied chairman F. Edward Hebert and speaker Carl Albert for their support; but she also went public, obtaining interviews in the press and on radio and television across the country, and taking the fight to the House Democratic Caucus after she was turned down by the Committee on Committees. She lost, but the pressure she generated did lead to the assignment of two other liberals, Michael Harrington (D- Mass.) and Les Aspin (D-Wis.) to Armed Services.[15]

Being a member of Congress helped Abzug amplify her already outspoken voice, and she was adept at maximizing her newfound leverage for mobilizing the public. This was not just a matter of speaking out but also one of mastering the rules of the House. She was critical of House liberals for not doing the latter:

> I'm convinced that the only way to fight the inflexibility of Congress is to turn the system against itself. There must be a way, somehow, to take all these damn rules and regulations and limitations—which the power structure now uses to squelch anything that sounds too liberal—and turn them around to our advantage.

> As far as I can tell, there are very few experts on procedure in the House. Those few experts we do have are old-timers, and not liberals. The average liberal thinks up what he wants to do and then runs off to somebody else to ask, "Now what procedural step do I take in order to do this?" Consequently, liberals rarely get anything significant accomplished.
>
> I'm determined to become an expert on procedure, but unfortunately it takes time. Most of the rules and regulations are so cumbersome and so complicated that even when you learn them, which in itself is not easy, it's still a whole other matter to know how to *use* them. (Abzug 1972, 11)

By June 1971 Abzug had made substantial strides forward in this task. She discovered a little-known procedure, the resolution of inquiry; this was basically a request by the House to the executive branch for information, but it had the great advantage of being privileged. Committees were required to report such resolutions, favorably or unfavorably, within seven days, and the resolutions could then be called up for a vote. At that time House doves were having a great deal of difficulty getting the House to vote on the Vietnam War,[16] and these resolutions provided a small step (albeit one with little legislative impact) in that direction. On June 21, 1971, Abzug introduced a resolution calling for the Pentagon Papers to be given to Congress, and similar resolutions by her and other antiwar members of Congress became a regular feature of the House. She also began to learn the tactics of delay, arguing that:

> by tying up the House you're *buying time* to allow pressure to build from the outside. . . . I feel that if you push and push and push without compromise for the right position, then you're serving the function of drawing attention to the politicians who are acting outside the public interest by supporting legislation that ignores the needs of human beings.

By June 16, 1971, she had developed

> a list of forty-eight tactics to delay proceedings, such as calling quorums, objecting to dispensing with the reading of bills, demanding the reading of the previous day's journal (which is similar to the minutes of a meeting), objecting to every single "unanimous consent" request, asking for roll call votes and so on. (Abzug 1972, 185)

Abzug made a major contribution to the development of the anti-war, women's, and other social movements, first through her victory over Leonard Farbstein, one of a few crucial races that demonstrated those movements' electoral power to the rest of Congress, and then through her astute use of the powers of the office to dramatize issues and mobilize constituencies. She was the first member of Congress to call for the impeachment of President Richard Nixon, and she wrote the law to fund the Houston National Women's Conference of 1977 (Baer 1991, 8). Like

Rankin before her, she left the House to run unsuccessfully for the Senate, in 1976; but unlike Rankin, she first served three terms and could certainly have retained her House seat if she had chosen to do so. She has remained active in politics, but with the Vietnam War over and the aforementioned movements in decline, her subsequent attempts to return to Congress have failed. Her six years in the House remain one of the best examples we have of how congressional office can be used to work with and support popular movements.

Ronald V. Dellums (D-Cal.) was, like Abzug, first elected as a protest candidate in 1970; as a member of the Berkeley City Council he had been a crusading activist and a frequent speaker at antiwar and civil rights protest rallies, including the long, militant strike at San Francisco State College in 1968. Like Powell, Dellums has stayed in the House to climb the seniority ladder, becoming chair of the House Armed Services Committee in 1993. But unlike Powell, Dellums, an African American, has not had the security of broad support from an all-black district. He represents Berkeley, Oakland, and their affluent suburbs, a district that in 1980 was 62 percent white, 24 percent African American, 8 percent Asian, and 6 percent Latino, and which contains what the authors of the *Almanac of American Politics* call "a rock-solid 40% anti-Dellums vote."[17] Dellums has survived because of his strong links with activist movements in the African American community in Oakland and the university community in Berkeley.

Dellums's career shows both the possibilities and the limits of congressional office as a resource for the left.[18] He helped to create the idea of an annual Congressional Black Caucus Alternative Budget (see Chapter 6) and influenced the caucus to make that budget call for drastic cuts in the military budget throughout the Reaganite spending frenzy of the 1980s. He worked with national advocacy groups to provide a congressional focus for such seemingly utopian issues as socialized medicine by sponsoring model bills that could serve as a rallying point. And he played a major role in pushing for stronger sanctions against the apartheid regime in South Africa. However, he has outlasted the movements that brought him to office; indeed, he has seen the Congressional Black Caucus move from a strategy of protest to one of accommodation as its other members, too, have climbed the seniority ladder and sought to deal for power as conventional politicians.

Without the support of a militant mass movement, Dellums has not been able to force the press to cover his policy alternatives, and thus his ability to mobilize the public has been limited. But he has at least kept alive the possibility and awareness of a more progressive alternative.

Victor Berger, Jeannette Rankin, Vito Marcantonio, Adam Clayton Powell, Jr., Bella Abzug, and Ron Dellums were very different from each other, in their politics, their personal character, their length of service, and their attainment of power and position within the House; but their careers had certain common elements. Each came (or was sent) to Congress as representative of a social movement and saw service in Congress as part of a two-way relationship with that movement whereby, in one direction, action within Congress could be used to publicize and strengthen the movement and, in the other, mobilization of the movement could generate pressure for legislative action. Each realized that, notwithstanding the powers and privileges of the office, a single member of Congress was relatively powerless to effect social change without such external support. Accordingly, each sought to stand on principle, advocating policies that could solve problems and meet people's needs whether or not those policies seemed likely to pass; and in consequence each was denounced and derided at one time or another for being uncompromising, obstructive, utopian, unrealistic, or even traitorous.[19]

In a sense, each of these exemplary representatives achieved personal success. They will be remembered long after many of their colleagues have been forgotten, and will continue to provide models for future activists. But in another sense they failed. None was able to create, or even to maintain, the social movement—whether of the working class, women, or African Americans—that put him or her in office. Although they demonstrated the possibilities of Congress, they also proved one of its limits. Ultimately, progressive congressional action requires a strong social movement—and the *creation* of such a movement is beyond the capacities of an individual member of Congress.

Taken collectively, these six careers provide the elements of a strategy for combining congressional action with social protest, but they do not prove that such a strategy will work. Since it has not worked yet, no such proof is available. My argument is a lesser one—that the failure of accommodationist politics to secure permanent improvements in the position of the working class, women, or African Americans (as detailed in Chapters 4, 5, and 6) may be due to the restraining effects of the economic on the political structure; and, if so, that the protest strategy modeled by these six members of Congress may be worth trying.

However, this has not been the approach taken by many progressive activists during the last two decades. The protest movements of the 1960s[20] declined during the late 1970s and the 1980s, but not before they had left their mark on the state structure. As their mass support dwindled, activists in and out of government made use of the tools that remained available to them, particularly lawsuits and lobbying. The complex and fascinating story of the left's use of the law is beyond the scope of this particular study; but I wish to close with some observations on left-wing lobbying.

For radical activists, many of whom had been trained in Marxist analysis, it was startling to discover that lobbying could work. The Civil Rights Act and the Great Society programs that followed could be seen to result from the pressure of mass movements and the fear of urban insurrection; but during the mid-1970s the situation became less clear. For example, in 1975 Congress forced an end to covert U.S. intervention in Angola, over the strenuous objections of the Ford administration, with little public pressure at all;[21] and Congress continued to defend some of the gains of the civil rights movement for several years after that movement had become less active (Orfield 1975). Heartened by these successes, and inspired by the record of such left-liberal organizations as Common Cause, organizations on the radical left began to establish Washington offices and hire full-time lobbyists.

Most of these lobbyists were not Capitol Hill veterans but were drawn from the ranks of activist organizers. Like more conventional interest groups, though, they had to face the problems associated with organizational maintenance; and they were part of the same Washington community, interacting daily with members of Congress, congressional staff, the press, and other lobbyists. It used to be said in France that two Deputies, one of whom was a Communist, had more in common than two Communists, one of whom was a Deputy; in the United States, with fewer Communists and even fewer left- wing members of Congress, something of the same logic applied to Marxist lobbyists.

The effects of this logic can be seen in the lobbying of the Central America solidarity movement, which sought to defend the Sandinista revolution in Nicaragua and promote the interests of *campesino*- and worker-based guerrilla movements in El Salvador and Guatemala. This movement differed in many ways from the anti-Vietnam War movement of the 1960s and 1970s; among other things, whereas the earlier movement had focused its energies on mass demonstrations in Washington and other cities, and regarded almost all members of Congress as captives of the imperialist establishment, the later one put considerable effort into lobbying Congress. There were valid reasons for this difference. On the one hand, with only a handful of U.S. troops involved in Central America, the organization of truly massive marches on Washington was probably not possible. On the other, large numbers of veterans of the student Vietnam movement were now older, settled, educated, and ready and willing to write and telephone their representatives in Washington. Lobbying Congress was one of the most available and effective means of mobilizing this force. Congressional action thus became an organizing focus for the movement.[22] Foreign aid authorization and appropriations bills became sites for battles over riders to ban or limit military aid to El

Salvador and Guatemala, and to prohibit covert action against the regime in Nicaragua.

Some of these riders passed but had little impact on the actions of the Reagan and Bush administrations. Sometimes the reason was that political compromises had left loopholes in the legislation. For example, the International Security and Development Cooperation Act of 1981 provided that military aid could be given to El Salvador only if the president first certified—and recertified every six months—that that government was "making a concerted and significant effort to comply with recognized human rights" and "achieving substantial control over all elements of its armed forces, so as to bring an end . . . [to] indiscriminate torture and murder." Despite massive evidence that this was not the case, President Reagan made such a certification four times during 1982 and 1983. Even easier to evade was the first Boland Amendment, added to a foreign aid appropriations bill signed into law in December 1982; this amendment provided that funds could not be used to support military activities by the right-wing terrorists operating in Nicaragua (often referred to as *contras*) if those activities were "for the purpose of overthrowing the government of Nicaragua or provoking a military exchange between Nicaragua and Honduras."[23] Since activities for other purposes were permitted, the administration simply announced that it was funding the *contras* for the purpose of interfering with weapons shipments from Nicaragua to the rebels in El Salvador.

However, such loopholes proved unnecessary. When Congress finally strengthened the Boland Amendment to prohibit aid to the *contras* outright, the administration simply continued it anyway, using—as we now know—funds obtained through the illegal sale of weapons to the Khomeini regime in Iran. Eventually a scandal and some criminal prosecutions were provoked; but this outcome had no influence on the flow of arms to right wing forces in Central America.

This pattern echoed that of congressional attempts to end the war in Vietnam; at that time, too, successive antiwar amendments had been evaded or ignored by the executive branch. But in that case the result had been disillusionment with Congress and with lobbying, an increase in street demonstrations, and a series of electoral challenges that brought newcomers such as Abzug and Dellums to Congress and warned incumbents that failure to act against the war might end their congressional careers. There were few such challenges in the 1980s.[24] Lobbyists for the solidarity movement began to put more emphasis on winning votes, even at the cost of principle. In March 1988, the Washington offices of several solidarity organizations supported a Democratic Party plan to give $16 million in "nonlethal" supplies—that is, everything but actual weapons—to the *contras*. They argued that this tactic was necessary in order to defeat a Republican proposal that would have been worse. This unprincipled compromise was too much for the grassroots members of some of the anti-*contra* lobbying groups, who called their representatives to repudiate the stand of their own national offices. Partly as a result of these calls, 15 anti-*contra* Democrats joined the Republicans to vote against the "nonlethal" aid, and the measure was defeated, 216 to 208. Since the Republican proposal was also defeated, *contra* aid was eliminated completely for the time being (Felton and Hook 1988, 558). But the trend toward compromise and manipulation, rather than principle, continued, and mass demonstrations themselves came to be seen as an adjunct to lobbying. By the end of the decade—and further demoralized by the electoral defeat of the Sandinista government in Nicaragua that summer—the Committee in Solidarity with the People of El Salvador (CISPES) had backed away from attempts to ban military aid, describing a Senate vote to cut the amount of such aid requested by the president by 50 percent ($43 million) as "the culmination of ten years of CISPES' work to change U.S. policy." CISPES further described the marches and sit-ins occurring across the country as efforts "to bring visibility to the war in El Salvador and pressure Congress to cut aid."[25] The possibility that the president's request had been inflated in anticipation of such a percentage cut was never considered; and in any case the cut had no material effect, since there was always enough money in what came to be called the "pipeline"—that is, money left over from past appropriations—to keep the Salvadoran military forces fully supplied.

Why did the solidarity movement work for such unsatisfactory legislation? Various reasons can be offered. On the one hand, activists in the movement believed that votes to limit the *contras* or to cut aid to El Salvador had a psychological force which went beyond their actual provisions. They hoped that Salvadoran officers and Nicaraguan terrorists would be more willing to compromise if they believed that Congress was against them. This may well have been true, at least in the short run—although no one would have taken such an argument seriously in the case of Vietnam. In addition, lobbying for amendments to foreign aid bills came to play an important part in the fund-raising campaigns of the organizations involved. No doubt many readers have shared this author's experience of receiving telephone calls from Neighbor to Neighbor, the Central America Solidarity Association, CISPES, and other organizations that began with a discussion of pending legislation and ended with an appeal for funds. Fund raising of this sort did make it possible for many able people to devote themselves to educating and organizing about Central America; but it also provided lobbying organizations with a reason for creating roll-call votes that they could hope to win, whatever the effect of those votes on the war in Central America might really be.

The point I wish to make, though, is that this lobbying effort was misdirected, and thus ineffective, because it arose from a naive view of the structure of power in Congress. As we have seen, this structure reflects the underlying economic terrain, and makes it easy for Congress to move in some directions and very hard to move in others. In the case of Central America, the main feature of that terrain is the interest of the financial community in freedom of movement and security for its capital. That interest is built into the structure of the International Monetary Fund, the World Bank, and a host of other financial institutions, and it is protected by military and diplomatic action. As with Vietnam and elsewhere, the state institutions which further this interest are difficult for Congress, and still more for the public, to control. Firm congressional action, such as a ban on all military aid to El Salvador, might have worked; however, winning such action would have required even greater public pressure. But partial, qualified, or symbolic cuts, though easier to enact, were doomed to fail to achieve their intended purpose.

Conclusion

My aim has been to develop a Marxist theory of Congress and to suggest the implications of such a theory for the strategy of political progressives. I am painfully aware of the preliminary nature of my effort. Much remains to be done in the way of tying up loose ends, working out details, and supporting postulates and suggestions with more convincing evidence. However, I hope that I have convinced the reader of the following points.

1. Neither the pluralist claim that Congress responds to group pressures nor the institutionalist claim that Congress has won the ability to act autonomously provides a satisfactory explanation of congressional action. Each appears to be true in some instances but not in others, so a more general theory is needed. Marxism provides such a theory: Congress acts autonomously when the views of its leaders correspond with the interests of the hegemonic interests in the capitalist economic structure, as in the case of the savings and loan bailout; it responds to group pressure when different nonhegemonic capitalist interests contend for advantage, as in the case of cable television regulation; and it responds more slowly and less strongly than pluralist pressure would suggest when action is sought by the working class, women, or African Americans, as in the cases of labor law reform, family leave, or the Congressional Black Caucus Alternative Budget.

2. The structure of Congress, which gives differing amounts of power to different interests, reflects the structure of the capitalist economy, but it can be changed by political struggle. Consider, for example, the civil

rights and anti-Vietnam War movements, which (among other things) modified the seniority rule, changed the nature of the Senate filibuster, and made it easier to force recorded teller votes in the House. However, in the absence of basic economic change, such political reforms always turn out to be less than they seem and tend to be eroded by the continuing pressure of the economic structure. The clearest example of this phenomenon was the inability of African Americans to hold on to congressional representation and the franchise after Reconstruction, but it can also be seen in the declining congressional power of the labor movement. (Owing to the differences between gender and class, however, it is possible—though very far from certain—that the current movement for women's equality may actually lead to basic change in the structure of the family and thence to equal inclusion of women in Congress.)

3. Subordinate social groups, such as the working class, women, and African Americans, tend to ride into Congress on a groundswell of social protest; but once there, their representatives tend to move to an accommodationist strategy as they acquire seniority and position. Such a strategy can benefit the individual representative. It can also benefit a privileged stratum within the represented group—highly skilled workers in craft unions, professional women, African American contractors—but not the great mass of that group, whose interests require fundamental change in the structure of capitalism and/or patriarchy.

4. The alternative to accommodationism is the strategy of protest: using membership in Congress to educate the public and stimulate the growth of a broad movement for social change. We can see the possibilities of such a strategy in the congressional careers of Victor Berger, Jeannette Rankin, Victor Marcantonio, Adam Clayton Powell, Jr., Bella Abzug, and Ronald Dellums. However, they are still only possibilities, because this strategy, too, has always failed in the long run. It can succeed only if protest activity in Congress remains linked to a broad social coalition that develops and voices a vision of what it stands for, a vision that meets the needs of the working class, women, African Americans, Latinos, and other social classes and groups oppressed by capitalism. I have argued that although compromise, choice of the lesser evil, and conventional politics are sometimes necessary, they do not have the potential to mobilize such a coalition. My admiration for Berger, Rankin, Marcantonio, Powell, Abzug, and Dellums is rooted in their grasp of this essential truth.

I have not shown that such a movement can actually be built; that is a topic for another book. I do hope to have shown that if it can be built at all, it will need to make use of activist congressional representation without being deceived by the illusion that congressional power is independent of the economic structure.

Notes

Introduction: Congress in the Public Mind

1. There has been considerable controversy over this question, of course. For a good introduction to the debate about race, see Robinson 1983; on the subject of gender, see Sargent 1981 and the classic statement by Shulamith Firestone (1970).

Chapter 1

1. For example, Keefe (1980, 121-23) asserts that "Congress is built to order for interest-group politics" because of the structure of the standing committees. Writing after the 1975 reforms, he adds, "If members cannot defy party leaders with impunity, they nonetheless can often go their own way, supporting legislation that seems likely to satisfy their constituencies, including the organized elements in them."

2. Mayhew (1974) argues that although such considerations are the dominant force in Congress, they are restrained by such institutions as leadership and the House Rules Committee; Fiorina (1977) sees them as operating with little if any restraint.

3. Krehbiel (1991, 141-43) argues, on the one hand, that committees were never as independent of floor majorities as has been claimed and, on the other, that the few senior members who actually lost chairs were "preference outliers"—seriously out of step with party majorities—and that their cases were not much different from such cases as those of Thomas Morgan or Graham Barden, discussed earlier in the chapter.

4. Kann (1980, 79-85) gives a cogent summary of "new pluralism."

5. See, in particular, the many works of Michel Foucault and Jacques Derrida, which have inspired many ex-Marxists and captured the imagination of many who might otherwise have become Marxists. The writings of Ernesto Laclau and Chantal Mouffe (1985) illustrate the trajectory of those who moved from a desire to give more stress to the ideological side of the class struggle to an abandonment of the centrality of class exploitation as an organizing concept. And Unger (1987) comes as close as possible, from the non-Marxist side, to the dividing line between a Marxist and a non-Marxist theory of revolutionary social change.

6. See Jessop (1982) for the best attempt so far.

7. This analytic effort can be fascinating, all the same. See de Duve 1984, Hubel 1988, and Snyder 1986 for some partial accounts of the molecule-animal linkage.

8. The details of this structure as it applies to the United States will be examined in the next chapter.

9. The concept of level of society is distinct from, and not particularly related to, the concept of level of analysis discussed in the preceding paragraph.

10. Similarly, the notion of relative autonomy allows one to think critically about the Soviet state, breaking through the Stalinist argument that every socialist society necessarily has a socialist state (since the base determines the superstructure), a principle formerly used to assert that the problems of the USSR need not be considered serious as long as the means of production continued to be publicly owned. Althusser, a dissident member of the Communist Party of France, sought to legitimize such criticism within the Communist movement.

11. Orthodox Marxist critics of Althusser often seize on a phrase of his, "the lonely hour of the last analysis never comes," as evidence that he himself was a pluralist at heart. But Althusser meant something different: not that relative autonomy was infinitely malleable, but that the economic structure *always* underlay the superstructure, with its effects *always* modified by other influences, rather than "determining" some things but not others.

12. The term *biased pluralism* was suggested by an anonymous reviewer of this manuscript. The concept has also been called *Pluralism II* (Manley 1983, 368-83) and *neo-pluralism* (Kann 1980).

13. I owe this insight to Nancy Perkins, who once remarked to me, "All great theories are circular." She was defending learning theory at the time. Learning theory holds that animals increase the frequency of behavior that is rewarded and decrease the frequency of behavior that is punished. However, when we try to apply this concept to real-life human situations, we find it difficult to construct an objective definition of "reward"—except that a reward is anything that causes organisms to alter their behavior in order to receive it! She pointed out that the same could be said of the Darwinian criterion of survival of the fittest—since we know what fitness is only in that individual organisms that possess it survive.

Actually, in both these cases the circularity is superficial; or perhaps I should say that it is so fundamental as to be irrelevant to the purposes for which each theory is used. The real point of both Darwinism and learning theory is that change occurs gradually, rather than all at once—even when the end result is something as clear-cut as a new species. The mechanism by which such change occurs is interesting but can be set aside in applying the theory.

14. This proposition has a fascinating implication: that the societies of Eastern Europe, now undergoing a reform in which democracy and capitalism are often portrayed as inseparable companions, will find it difficult to change their economic structures, to the extent that these are really socialist. If so, we may expect these countries either to wind up with some sort of democratic socialist system, despite the current enthusiasm for the free market, or to attain working capitalist economies only after long, bitter, and probably bloody struggle. The developments of the next few years will provide an important test of this theory.

15. This admittedly vague term, *large capital*, will be expanded upon later.

16. Hinckley (1971, 113) concludes, "Both leaders and ordinary members of Congress are attached to the seniority system because they profit by the stability, predictability, and maintenance of traditional power alignments which it fosters. And by contributing this stability, predictability, and support of decentralized leadership, the seniority system helps to support the larger congressional system which has produced and is nourishing it." She adds that the system's opponents "constitute a small minority of congressmen, supported by some outsiders." See also Davidson, Kovenock, and O'Leary 1966, 101. In the second

edition of her *Stability and Change in Congress* (1978, 80-82), Hinckley acknowledges, "Against this pattern of support, the House challenges of 1975 require some attention," concluding that they succeeded due to the declining proportion of Southerners among House Democrats and overall membership turnover, with "government scandals" as a contributing factor.

17. See Ste. Croix (1984, 94-111) for a discussion of the relation of class and class struggle to class consciousness.

Part One Introduction

1. Consider, for example, the Washington bureau chief for the *Wall Street Journal*, Albert R. Hunt, who observed that "money is the engine that fuels much of our politics" (quoted in Birnbaum and Murray 1987, xii).

2. I use the phrases *to the extent* and *seems to imply* here because it is not at all clear either that Lindblom does stop short of economic determinism or that he believes basic change to be possible.

3. The influence of campaign contributions, particularly those from political action committees (PACs) is discussed more fully in Chapter 3.

4. Estimates have continued to grow; in April 1990, the General Accounting Office predicted a cost of $385 billion over forty years, with $185 billion recouped through sale of the assets of the failed institutions and increased deposit insurance premiums, leaving $200 billion to be paid by the taxpayers or added to the deficit. See *Congressional Quarterly Weekly Report*, April 7, 1990, p. 1056.

5. This point is so absurd that it demands explanation. The Gramm-Rudman-Hollings Act (GRH) prescribes automatic budget cuts, known as sequestration, if the director of the Office of Management and Budget determines that the budget for the next fiscal year does not meet specified deficit reduction targets, which are lower each year. However, this determination is made only once a year; once made it is not changed, even if the deficit grows to be more than had been predicted. The bailout bill increased the deficit for fiscal year 1989 by $20 billion, but this outcome did not trigger sequestration because fiscal 1989 had already passed the GRH test. See Penner and Abramson 1988, 95-98, for an explanation of the sequestration process.

6. In some more contemporary sociology textbooks, Federico and Schwartz say that "groups who share the same characteristics of economic resources, prestige, and power and are aware of their common situation constitute a *social class*" (1983, 229); and Kammeyer, Ritzer, and Retman gesture weakly toward Marxism with their definition, "social ranking in a stratification system based on one's relationship to the means of production; more commonly, social ranking based on economic factors such as income and wealth" (1990, 678). In *The Analysis of Political Structure*, David Easton recognizes the inadequacy of the usual sociological definition of class; however, he does not realize that Marxists generally define the term otherwise, so that for Marxists the use of *class* to refer to class structure is not metonymy (as Easton maintains) but, rather, application of the literal definition (1990, 54).

7. John Roemer (1982) has attempted to redefine the Marxist concept of exploitation without reference to the appropriation of surplus labor. The resulting controversy has important implications for Marxist theory; however, we can ignore it for our present purposes, because Roemer and those who use his method still posit the same basic set of classes. Erik Olin Wright (1985, 106-08) gives an excellent summary of the differences between Marxist and non-Marxist concepts of class.

8. Poulantzas uses the term *social formation* to refer to the structure of an actual society; but this extra layer of abstraction, though more precise, is not really needed for our purposes here.

9. Poulantzas (1974, 13-19) discusses the technical derivation of class difference from the relations of production.

Chapter 2

1. Transcript of hearings before the Senate Armed Services Committee, January 15, 1983, printed in *New York Times*, January 24, 1953, p. 8.

2. The automobile companies, though still very powerful, are no longer in as central a position as they were during the 1950s. Since their decline was associated with national economic stagnation, it may be said to have proved Wilson right.

3. This trend, too, was the result of class struggle, particularly during Franklin Roosevelt's second term.

4. The president appoints the members of the Federal Reserve Board, who must be confirmed by the Senate. However, important policy decisions are made by the Federal Open Market Committee, many of whose members are elected directly by the system's member banks.

5. I discuss war powers more fully in Berg 1979 and 1985.

6. Nonhegemonic social forces have also gained footholds in other parts of the executive branch, such as the Departments of Agriculture, Interior, and Labor; but none of these is in an area crucial to hegemonic interests. The question of subfederal layers of government is also important but will not be taken up here.

7. For example, oil companies managed to retain important tax breaks under the Tax Reform Act of 1986, which repealed many special deductions and raised corporate taxes overall by an estimated $120 billion (Conlan, Wrightson, and Beam 1990, 232).

8. The technical term for this option is *disintermediation*—since the thrifts were being eliminated as an intermediary between the small saver and the mortgage market.

9. Mayer 1990 describes the important provisions of the law and their effect on the thrift industry.

Chapter 3

1. Lowi (1970, 1972) later added some additional categories.

2. This is a partial example of what Peter Bachrach and Morton Baratz (1962, 947-52) have called a *nondecision*—that is, a real issue that is kept off the decision agenda.

3. Chamber of Commerce of the United States, *Minutes of the 26th Annual Meeting* May 2, 1938, p. 35; quoted in Collins 1981, 46.

4. See Chapters 4-6.

5. Bernstein 1955 provides the classic description of this phenomenon.

6. See Chapter 2.

7. The data for 1988 are taken from Jacobson 1992, 67; and those for 1990, from Alston 1991, 2313-18. See also the characterization of "trade/membership/health" PACs in H. Alexander 1983, 372.

8. Studies that find significant PAC influence include Stratmann 1991; Brown 1983; Frendreis and Waterman 1985; Ginsberg and Green 1986; Gleiber, King, and Mahood 1987; Silberman and Durden 1976; Kau and Rubin 1982; Wilhite and Theilmann 1987; and Schroedel 1986. Studies that find little or no PAC influence include Evans 1986; Nelson 1982; Wayman and Kutler 1985; Welch 1982; J. Wright 1985; Chappell 1982; and Grenzke 1989.

9. See Chapter 4.

10. A cable television regulation bill was enacted in 1993, the first year of the next administration.

11. The figure cited includes contributions only from PACs, not from individuals, although the latter may be significant as well. For example, the Congressional Quarterly (1991a) study found that Mike Synar (D-Okla.), who refuses all PAC contributions, received at least $16,375 in personal contributions from executives in the energy industry and other companies interested in clean air legislation.

12. See Surrey 1957, 1981; Simons 1938, 1950; Pechman 1957, 1959. The intellectual campaign for the principle of horizontal equity is described in Conlan, Wrightson, and Beam 1990, 25-38; see also Strahan 1990, 152. Martin (1991, 194-95 and *passim*) argues that state officials with a theory of what would be good for the national economy have generally been able to mobilize business coalitions around that theory; her argument provides a good illustration of Poulantzas's (1978c, 123-60) concept of the state as the *condensation* of a pattern of class relations.

13. See the estimates from the U.S. Congress Joint Committee on Taxation 1986, cited in Strahan 1990, 141-42.

Part Two Introduction

1. Many such books have been written. See, in particular, Marx [1867-1894] 1967. See also McDermott 1991; McConnell 1966; Katznelson and Kesselman 1987; Greenberg 1974; Parenti 1978, 1980.

2. This ideal underlies much of *The Federalist*; see, for example, Numbers 55 and 62, both by Madison.

3. See the letter from Abigail Adams to John Adams, March 31, 1776, and that from John Adams to Abigail Adams, April 14, 1776; both are reprinted in Dolbeare 1984.

4. From a document entitled "The petition of a great number of blacks detained in a state of slavery in the bowels of a free and Christian country," reprinted in *Annals of America* 1968, 1:113.

5. As the Cuffe brothers' mother, Ruth Moses, was a Gay Head Indian, the brothers also claimed exemption from taxes as Indians; they lost on both grounds.

6. Along with these political arguments, Jefferson added all the standard claims that black people were physically inferior to whites. Takaki (1990, 1-65) gives a fuller presentation of the framers' views on race and citizenship.

7. The Seneca Falls Declaration is reprinted in Dolbeare 1984, 255-57. See also David Buel, Jr., "Speech in Support of Universal Suffrage Delivered at the New York Constitutional Convention (1821)," in Levy 1982, 145, 149; note, however, that Buel's reference to the principles of human equality in the Declaration is less explicit.

Chapter 4

1. For example, Van Horn, Baumer, and Gormley (1992, 162) assert, with no further explanation, definition, or evidence, that "because most Americans belong to the middle class, U.S. politics tends to revolve around issues that most directly affect the middle class."

2. See Chapter 1.

3. See Goldfield (1987, 85-87) for a fuller description of this process.

4. See Chapter 2.

5. Section 14-B gives state governments the option to outlaw union shop contracts—contracts that require union membership as a condition of employment—within their states. Unions believe that such contracts are needed to prevent "free riders"—workers who get the benefits that unions bargain for, but who refuse to join and pay dues—and have periodically sought to repeal 14-B ever since it was adopted in 1947.

6. These job loss estimates are taken from a study conducted by Data Resources, Incorporated, for the Congressional Budget Office, reported in the *New York Times*, August 12, 1979, p. 33.

7. *New York Times*, December 21, 1979, p. 1.

8. *New York Times*, October 26, 1979, section IV, p. 3.

9. See *New York Times*, December 11, 1979, section IV, p. 1, for a description of the lobbying campaign.

10. For example, see Foner (1980, 66-84) for discussion of the attempts made to move toward socialism through municipal ownership of utilities.

11. See Lynd 1990, 85; Lynd cites Montgomery 1987.

12. Gompers was quoted in the AFL's *Weekly News Letter*, April 8, 1911; the same quotation appears in Foner 1980, 98.

13. According to David Montgomery, Wilson used his position to promote "the consistent theme . . . that employers should be encouraged to negotiate with legitimate unions and to shun the IWW and other groups deemed 'outlaw' by the AFL" (Montgomery 1987, 357).

14. To their credit, Wilson and Post of the Labor Department did play a moderating role, insisting that some procedural standards be applied to the deportations carried out during the Palmer raids. This fact might be used to argue that "futile" is too strong a word; but given the magnitude of the repression that occurred in spite of their efforts, I do not apologize for using it. See Berg 1991a.

15. Howe and Widick (1949, 55-62) give a good brief account of the Flint strike, as does Zinn (1980, 390-91). For a full account, see Fine 1969.

16. Moreover, this hope was sometimes dashed, as when the Landrum-Griffith Act was passed by a Democratic Congress in 1959 (see Draper 1989, 73-76). Goldfield (1989, 106-07) points out that in addition to authorizing government intervention in unions' internal affairs, the act also "[eliminated] . . . some of the most powerful weapons [of unions, including] . . . the secondary boycotts and 'hot cargo' agreements."

Chapter 5

1. See *New York Times*, November 22, 1922, p. 10. See also Chamberlin 1973, 19-22, 31-37.

2. Kincaid 1979, 7. The phrase quoted earlier in the paragraph is taken from the *Arkansas Gazette*, November 28, 1931.

3. Kincaid 1979, 10-11. McClellan's slogan is quoted in Young 1971, 286.

4. See Notes 20 and 21 below for some examples of studies that make this argument.

5. For example, see Hartman 1981 on the use of the concept of "the family wage" to exclude women from employment in the late nineteenth and early twentieth centuries.

6. See especially Sargent 1981; Weinbaum 1978; Delphy 1984; and Hartsock 1983.

7. This argument is also factually incorrect. Delphy shows that women often work without pay in family businesses, producing goods or services that are sold for money (1984, 60-63).

8. Iris Young has argued that contemporary society can be best understood by abandoning the concept of mode of production and going back to a more fundamental analysis based on the division of labor. In her view, positing the simultaneous existence of two distinct modes of production implies the possibility, or even the inevitability, of separate struggles against each. She insists that, to the contrary, "the project of socialist feminism should be to develop a single theory out of the best insights of both marxism and radical feminism, which can comprehend capitalist patriarchy as one system in which the oppression of women is a *core* attribute" (Young 1981, 44).

The search for a single theory is seductive. However, it does not follow from the desirability of such a theory that one is necessarily available. There are many aspects of life—sexuality, for example—that do not seem explicable by the division of labor. Moreover, the basic purpose of theoretical abstraction is to simplify. A theory that is as complex as life itself must also be as difficult to comprehend, thereby failing of this purpose. To pose theoretically the existence of two modes of production is not to suppose that the two are separable, nor that both together explain everything that there is to be explained; rather, doing so enables us to simplify the reality of our society to the point where it can be easily grasped. Our task is to find a means of simplification that distorts as little as possible.

9. For 1987, the Census Bureau estimated a U.S. population of 101 million men and 105 million women (U.S. Department of Commerce 1989, 17).

10. For some elections Wilhite found that female candidates actually did better than men in similar situations.

11. Although the U.S. Senate does have two-member districts, each Senate seat is chosen in a separate election, so the same winner-take-all logic applies.

12. Jacobson (1992, 26-37) summarizes the literature on incumbent advantage.

13. As Burrell (1992, 505) argues, there are few enough female state legislators— particularly state senators—that the odds that one of them would be living in an open-seat House district are relatively low. But many nonlegislators, too, have run effective campaigns, often victorious ones.

14. Tamposi was later appointed to a State Department post, from which she was forced to resign when it became publicly known that she had revealed the contents of Democratic candidate Bill Clinton's passport records to President George Bush's reelection campaign.

15. Preston (1978, 197) makes a similar point about African American representation.

16. The Lever Bill authorized the Department of Agriculture to ensure the wartime food supply.

17. See Whalen and Whalen 1985 for a full account of the Congressional passage of the Civil Rights Act; Charles Whalen (R-Ohio) was a member of Congress at the time.

18. Griffiths told Bird that she had meant to offer a similar amendment herself but refrained because of the tactical advantages of Smith's sponsorship.

19. Of course, this success was more limited than that of the Civil Rights Act, since the ERA was never ratified. For accounts of the campaign for and defeat of the ERA, see Mansbridge 1986; Hoff-Wilson 1986; and Berry 1986.

20. See Frankovic 1977; Gehlen 1977; Leader 1977; Welch 1985; and Thomas 1991.

21. See also Gehlen 1977; Mezey 1978; Saint-Germain 1989; Reingold 1990; Thomas 1991; and Thomas and Welch 1991.

22. In 1980, the Roper Organization found that 75 percent of women and 66 percent of men wanted more day-care facilities; these figures indicate a sizable increase over the support in 1970 (Boneparth 1982, 120-21).

23. Roper Organization, *The 1980 Virginia Slims American Women's Opinion Poll*, p. 12, cited in Boneparth 1982, 121.

24. The Comprehensive Child Development Act was part of an omnibus bill that also included reauthorization of the Office of Economic Opportunity and establishment of the Legal Services Corporation, and Nixon objected to all three parts; however, he concluded his veto message with a plea for "Congress to act now to pass the OEO extension and to create the legal services corporation along the lines proposed in our original legislation," although he made no such plea for the Child Development Act.

25. George Bush, "Memorandum of Disagreement," reprinted in *Congressional Quarterly Weekly Report* 50 (October 3, 1992), p. 2976.

26. *Congressional Quarterly Weekly Report* 50 (October 3, 1992), p. 3059. See also Mezey 1992, 134-37.

27. See Klein 1984 for a description of the women's vote through the 1982 elections.

28. See Duverger 1955; Means 1972; Currell 1974; Rule 1981, 77, and 1987; Matland and Brown 1992, 488-89; Norris 1985; Lovenduski 1986; Haavio-Mannila, Dahlerup, Edwards et al. 1985; and Phillips 1991, 80-88.

Chapter 6

1. See Davis 1991 for a fuller discussion of these complexities and their historical evolution.

2. Since my purpose here is discuss the possible uses of membership in Congress by members of oppressed groups, I have not included in this count those who were never seated in Congress, whether they were elected, appointed, or claimed victory in a disputed election.

3. After he became President, Wilson ordered the racial segregation of the federal civil service.

4. Blaine is quoted in Foner 1988, 555; Foner cites Lynch 1970, 160.

5. Taylor 1922, 168-71. Taylor cites a letter from John E. Bruce, who was living in Brooklyn, New York, in support of his contention that the African American members of Congress were held in suspicion by their fellow Republicans.

6. White is quoted in Logan 1954, 92; see also Christopher 1971, 160-67.

7. Gosnell (1935, 163-95) gives a brief political biography of DePriest; Pinderhughes (1987, 63-65) describes the strategic importance of Dawson's switch. Dawson switched again to run against Mitchell as a Republican in 1938 but then returned to the Democratic fold

permanently (Congressional Quarterly 1985b, 932-52). See also Marable 1985, 157-82; and Rakove 1975, 256-59.

8. Wilson (1960) describes the stylistic differences between Dawson and Powell. Pinderhughes (1987, 124-27) criticizes Wilson for oversimplification of the link between leadership style and political ends, and points out the importance of resource limitations and other aspects of the political context.

9. Walton (1972, 171) overlooked the relationship of the Powell Amendment to the Civil Rights Act when he charged that "Powell, before losing his position, advanced black issues and legislation in only a minimal and rhetorical fashion," and reported his "casual observation . . . that no significant piece of civil rights legislation authored by a black congressman has been passed."

10. The text of the Black Agenda is quoted in Marable 1980, 77-78.

11. Interview with Daniel Lindheim, assistant to Ronald Dellums (D-Cal.), Washington, D.C., October 20, 1988.

12. See, for example, the speech by Harold Ford (D-Tenn.) quoted in *Congressional Record*, May 6, 1981, p. 8693.

13. *Congressional Record*, May 5, 1981, p. 8508.

14. *Congressional Record*, May 6, 1981, p. 8671.

15. *Congressional Record*, May 5, 1981, p. 8510.

16. *Congressional Record*, May 6, 1981, p. 8685.

17. *Congressional Record*, May 6, 1981, p. 8671.

18. *Congressional Record*, May 5, 1981, p. 8512.

19. *Congressional Record*, May 6, 1981, p. 8682.

20. See the speech by Delbert Latta (R-Ohio) quoted in *Congressional Record*, March 22, 1983, p. H1495.

21. *Congressional Record*, daily edition, March 22, 1983, pp. H1499-H1500.

22. *Congressional Record*, daily edition, March 22, 1983, p. H1502.

23. *Congressional Record*, daily edition, April 5, 1984, p. H2388.

24. Interviews with Daniel Lindheim, October 20, 1988; and Amelia Parker, executive director of the Congressional Black Caucus, August 4, 1988.

25. In 1993 the American Friends Service Committee and other leftist lobbying groups made some attempt to gather national support for the CBC Budget. It is possible that this effort may grow in the future.

26. *Congressional Record*, May 24, 1982, p. 11533.

27. A member's ADA rating is simply the percentage of those votes designated by the ADA on which the member voted for the ADA position.

28. Barnett 1977, 23-24; interview with Walter Fauntroy, November 3, 1988.

29. Interview with Daniel Lindheim, October 20, 1988.

30. Interview with Frank Clemente, former lobbyist for Jobs With Peace, July 13, 1989.

31. Interview with Ruth Flower, staff member of Friends Committee on National Legislation, July 13, 1989.

32. Interviews with John Balder, aide to Walter Fauntroy (D-D.C.), September 1, 1988; and Daniel Lindheim, aide to Ronald Dellums (D-Cal.), October 20, 1988.

Chapter 7

1. Here and elsewhere, I use *socialist* in the same way as *democratic*. When capitalized, it refers to the party of that name; in lower case, it refers to the broader political position.

2. Socialist Party, *Proceedings of the 1912 National Convention*, p. 234, quoted in Miller 1973, 74-75.

3. Berger is cited by Miller (1973, 73), who in turn quotes from the *Social-Democratic Herald*, November 12, 1910.

4. Berger had already worked with Haywood in 1911, forcing the resignation of a federal judge in Seattle who had denied an application for citizenship because of the applicant's IWW membership (Kipnis 1952, 333-34; Haywood 1929, 249-50).

5. See Chapter 4.

6. An example of Wilson's use of his office to hurt the Socialists can be found in the correspondence in 1918 between Wilson and W. B. Rubin, a labor attorney, about how to undermine Berger's support by awarding defense contracts to Milwaukee firms with anti-Socialist unions. (See the General Records of the Department of Labor, Record Group 174, Office of the Secretary, William B. Wilson, General Subject Files, 1913-1921, Box No. 2, File 13/121, "William B. Rubin, 1918-19.")

7. This was the case except for a few months in 1948, when Leo Isaacson also served as an ALP member of Congress.

8. A week earlier, the AYC had defeated a motion to ban young Communists from membership.

9. Richard Rovere in *Harpers*, April, 1944, cited by Rubinstein (1956, 6).

10. The charge that Marcantonio was "Moscow's mouthpiece," made by his opponent John Ellis, was printed in the *New York Times*, July 13, 1948; Marcantonio's response—to a *Times* editorial, not directly to Ellis—was in a letter to the editor in the *New York Times*, October 30, 1948. Both are quoted in Schaffer 1966, 188-90.

11. The "red Vito" statement was made by the New York Young Republican Club.

12. Examples can be found in Walton 1972, 171; and Fenno 1973, 131-32. For general criticism of Powell along these lines, and praise of the machine hack Dawson, see Wilson 1960.

13. It is worth noting that the initial charge against Powell—that he had libeled a political opponent—was not a matter of personal corruption. However, this charge was followed by others, including some concerning payroll irregularities (Christopher 1971, 203-08).

14. Wilson (1960) criticizes Powell for what he considers ineffective grandstanding; but Wilson's analysis is refuted by Dianne M. Pinderhughes (1987, 124-27). See also Powell 1971; and Hamilton 1991.

15. Abzug's campaign for the seat in question is described in Abzug 1972, 14-28. This memoir, in the form of a diary of her first year in office, was obviously written to be published, and may have been revised by the author or her editor between the events described and the book's publication in 1972. It certainly represents her real opinions, but some of the analysis may have benefited from hindsight. In any case, she was at times remarkably candid in her contributions to what was in part a campaign book; for example, she complained about what she considered to be excessive demands on her time made by Women Strike for Peace, part of her core constituency (see pp. 177-78).

16. See Berg 1975 for a fuller account of congressional attempts at action against the Vietnam War.

17. Barone and Ujifusa 1987, 96. Since its acquisition by the Dow Jones Co., the *Almanac's* opinions have taken on a right-wing slant, but its quantitative estimates are usually reliable. Dellums's general election margins were 60 percent to 40 percent in 1984, and 60 percent to 38 percent in 1986, but 67 percent to 31 percent in 1988. In that last year he outspent his Republican opponent, John J. Cuddihy, by a ratio of $1.1 million to $7,000; (Barone and Ujifusa 1989, 103).

18. I owe this phrase, of course, to Brenner 1983.

19. Bernard Sanders (I-Vt.), an unaffiliated socialist representative, clearly belongs in this list, but was elected too recently to be fully studied for this book. See Grover 1994 for a good first account of Sanders's impact on Congress.

20. By "the 1960s" I mean the period which lasted from 1954 to 1974.

21. I discuss congressional action on Angola at greater length in Berg 1985.

22. Congressional action was not the only focus; considerable effort was also put into raising money for direct aid to Nicaraguan development projects and Salvadoran base communities, and into what came to be known as "accompaniment"—sending delegations of U.S. citizens either into areas where there was particular danger of right-wing terrorism, or to accompany activists who might be in particular danger from terrorists wherever they went. It was hoped that the publicity resulting from such accompaniment might serve as some protection to those accompanied.

23. Both laws are quoted in Central America Crisis Monitoring Team (1985, 67).

24. A friend who is a full-time organizer in the Central America solidarity movement told me in the mid-1980s that it would be a bad idea to run a protest candidate against our local representative, at that time the conservative Democrat Brian Donnelly (Mass.), because it might make him mad and harder to influence in the future. This thinking seemed to typify the movement.

25. The quoted passages are taken from Committee in Solidarity with the People of El Salvador (1991) and from the letter written by Angela Sanbrano, CISPES executive director, that was mailed with it.

Bibliography

Abzug, Bella S. 1972. *Bella! Ms. Abzug Goes to Washington*. Ed. Mel Ziegler. New York: Saturday Review Press.

Alexander, E. Curtis. 1983. *Adam Clayton Powell Jr.: A Black Power Political Educator*. African American Educator Series, Vol. 2. Chesapeake, Va.: ECA Associates.

Alexander, Herbert E. 1983. *Financing the 1980 Election*. In collaboration with Brian A. Haggerty. Lexington, Mass.: Heath-Lexington.

____. 1992. *Financing Politics: Money, Elections, and Political Reform*. 4th ed. Washington, D.C.: CQ Press.

Alexander, Herbert E., and Brian A. Haggerty. 1984. *PACs and Parties: Relationships and Interrelationships*. Los Angeles: Citizens' Research Foundation.

Alston, Chuck. 1990. "As Clean-air Bill Took Off, So Did PAC Donations." *Congressional Quarterly Weekly Report*, March 17, pp. 811-17.

____. 1991. "Lobbyists Storm Capitol Hill, Clash Over Banking Bill." *Congressional Quarterly Weekly Report*, August 24, pp. 2313-18.

Annals of America. 1968. 18 vols. Chicago: Encyclopaedia Brittanica.

Aronowitz, Stanley. 1973. *False Promises: The Shaping of American Working Class Consciousness*. New York: McGraw-Hill.

Atkinson, Charles Raymond. 1911. *The Committee on Rules, and the Overthrow of Speaker Cannon*. New York: Columbia University Press.

"At Last, Profits Worth Savoring: The Service 500." 1989. *Fortune*, June 5, p. 364.

Bachrach, Peter, and Morton S. Baratz. 1962. "The Two Faces of Power." *American Political Science Review* 57:947-52.

Baer, Denise L. 1991. "Bella S. Abzug (1920-)." In *Political Parties & Elections in the United States: An Encyclopedia*, pp. 8-9. Ed. L. Sandy Maisel. New York: Garland.

Barnett, Marguerite Ross. 1975. "The Congressional Black Caucus." *Proceedings of the Academy of Political Science* 32:34-50.

____. 1977. "The Congressional Black Caucus: Symbol, Myth, and Reality." *The Black Scholar*, January/February, pp. 17-26.

Barone, Michael, and Grant Ujifusa. 1987. *The Almanac of American Politics 1988: The President, the Senators, the Representatives, the Governors: Their Records and Elections Results, Their States and Districts*. Washington, D.C.: National Journal.

____. 1989. *The Almanac of American Politics 1990: The Senators, the Representatives and the Governors: Their Records and Election Results, Their States and Districts*. Washington, D.C.: National Journal.

Barrett, Michele. 1980. *Women's Oppression Today: Problems in Marxist Feminist Analysis*. London: NLB.

Bebel, August. 1910. *Woman and Socialism*, Jubilee 50th Edition. Trans. Meta L. Stern. New York: Socialist Literature Co.

Bentley, Arthur F. 1967. *The Process of Government*. Ed. Peter H. Odegard. Cambridge, Mass.: Harvard University Press/Belknap.

Berg, John C. 1975. "Why the Congressional Doves Failed to End United States Participation in the Vietnam War." Ph.D. Dissertation, Harvard University.

____. 1977. "Reforming Seniority in the House of Representatives: Did It Make any Difference?" *Policy Studies Journal* 5 (Summer):437-43.

____. 1978a. "The Effects of Seniority Reform on Three House Committees in the Ninety-Fourth Congress." In *Legislative Reform: The Policy Impact*, pp. 49-59. Ed. Leroy N. Rieselbach. Lexington, Mass.: Heath-Lexington.

____. 1978b. "What Did Congress Learn from Vietnam?" Paper presented at the annual meeting of the New England Political Science Association, Chestnut Hill, Mass.

____. 1979. "Resistance to Limited War in the United States Congress." Paper submitted to the triennial congress of the International Political Science Association, Moscow.

____. 1985. "Vietnam, Angola, Lebanon, and Central America: Many Limits, Limited Possibilities for Congressional Control of Military Intervention." Paper presented at the annual meeting of the American Political Science Association, New Orleans.

____. 1987. "The Congressional Black Caucus Budget and the Representation of Black Americans." Paper presented at the annual meeting of the American Political Science Association, Chicago.

____. 1991a. "Red Scare." In *Political Parties & Elections in the United States: An Encyclopedia*, pp. 921-23. Ed. L. Sandy Maisel. New York: Garland.

____. 1991b. "Vito Marcantonio (1902-1954)." In *Political Parties & Elections in the United States: An Encyclopedia*, pp. 636-37. Ed. L. Sandy Maisel. New York: Garland.

Bernstein, Marver. 1955. *Regulating Business by Independent Commission*. Princeton: Princeton University Press.

Berry, Mary Frances. 1986. *Why ERA Failed: Politics, Women's Rights, and the Amending Process of the Constitution*. Bloomington: Indiana University Press.

"The Biggest Blowout Ever: The Fortune 500 Largest U.S. Industrial Corporations." 1989. *Fortune* April 24, pp. 349-401.

Bird, Caroline (assisted by Sara Welles Briller). 1974. *Born Female: The High Cost of Keeping Women Down*, rev. ed. New York: David McKay.

Birnbaum, Jeffrey H., and Alan S. Murray. 1987. *Showdown at Gucci Gulch; Lawmakers, Lobbyists, and the Unlikely Triumph of Tax Reform*. New York: Vintage.

Bolling, Richard. 1965. *House Out of Order*. New York: E. P. Dutton.

____. 1968. *Power in the House: A History of the Leadership in the House of Representatives*. New York: E. P. Dutton.

Boneparth, Ellen, ed. 1982. *Women, Power and Policy*. New York: Pergamon.

Boyer, Richard O., and Herbert M. Morais. [1955] 1970. *Labor's Untold Story*. New York: United Electrical Workers.

Brecher, Jeremy. 1977. *Strike!* Boston: South End.

Brenner, Philip. 1983. *The Limits and Possibilities of Congress*. New York: St. Martin's.

Brown, Kirk F. 1983. "Campaign Contributions and Congressional Voting." Paper presented at the annual meeting of the American Political Science Association, Chicago.

Burns, James McGregor. 1963. *The Deadlock of Democracy: Four-party Politics in America*. Englewood Cliffs, N.J.: Prentice-Hall.

____. 1972. *Uncommon Sense*. New York: Harper & Row.

Burrell, Barbara. 1992. "Women Candidates in Open-seat Primaries for the U.S. House: 1968-1990." *Legislative Studies Quarterly* 17:493-508.

Cain, Bruce, John Ferejohn, and Morris Fiorina. 1987. *The Personal Vote: Constituency Service and Electoral Independence.* Cambridge, Mass.: Harvard University Press.

Cavanagh, Thomas E. 1984. *The Impact of the Black Electorate.* JCPS Election '84 Report, No. 1. Washington, D.C.: Joint Center for Political Studies.

Central America Crisis Monitoring Team. 1985. *In Contempt of Congress: The Reagan Record of Deceit & Illegality on Central America.* Washington, D.C.: Institute for Policy Studies.

Chamberlin, Hope. 1973. *A Minority of Members: Women in the U.S. Congress.* New York: Praeger.

Chappell, Henry. 1982. "Campaign Contributions and Congressional Voting: A Simultaneous Probit-Tobit Model." *Review of Economics and Statistics* 64:77-83.

Cheney, Richard B., and Lynne V. Cheney. 1983. *Kings of the Hill: Power and Personality in the House of Representatives.* New York: Continuum.

Chepaitis, Joseph B. 1972. "Federal Social Welfare Progressivism in the 1920s." *Social Service Review* 46:213-29.

Christopher, Maurine. 1971. *America's Black Congressmen.* New York: Thomas Y. Crowell.

Clapp, Charles L. 1963. *The Congressman: His Work as He Sees It.* Washington, D.C.: Brookings Institution.

Clark, Janet. 1991. "Getting There: Women in Political Office." *Annals of the American Academy of Political and Social Science* 515 (May):63-76.

Clark, Joseph. 1964. *Congress: The Sapless Branch.* New York: Harper & Row.

Clawson, Dan, and Tie-ting Su. 1990. "Was 1980 Special? A Comparison of 1980 and 1986 Corporate PAC Contributions." *The Sociological Quarterly* 21:371-87.

Cohodas, Nadine. 1985. "Black House Members Striving for Influence." *Congressional Quarterly Weekly Report,* April 13, p. 675.

Collins, Robert M. 1981. *The Business Response to Keynes, 1929-1964.* New York: Columbia University Press.

Committee in Solidarity with the People of El Salvador. 1991. "CISPES 1990 Year in Review." Washington.

Conable, Barber B., Jr. 1989. *Congress and the Income Tax.* Norman: University of Oklahoma Press.

Congressional Quarterly. 1981. *Congress and the Nation: A Review of Government and Politics, 1977-1980,* Vol. 5. Ed. Martha V. Gottrow. Washington, D.C.: Congressional Quarterly.

_____. 1982. *Congressional Quarterly Almanac 1981.* Washington, D.C.: Congressional Quarterly.

_____. 1983. *Congressional Quarterly Almanac 1982.* Washington, D.C.: Congressional Quarterly.

_____. 1984. *Congressional Quarterly Almanac 1983.* Washington, D.C.: Congressional Quarterly.

_____. 1985a. *Congressional Quarterly Almanac 1984.* Washington, D.C.: Congressional Quarterly.

_____. 1985b. *Guide to U.S. Elections.* 2d ed. Washington, D.C.: Congressional Quarterly.

_____. 1986. *Congressional Quarterly Almanac 1985.* Washington, D.C.: Congressional Quarterly.

_____. 1987. *Congressional Quarterly Almanac 1986.* Washington, D.C.: Congressional Quarterly.

_____. 1988. *Congressional Quarterly Almanac 1987.* Washington, D.C.: Congressional Quarterly.

_____. 1989. *Congressional Quarterly Almanac 1988.* Washington, D.C.: Congressional Quarterly.

_____. 1990. *Congressional Quarterly Almanac 1989.* Washington, D.C.: Congressional Quarterly.

_____. 1991a. "Clean Air Act Rewritten, Tightened." In *Congressional Quarterly Almanac 1990,* pp. 229-79. Washington, D.C.: Congressional Quarterly.

_____. 1991b. "Oil Spill Liability, Prevention Bill Enacted." In *Congressional Quarterly Almanac 1990,* pp. 283-87. Washington, D.C.: Congressional Quarterly.

____. 1993. *Congressional Quarterly Almanac 1992*. Washington, D.C.: Congressional Quarterly.

Conlan, Timothy J., Margaret T. Wrightson, and David R. Beam. 1990. *Taxing Choices: The Politics of Tax Reform*. Washington, D.C.: CQ Press.

Currell, Melville E. 1974. *Political Woman*. London: Croom Helm.

Dahl, Robert A. 1982. *Dilemmas of Pluralist Democracy*. New Haven: Yale University Press.

Darcy, R., and James R. Choike. 1986. "A Formal Analysis of Legislative Turnover: Women Candidates and Legislative Representation." *American Journal of Political Science* 30:237-55.

Darcy, R., and Sarah Slavin Schramm. 1977. "When Women Run Against Men: The Electorate's Response to Congressional Contests." *Public Opinion Quarterly* 41:1-12.

Davidson, Roger H., David M. Kovenock, and Michael K. O'Leary. 1966. *Congress in Crisis: Politics and Congressional Reform*. Belmont, Cal.: Wadsworth.

Davies, David G. 1986. *United States Taxes and Tax Policy*. Cambridge, England: Cambridge University Press.

Davis, F. James. 1991. *Who is Black? One Nation's Definition*. University Park: Pennsylvania State University Press.

de Duve, Christian. 1984. *A Guided Tour of the Living Cell*. New York: Scientific American Library.

Delphy, Christine. 1984. *Close to Home: A Materialist Analysis of Women's Oppression*. Ed. and trans. Diana Leonard. Amherst: University of Massachusetts Press.

Dodd, Lawrence C. 1977. "Congress and the Quest for Power." In *Congress Reconsidered*. Ed. Lawrence C. Dodd and Bruce I. Oppenheimer. New York: Praeger.

____. 1986. "A Theory of Congressional Cycles: Solving the Puzzle of Change." In *Congress and Policy Change*, pp. 3-44. Eds. Gerald C. Wright, Leroy N. Rieselbach, and Lawrence C. Dodd. New York: Agathon Press.

Dolbeare, Kenneth M., ed. 1984. *American Political Thought*, rev. ed. Chatham, N.J.: Chatham House.

Domhoff, G. William. 1983. *Who Rules America Now? A View for the '80s*. Englewood Cliffs, N.J.: Prentice-Hall.

Draper, Alan. 1989. *A Rope of Sand: The AFL-CIO Committee on Political Education, 1955-1967*. New York: Praeger.

DuBois, W.E.B. [1953] 1963. *Black Reconstruction in America: An Essay Toward a History of the Part Which Black Folk Played in the Attempt to Reconstruct Democracy in America, 1860-1880*. New York: Russell and Russell.

____. [1903] 1969. *The Souls of Black Folk*. New York: New American Library, Signet Classic.

Dunning, William A. 1898. *Essays on the Civil War and Reconstruction*. New York: Macmillan.

____. 1907. *Reconstruction, Political and Economic 1865-1877*. New York: Harper & Brothers.

Duverger, Maurice. 1955. *The Political Role of Women*. Paris: UNESCO.

Easton, David. 1965. *A Systems Analysis of Political Life*. New York: John Wiley.

____. 1990. *The Analysis of Political Structure*. New York: Routledge.

Engels, Friedrich. [1942] 1972. *The Origin of the Family, Private Property, and the State, in the Light of the Researches of Lewis H. Morgan*. Introd. by Eleanor Burke Leacock. New York: International Publishers.

____. [1848] 1978. "Socialism: Utopian and Scientific." In *The Marx-Engels Reader*, 2d ed., pp. 683-717. Ed. Robert C. Tucker. New York: W. W. Norton.

Evans, Diana M. 1986. "PAC Contributions and Roll-call Voting: Conditional Power." In *Interest Group Politics*. Eds. Allen J. Cigler and Burdett Loomis. Washington, D.C.: CQ Press.

Federico, Ronald C., and Janet S. Schwartz. 1983. *Sociology*, 3d ed. Reading, Mass.: Addison-Wesley.

Felton, John, and Janet Hook. 1988. "House Defeat Clouds Outlook for Contra Aid." *Congressional Quarterly Weekly Report*, March 5, pp. 555-58.

Fenno, Richard F., Jr. 1969. "The Appropriations Committee as a Political System." In *New Perspectives on the House of Representatives*, Eds. Robert L. Peabody and Nelson W. Polsby. Chicago: Rand McNally.

———. 1973. *Congressmen in Committees*. Boston: Little, Brown and Co.

———. 1978. *Home Style: House Members in Their Districts*. Boston: Little, Brown.

Ferguson, Thomas. 1983. "Party Realignment and American Industrial Structure: The Investment Theory of Political Parties in Historical Perspective." *Research in Political Economy* 6:1-82.

Ferguson, Thomas, and Joel Rogers. 1979. "Anti-union Alliance: Labor Law Reform and Its Enemies." *The Nation* 228 (6-13 January):1, 17-20.

———. 1986. *Right Turn: The Decline of the Democrats and the Future of American Politics*. New York: Hill and Wang.

Fine, Sidney. 1969. *Sit-down: The General Motors Strike of 1936-1937*. Ann Arbor: University of Michigan Press.

Fiorina, Morris P. 1977. *Congress: Keystone of the Washington Establishment*. New Haven: Yale University Press.

Firestone, Shulamith. 1970. *The Dialectic of Sex: The Case for Feminist Revolution*. New York: Morrow.

Foner, Eric. 1988. *Reconstruction: America's Unfinished Revolution 1863-1877*. New York: Harper & Row.

Foner, Philip S. 1964. *History of the Labor Movement in the United States. Vol. 3: The Policies and Practices of the American Federation of Labor, 1900-1909*. New York: International Publishers.

———. 1980. *History of the Labor Movement in the United States. Vol. 5: The AFL in the Progressive Era, 1910-1915*. New York: International Publishers.

Frankfurter, Felix, and Nathan Greene. 1930. *The Labor Injunction*. New York: Macmillan.

Frankovic, K. A. 1977. "Sex and Voting in the U.S. House of Representatives 1961-1975." *American Politics Quarterly* 5:315-31.

Freeman, Jo. 1975. *The Politics of Women's Liberation: A Case Study of an Emerging Social Movement and Its Relation to the Policy Process*. New York: David McKay.

Frendreis, John, and Richard Waterman. 1985. "PAC Contributions and Legislative Behavior: Senate Voting on Trucking Deregulation." *Social Science Quarterly* 66:401-12.

Galbraith, John Kenneth. [1956] 1980. *American Capitalism: The Concept of Countervailing Power*. White Plains, N.Y.: M. E. Sharpe.

———. 1985. *The New Industrial State*, 4th ed. Boston: Houghton Mifflin.

Gallup, George. 1978. *The Gallup Poll: Public Opinion 1972-1977*. Wilmington, Del.: Scholarly Resources.

———. 1983. *The Gallup Poll: Public Opinion 1982*. Wilmington, Del.: Scholarly Resources.

Gehlen, Frieda L. 1977. "Women Members of Congress: A Distinctive Role." In *A Portrait of Marginality: The Political Behavior of the American Woman*, pp. 304-19. Eds. Marianne Githens and Jewel L. Prestage. New York: David McKay.

Giles, Kevin S. 1980. *Flight of the Dove: The Story of Jeannette Rankin*. Beaverton, Ore.: Touchstone.

Ginsberg, Benjamin, and John Green. 1986. "The Best Congress Money Can Buy: Campaign Contributions and Congressional Behavior." In *Do Elections Matter?* Armonk, N.Y.: M. E. Sharpe.

Gleiber, Dennis, James King, and H. R. Mahood. 1987. "PAC Contributions, Constituency Interest and Legislative Voting: Gun Control Legislation in the U.S. Senate." Paper presented at the annual meeting of the American Political Science Association, Chicago.

Goldfield, Michael. 1987. *The Decline of Organized Labor in the United States.* Chicago: University of Chicago Press.

Goldstein, Robert J. 1978. *Political Repression in Modern America: From 1870 to the Present.* Cambridge, Mass.: Schenkman.

Gompers, Samuel. [1925] 1984. *Seventy Years of Life and Labor: An Autobiography.* Ed. Nick Salvatore. Ithaca, N.Y.: ILR Press.

Goodwin, George, Jr. 1970. *The Little Legislatures: Committees in Congress.* Amherst: University of Massachusetts Press.

Gordon, David M., Richard Edwards, and Michael Reich. 1982. *Segmented Work, Divided Workers: The Historical Transformation of Labor in the United States.* Cambridge, England: Cambridge University Press.

Gosnell, Harold F. 1935. *Negro Politicians: The Rise of Negro Politics in Chicago.* Introd. by Robert E. Park. Chicago: University of Chicago Press.

Greenberg, Edward S. 1974. *Serving the Few: Corporate Capitalism and the Bias of Government Policy.* New York: John Wiley & Sons.

———. 1979. *Understanding Modern Government: The Rise and Decline of the American Political Economy.* New York: John Wiley & Sons.

———. 1985. *Capitalism and the American Political Ideal.* Armonk, N.Y.: M. E. Sharpe.

Greenstone, J. David. [1969] 1977. *Labor in American Politics.* With a New Introduction by the author. Chicago: University of Chicago Press.

Grenzke, Janet. 1989. "PACs in the Congressional Supermarket: The Currency Is Complex." *American Journal of Political Science* 33:1-24.

Griffith, Ernest S. 1939. *The Impasse of Democracy.* New York: Harrison Hilton.

Griffith, Ernest S., and Francis R. Valeo. 1975. *Congress: Its Contemporary Role.* 5th ed. New York: New York University Press.

Gross, James A. 1974. *The Making of the National Labor Relations Board: A Study in Economics, Politics, and the Law.* Albany: State University of New York Press.

Grover, William F. 1994. "In the Belly of the Beast: Bernie Sanders, Congress and Political Change." *New Political Science,* Nos. 28-29 (Winter-Spring), pp. 31-51.

Haavio-Mannila, Elina, Drude Dahlerup, Maud Eduards, et al. 1985. *Unfinished Democracy: Women in Nordic Politics.* Trans. Christine Badcock. Oxford: Pergamon.

Hamilton, Alexander. [1791] 1966. *The Papers of Alexander Hamilton,* Vol. 10. *Alexander Hamilton's Final Version of the Report on the Subject of Manufactures.* Ed. Harold C. Syrett. New York: Columbia University Press.

Hamilton, Alexander, James Madison, and John Jay. [1791] 1961. *The Federalist Papers.* Ed. Clinton Rossiter. New York: New American Library.

Hamilton, Charles V. 1991. *Adam Clayton Powell, Jr.: The Political Biography of an American Dilemma.* New York: Atheneum.

Harris, Sheldon H. 1972. *Paul Cuffe: Black America and the African Return.* New York: Simon and Schuster.

Harris, William C. 1982. "Blanche K. Bruce of Mississippi: Conservative Assimilationist." In *Southern Black Leaders of the Reconstruction Era*, pp. 3-38. Ed. Howard N. Rabinowitz. Urbana: University of Illinois Press.

Hartman, Heidi. 1981. "The Unhappy Marriage of Marxism and Feminism." In *Women and Revolution*. Ed. Lydia Sargent. Boston: South End.

Hartsock, Nancy C.M. 1983. *Money, Sex, and Power: Toward a Feminist Historical Materialism*. New York: Longman.

Haygood, Wil. 1993. *King of the Cats: The Life and Times of Adam Clayton Powell Jr*. Boston: Houghton Mifflin.

Haywood, William D. 1929. *Bill Haywood's Book: The Autobiography of William D. Haywood*. New York: International Publishers.

Hinckley, Barbara. 1971. *The Seniority System in Congress*. Bloomington: Indiana University Press.

———. 1978. *Stability and Change in Congress*. 2d ed. New York: Harper & Row.

Hine, William C. 1982. "Dr. Benjamin A. Boseman, Jr.: Charleston's Black Physician-Politician." In *Southern Black Leaders of the Reconstruction Era*. Ed. Howard N. Rabinowitz. Urbana: University of Illinois Press.

Hoff-Wilson, Joan, ed. 1986. *Rights of Passage: The Past and Future of the ERA*. Bloomington: Indiana University Press.

Hook, R. 1982. "The Timetable of Delay: The Unfair Labor Practice Process." *Labor Update* 3:6-7.

Howe, Irving, and B. J. Widick. 1949. *The UAW and Walter Reuther*. New York: Random House.

Hubel, David H. 1988. *Eye, Brain, and Vision*. New York: Scientific American Library.

Humphries, Craig. 1991. "Corporations, PACs, and the Strategic Link Between Contributions and Lobbying Activities." *Western Political Quarterly* 44:353-72.

Jackson, Brooks. 1988. *Honest Graft: Big Money and the American Political Process*. New York: Alfred A. Knopf.

Jacobson, Gary C. 1992. *The Politics of Congressional Elections*. 3d ed. New York: HarperCollins.

Jefferson, Thomas. [1785] 1972. *Notes on the State of Virginia*. Ed. William Peden. New York: W. W. Norton. (Also published in 1954 by University of North Carolina Press.)

Jennings, James. 1983-84. "America's New Urban Politics: Black Electoralism, Black Activism." *Radical America*, Vol. 17, No. 6-Vol. 18, No. 1.

———. 1984. "Boston: Blacks and Progressive Politics." In *The New Black Vote: Politics and Power in Four American Cities*, pp. 199-313. Ed. Rod Bush. San Francisco: Synthesis.

Jessop, Bob. 1982. *The Capitalist State: Marxist Theories and Methods*. New York: New York University Press.

Jones, Charles O. 1968. "Joseph G. Cannon and Howard W. Smith: An Essay on the Limits of Leadership in the House of Representatives." *Journal of Politics* 30:617-46.

———. 1969. "The Agriculture Committee and the Problem of Representation." In *New Perspectives on the House of Representatives*, 2d ed., pp. 155-73. Eds. Robert L. Peabody and Nelson W. Polsby. Chicago: Rand McNally.

Josephson, Hannah. 1974. *Jeannette Rankin: First Lady in Congress: A Biography*. Indianapolis: Bobbs-Merrill.

Kammeyer, Kenneth C.W., George Ritzer, and Norman W. Retman. 1990. *Sociology: Experiencing Changing Societies*, 4th ed. Boston: Allyn and Bacon.

Kann, Mark. 1980. *Thinking About Politics: Two Political Sciences*. St. Paul: West.

Kaplan, Dave. 1993. "Constitutional Doubt Is Thrown on Bizarre-shaped Districts." *Congressional Quarterly Weekly Report*, July 3, pp. 1761-63.

Kariel, Henry S. 1961. *The Decline of American Pluralism*. Stanford: Stanford University Press.

Katznelson, Ira, and Mark Kesselman. 1987. *The Politics of Power: A Critical Introduction to American Government*. 3d ed. San Diego: Harcourt Brace Jovanovich.

Kau, James B., and Paul Rubin. 1982. *Congressmen, Constituents, and Contributors*. Boston: Martinus Nijhoff.

Keefe, William J. 1980. *Congress and the American People*. Englewood Cliffs, N.J.: Prentice-Hall.

Kennon, Donald R. 1986. *The Speakers of the House of Representatives*. Baltimore: Johns Hopkins University Press.

Key, V. O., Jr. 1964. *Politics, Parties, & Pressure Groups*, 5th ed. New York: Thomas Y. Crowell.

Kincaid, Diane D., ed. 1979. *Silent Hattie Speaks: The Personal Journal of Senator Hattie Caraway*. Contributions in Women's Studies, No. 9. Westport, Conn.: Greenwood.

King, Ronald F. 1984. "Tax Expenditures and Systematic Public Policy: An Essay on the Political Economy of the Federal Revenue Code." *Public Budgeting and Finance* (Spring), pp. 14-31.

Kipnis, Ira. 1952. *The American Socialist Movement 1897-1912*. New York: Columbia University Press.

Kirkpatrick, Jeane J. 1974. *Political Woman*. New York: Basic Books.

Klein, Ethel. 1984. *Gender Politics*. Cambridge, Mass.: Harvard University Press.

Knight, T. R. 1979. "Procedure and Delay in NLRB Representation Elections: Is Remedial Legislation Justified?" *Industrial and Labor Relations Forum* 13:3-43.

Kolko, Gabriel. 1967. *The Triumph of Conservatism: A Reinterpretation of American History, 1900-1916*. Chicago: Quadrangle.

Kollontai, Alexandra. 1977. *Selected Writings of Alexandra Kollontai*. Trans. Alix Holt. New York: W. W. Norton.

Kong, Dolores. 1991. "Age-old Illnesses Making Comeback." *Boston Globe*, September 9, p. 46.

Krehbiel, Keith. 1991. *Information and Legislative Organization*. Ann Arbor: University of Michigan Press.

Laclau, Ernesto, and Chantal Mouffe. 1985. *Hegemony and Socialist Strategy: Towards a Radical Democratic Politics*. Trans. Winston Moore and Paul Cammack. London: Verso.

Lamson, Peggy. 1968. *Few Are Chosen: American Women in Political Life Today*. Boston: Houghton Mifflin.

Leader, S. G. 1977. "The Policy Impact of Elected Women Officials." In *The Impact of the Electoral Process*, pp. 265-84. Eds. L. Sandy Maisel and Joseph Cooper. Beverly Hills: Sage.

Levy, Michael B., ed. 1982. *Political Thought in America: An Anthology*. Homewood: Dorsey.

Lindblom, Charles E. 1977. *Politics and Markets: The World's Political-Economic Systems*. New York: Basic Books.

———. 1983. "Comment on Manley." *American Political Science Review* 77:384-86.

Logan, Rayford W. 1954. *The Negro in American Life and Thought: The Nadir 1877-1901*. New York: Dial.

Lovenduski, Joni. 1986. *Women and European Politics: Contemporary Feminism and Public Policy*. Brighton, England: Wheatsheaf.

Lowi, Theodore J. 1964. "American Business, Public Policy, Case-studies, and Political Theory." Review. *World Politics*, July, pp. 677-715.

____. 1970. "Decision Making Vs. Policy Making: Toward an Antidote for Technocracy." *Public Administration Review* 30 (May/June).

____. 1972. "Four Systems of Policy, Politics, and Choice." *Public Administration Review* 32 (July/August):298-310.

____. 1979. *The End of Liberalism: The Second Republic of the United States*, 2d ed. New York: W. W. Norton.

Lynch, John R. 1970. *Reminiscences of an Active Life: The Autobiography of John Roy Lynch*. Ed. John Hope Franklin. Chicago: University of Chicago Press.

Lynd, Staughton. 1990. "Trade Unionism in the USA." *New Left Review*, No. 184 (November-December), pp. 76-87.

Lynn, Naomi, and Cornelia Butler Flora. 1977. "Societal Punishment and Aspects of Female Political Participation: 1972 National Convention Delegates." In *A Portrait of Marginality: The Political Behavior of the American Woman*, pp. 139-49. Ed. Marianne Githens and Jewel L. Prestage. New York: David McKay.

Maass, Arthur. 1983. *Congress and the Common Good*. New York: Basic Books.

Mandel, Ruth B. 1981. *In the Running: The New Woman Candidate*. New Haven: Ticknor & Fields.

Manley, John F. 1983. "Neo-pluralism: A Class Analysis of Pluralism I and Pluralism II." *American Political Science Review* 57:368-83.

Mansbridge, Jane J. 1986. *Why We Lost the ERA*. Chicago: University of Chicago Press.

Marable, Manning, Jr. 1980. "Black Nationalism in the 1970s: Through the Prism of Race and Class." *Socialist Review*, Nos. 50-51 (March- June), pp. 57-108.

____. 1985. "Black Power in Chicago: An Historical Overview of Class Stratification and Electoral Politics in a Black Urban Community." *Review of Radical Political Economics* 17:157-82.

____. 1993. "Racism and Multicultural Democracy." *Poverty & Race* 2 (September/October):1-4, 12.

Marcantonio, Vito. 1956. *I Vote My Conscience: Debates Speeches and Writings of Vito Marcantonio 1935-1950*. Eds. Annette T. Rubinstein and associates. New York: The Vito Marcantonio Memorial.

Marcus, Ruth. 1989. "Three Former Officials of Texas S&L Indicted." *Washington Post*, January 13.

Martin, Cathie J. 1991. *Shifting the Burden: The Struggle Over Growth and Corporate Taxation*. Chicago: University of Chicago Press.

Marx, Karl. [1867-1894] 1967. *Capital: A Critique of Political Economy*. Ed. Friedrich Engels. Trans. Edward Aveling and Samuel Moore. New York: International Publishers.

Marx, Karl, and Friedrich Engels. [1848] 1978. "Manifesto of the Communist Party." In *The Marx-Engels Reader*, 2d ed., pp. 469-500. Ed. Robert C. Tucker. New York: W. W. Norton.

Masters, Nicholas A. 1962. "The Organized Labor Bureaucracy as a Base of Support for the Democratic Party." *Law and Contemporary Problems* 27 (Spring).

____. 1969. "Committee Assignments." In *New Perspectives on the House of Representatives*, Eds. Robert L. Peabody and Nelson W. Polsby. Chicago: Rand McNally.

Matland, Richard E., and Deborah Dwight Brown. 1992. "District Magnitude's Effect on Female Representation in U.S. State Legislatures." *Legislative Studies Quarterly* 17:469-92.

Mayer, Martin. 1990. *The Greatest-ever Bank Robbery: The Collapse of the Savings and Loan Industry*. New York: Charles Scribner's Sons.

Mayhew, David R. 1974. *Congress: The Electoral Connection*. New Haven: Yale University Press.

McConnell, Grant. 1966. *Private Power and American Democracy*. New York: Vintage.

McDermott, John. 1991. *Corporate Society: Class, Property, and Contemporary Capitalism*. Boulder: Westview.

McGovern, George S., and Leonard F. Guttridge. 1972. *The Great Coalfield War*. Maps by Samuel H. Bryant. Boston: Houghton Mifflin.

Means, Ingun Norderval. 1972. "Political Recruitment of Women in Norway." *Western Political Quarterly* 25:491-521.

Mezey, Michael L. 1989. *Congress, the President, and Public Policy*. Boulder: Westview.

Mezey, Susan Gluck. 1978. "Women and Representation: The Case of Hawaii." *Journal of Politics* 40:369-85.

_____. 1992. *In Pursuit of Equality: Women, Public Policy, and the Federal Courts*. New York: St. Martin's.

Miller, Jake C. 1979. "Black Legislators and African-American Relations, 1970-1975." *Journal of Black Studies* 10 (December):245-61.

Miller, Sally M. 1973. *Victor Berger and the Promise of Constructive Socialism, 1910-1920*. Contributions in American History, No. 24. Westport, Conn.: Greenwood.

_____. 1990. "Berger, Victor L. (1860-1929)." In *Encyclopedia of the American Left*, pp. 84-85. Eds. Mary Jo Buhle, Paul Buhle, and Dan Georgakas. New York: Garland.

Mills, Mike. 1990a. "Cable Regulation Is Dead—Again." *Congressional Quarterly Weekly Report*, October 20, p. 3506.

_____. 1990b. "Cable Re-regulation Measures Would Add Few Strings." *Congressional Quarterly Weekly Report*, September 15, pp. 2910-12.

Moncrief, Gary F., and Joel A. Thompson. 1992. "Electoral Structure and State Legislative Representation: A Research Note." *Journal of Politics* 34:246-56.

Montgomery, David. 1987. *The Fall of the House of Labor: The Workplace, the State and American Labor Activism, 1865-1925*. Cambridge, England: Cambridge University Press.

Nelson, Candice. 1982. "Counting the Cash: PAC Contributions to Members of the House of Representatives." Paper presented at the annual meeting of the American Political Science Association, Washington, D.C.

Neustadtl, Alan. 1990. "Interest Group PACsmanship: An Analysis of Campaign Contributions, Issue Visibility, and Legislative Impact." *Social Forces* 69:549-64.

Neustadtl, Alan, and Dan Clawson. 1988. "Corporate Political Groupings: Does Ideology Unify Business Behavior?" *American Sociological Review* 53:172-90.

Nixon, Richard M. 1971. "Veto of Economic Opportunity Amendments of 1971." *Weekly Compilation of Presidential Documents*, December 13, pp. 1635-36.

Norgren, Jill. 1982. "In Search of a National Child-care Policy: Background and Prospects." In *Women, Power and Policy*, pp. 124-43. Ed. Ellen Boneparth. New York: Pergamon.

Norris, Pippa. 1985. "Women's Legislative Participation in Western Europe." In *Women and Politics in Western Europe*. Ed. Sylvia Bashevkin. London: Frank Cass.

Olson, Mancur. 1971. *The Logic of Collective Action: Public Goods and the Theory of Groups*, 2d ed. Cambridge, Mass.: Harvard University Press.

Orfield, Gary. 1975. *Congressional Power: Congress and Social Change*. New York: Harcourt Brace Jovanovich.

Ornstein, Norman. 1975. "Causes and Consequences of Congressional Change: Subcommittee Reform in the House of Representatives, 1970-1973." In *Congress in Change: Evolution and Reform*. Ed. Norman J. Ornstein. New York: Praeger.

Parenti, Michael. 1978. *Power and the Powerless*. New York: St. Martin's.

_____. 1980. *Democracy for the Few*, 3d ed. New York: St. Martin's.

Parker, Glenn R., and Roger Davidson. 1979. "Why Do Americans Love Their Congressman So Much More Than Their Congress?" *Legislative Studies Quarterly* 4:53-62.

Parsons, Talcott. 1951. *The Social System*. New York: Free Press.

Peabody, Robert L. 1969. "Research on Congress: A Coming of Age." In *Congress: Two Decades of Analysis*, pp. 3-73. Ralph K. Huitt and Robert L. Peabody. New York: Harper & Row.

Pechman, Joseph A. 1957. "Erosion of the Individual Income Tax." *National Tax Journal* 10:24.

____. 1959. "What Would a Comprehensive Individual Income Tax Yield?" In *Tax Revision Compendium*. Submitted to the House Committee on Ways and Means. Washington, D.C.: U.S. Government Printing Office.

Penner, Rudolph G., and Alan J. Abramson. 1988. *Broken Purse Strings: Congressional Budgeting 1974 to 1988*. Washington, D.C.: Urban Institute Press.

Peters, Ronald M., Jr. 1991. "Speaker of the House." In *Political Parties & Elections in the United States: An Encyclopedia*, pp. 1033-39. Ed. L. Sandy Maisel. New York: Garland.

Phillips, Anne. 1991. *Engendering Democracy*. University Park: Pennsylvania State University Press.

Pinderhughes, Dianne M. 1987. *Race and Ethnicity in Chicago Politics: A Reexamination of Pluralist Theory*. Urbana: University of Illinois Press.

Pitney, John J., Jr. 1991. "Joseph G. Cannon (1836-1926)." In *Political Parties & Elections in the United States: An Encyclopedia*, pp. 128-29. Ed. L. Sandy Maisel. New York: Garland.

Piven, Frances Fox, and Richard A. Cloward. 1971. *Regulating the Poor: The Functions of Public Welfare*. New York: Pantheon.

Poulantzas, Nicos. 1969. "The Problem of the Capitalist State." *New Left Review*, No. 58 (November-December), pp. 67-78.

____. 1974. *Les classes sociales dans le capitalisme aujourd'hui*. Paris: Editions Du Seuil.

____. 1978a. *L'état, le Pouvoir, le Socialisme*. Paris: Presses Universitaires de France.

____. [1975] 1978b. *Political Power and Social Classes*. Trans. Timothy O'Hagan. London: Verso.

____. 1978c. *State, Power, Socialism*. Trans. Patrick Camiller. London: NLB.

Powell, Adam Clayton, Jr. 1971. *Adam by Adam: The Autobiography of Adam Clayton Powell, Jr.* New York: Dial.

Preston, Michael. 1978. "Black Elected Officials and Public Policy: Symbolic or Substantive Representation?" *Policy Studies Journal* 7 (Winter):196-201.

Rabinowitz, Howard N., ed. 1982. *Southern Black Leaders of the Reconstruction Era*. Urbana: University of Illinois Press.

Rakove, Milton L. 1975. *Don't Make No Waves—Don't Back No Losers: An Insider's Analysis of the Daley Machine*. Bloomington: Indiana University Press.

Reingold, Beth. 1990. "Representing Women: A Comparison of Female and Male Legislators in California and Arizona." Paper presented at the annual meeting of the American Political Science Association, San Francisco.

____. 1992. "Concepts of Representation Among Female and Male State Legislators." *Legislative Studies Quarterly* 17:509-37.

Ripley, Randall B. 1975. *Congress: Process and Policy*. New York: W. W. Norton.

Ripley, Randall B., and Grace A. Franklin. 1976. *Congress, the Bureaucracy, and Public Policy*, 2d ed. Homewood, Ill.: Dorsey.

____. 1987. *Congress, the Bureaucracy, and Public Policy*. 4th ed. Homewood, Ill.: Dorsey.

Robertson, David Brian, and Dennis R. Judd. 1989. *The Development of American Public Policy: The Structure of Policy Restraint*. Glenview, Ill.: Scott, Foresman/Little, Brown.

Robinson, Cedric J. 1983. *Black Marxism: The Making of the Black Radical Tradition*. London: Zed.

Roemer, John E.. 1982. *A General Theory of Exploitation and Class.* Cambridge, Mass.: Harvard University Press.

Rubinstein, Annette T. 1956. "Vito Marcantonio, Congressman." In *I Vote My Conscience: Debates Speeches and Writings of Vito Marcantonio 1935-1950*, pp. 1-34. Vito Marcantonio. Eds. Annette T. Rubinstein and associates. New York: The Vito Marcantonio Memorial.

Rudwick, Elliott M. 1966. "Oscar DePriest and the Jim Crow Restaurant in the U.S. House of Representatives." *Journal of Negro Education* 35:77-82.

Rule, Wilma. 1981. "Why Women Don't Run: The Critical Contextual Factors in Women's Legislative Recruitment." *Western Political Quarterly* 34:60-77.

———. 1987. "Electoral Systems, Contextual Factors, and Women's Opportunity for Election to Parliament in Twenty-three Democracies." *Western Political Quarterly* 40:477-98.

Rule, Wilma, and Pippa Norris. 1992. "Anglo and Minority Women's Underrepresentation in the Congress: Is the Electoral System the Culprit?" In *United States Electoral Systems: Their Impact on Women and Minorities.* Ed. Wilma Rule and Joseph F. Zimmerman. New Haven: Greenwood.

Sabato, Larry J. 1984. *PAC Power: Inside the World of Political Action Committees.* New York: W. W. Norton.

Saint-Germain, Michelle. 1989. "Does Their Difference Make a Difference? The Impact of Women in Public Policy in the Arizona Legislature." *Social Science Quarterly* 70:956-68.

Salamon, Lester M., ed. 1975. *The Money Committees.* New York: Grossman.

Salamon, Lester M., and Alan J. Abramson. 1984. "Governance: The Politics of Retrenchment." In *The Reagan Record: An Assessment of America's Changing Domestic Priorities,* pp. 31-68. Eds. John L. Palmer and Isabel V. Sawhill. Cambridge, Mass.: Ballinger.

Sapiro, Virginia. 1981. "Research Frontier Essay: When Are Interests Interesting? The Problem of Political Representation of Women." *American Political Science Review* 75:703-04.

———. 1984. *The Political Integration of Women: Roles, Socialization, and Politics.* Urbana: University of Illinois Press.

Sargent, Lydia, ed. 1981. *Women and Revolution: A Discussion of the Unhappy Marriage of Marxism and Feminism.* Boston: South End.

Schaffer, Alan. 1966. *Vito Marcantonio, Radical in Congress.* Syracuse, N.Y.: Syracuse University Press.

Schattschneider, E. E. 1960. *The Semisovereign People: A Realistic View of Democracy in America.* New York: Holt, Rinehart and Winston.

Schlesinger, Arthur, Jr. 1974. *The Imperial Presidency.* New York: Popular Library.

Schroedel, Jean Reith. 1986. "Campaign Contributions and Legislative Outcomes." *Western Political Quarterly* 39:371-89.

Schwarz, John E., and L. Earl Shaw. 1976. *The United States Congress in Comparative Perspective.* Hinsdale, Ill.: Dryden Press.

Schweninger, Loren. 1982. "James T. Rapier and the Noble Cause of Reconstruction." In *Southern Black Leaders of the Reconstruction Era.* Ed. Howard N. Rabinowitz. Urbana: University of Illinois Press.

Silberman, Jonathan, and Garey C. Durden. 1976. "Determining Legislative Preferences on the Minimum Wage: An Economic Approach." *Journal of Political Economy* 84:317-29.

Simons, Henry C. 1938. *Personal Income Taxation: The Definition of Income as a Problem of Fiscal Policy.* Chicago: University of Chicago Press.

———. 1950. *Federal Tax Reform.* Chicago: University of Chicago Press.

Snyder, Solomon H. 1986. *Drugs and the Brain.* New York: Scientific American Library.

Ste. Croix, Geoffrey de. 1984. "Class in Marx's Conception of History, Ancient and Modern." *New Left Review*, No. 146 (July-August), pp. 94-111.

Stewart, Charles, III. 1991. "Thomas B. Reed (1839-1902)." In *Political Parties & Elections in the United States: An Encyclopedia*, pp. 923-24. Ed. L. Sandy Maisel. New York: Garland.

Stockwell, John. 1978. *In Search of Enemies: A CIA Story*. New York: W. W. Norton.

Stokes, Donald E., and Warren E. Miller. 1966. "Party Government and the Saliency of Congress." In *Elections and the Political Order*, pp. 194-211. Eds. Angus Campbell, Philip E. Converse, Warren E. Miller, and Donald E. Stokes. New York: John Wiley and Sons.

Stoper, Emily. 1977. "Wife and Politician: Role Strain Among Women in Public Office." In *A Portrait of Marginality: The Political Behavior of the American Woman*, pp. 320-37. Eds. Marianne Githens and Jewel L. Prestage. New York: David McKay.

Strahan, Randall. 1990. *New Ways and Means: Reform and Change in a Congressional Committee*. Chapel Hill: University of North Carolina Press.

Stratmann, Thomas. 1991. "What Do Campaign Contributions Buy? Deciphering Causal Effects of Money and Votes." *Southern Economic Journal* 57:606-20.

Surrey, Stanley S. 1957. "The Congress and the Tax Lobbyist—How Special Tax Provisions Get Enacted." *Harvard Law Review* 70:1145-82.

———. 1981. "Our Troubled Tax Policy." *Tax Notes*, February 2, pp. 179-97.

Swidorski, Carl. 1994. "The Law, Corporations, and the Left: Historical Lessons for Contemporary Decisions." *New Political Science*, Nos. 28-29 (Winter-Spring), pp. 167-90.

Takaki, Ronald. 1990. *Iron Cages: Race and Culture in 19th-Century America*. New York: Oxford University Press.

Taylor, Alrutheus A. 1922. "Negro Congressmen a Generation After." *Journal of Negro History* 7:127-71.

Teeters, Holly, and Jody Neathery, compilers. 1992. "Women Elected to National Legislatures." Table. *APSA Legislative Studies Section Newsletter* 16 (November):16-17.

Thomas, Lamont D. 1986. *Rise to Be a People: A Biography of Paul Cuffe*. Urbana: University of Illinois Press.

Thomas, Sue. 1991. "The Impact of Women on State Legislative Policies." *Journal of Politics* 53:958-76.

Thomas, Sue, and Susan Welch. 1991. "The Impact of Gender on Activities and Priorities of State Legislators." *Western Political Quarterly* 44:445-56.

Tomlins, Christopher L. 1985. *The State and the Unions: Labor Relations, Law, and the Organized Labor Movement in America, 1880-1960*. Cambridge, England: Cambridge University Press.

Truman, David B. 1971. *The Governmental Process: Political Interests and Public Opinion*, 2d ed. New York: Knopf.

Unger, Roberto Mangabeira. 1987. *Politics, a Work in Constructive Social Theory*. Cambridge, England: Cambridge University Press.

U.S. Congress, Joint Committee on Taxation. 1986. *General Explanation of the Tax Reform Act of 1986*. Washington, D.C.: U.S. Government Printing Office.

U.S. Department of Commerce, Bureau of the Census. 1989. *USA Statistics in Brief 1988: A Statistical Abstract Supplement*. Washington, D.C.: U.S. Government Printing Office.

U.S. National Commission on Excellence in Education. 1983. *A Nation at Risk: The Imperative for Educational Reform*. Report to the Nation and the Secretary of Education. Washington, D.C.: U.S. Government Printing Office.

Uya, Okon Edet. 1971. *From Slavery to Public Service: Robert Smalls 1839-1915*. London: Oxford University Press.

Van Horn, Carl E., Donald C. Baumer, and William T. Gormley. 1992. *Politics and Public Policy*, 2d ed. Washington, D.C.: CQ Press.

Verba, Sidney, and Norman H. Nie. 1972. *Participation in America: Political Democracy and Social Equality*. New York: Harper & Row.

Walsh, John. 1991. "Victor L. Berger (1860-1929)." In *Political Parties & Elections in the United States: An Encyclopedia*, pp. 67-68. Ed. L. Sandy Maisel. New York: Garland.

Walton, Hanes, Jr. 1972. *Black Politics: A Theoretical and Structural Analysis*. Philadelphia: Lippincott.

Wayman, Frank, and Edward Kutler. 1985. "The Changing Politics of Oil and Gas Price Deregulation: Ideology, Campaign Contributions, and Interests, 1973-1982." Paper presented at the annual meeting of the American Political Science Association, New Orleans.

Weinbaum, Batya. 1978. *The Curious Courtship of Women's Liberation and Socialism*. Boston: South End.

Weinstein, James. 1968. *The Corporate Ideal in the Liberal State: 1900-1918*. Boston: Beacon.

Welch, Susan. 1985. "Are Women More Liberal Than Men in the U.S. Congress?" *Legislative Studies Quarterly* 10:125-34.

Welch, William P. 1982. "Campaign Contributions and Legislative Voting: Milk Money and Dairy Price Supports." *Western Political Quarterly* 35:478-95.

Whalen, Charles, and Barbara Whalen. 1985. *The Longest Debate: A Legislative History of the 1964 Civil Rights Act*. Cabin John, Md.: Seven Locks.

Wilhite, Al. 1988. "Political Parties, Campaign Contributions and Discrimination." *Public Choice* 58:259-68.

Wilhite, Al, and John Theilmann. 1986. "Women, Blacks, and PAC Discrimination." *Social Science Quarterly* 67:283-98.

———. 1987. "Labor PAC Contributions and Labor Legislation: A Simultaneous Logit Approach." *Public Choice* 53:267-76.

Wilson, James Q. 1960. "Two Negro Politicians." *Midwest Journal of Political Science* 4:146-69.

Wilson, Woodrow. [1893] 1898. *Division and Reunion 1829-1889*, 10th ed. New York: Longmans, Green.

———. [1885] 1956. *Congressional Government: A Study in American Politics*. Cleveland: Meridian.

Witte, John F. 1985. *The Politics and Development of the Federal Income Tax*. Madison: University of Wisconsin Press.

Wright, Erik Olin. 1985. *Classes*. London: Verso.

Wright, John. 1985. "PACs, Contributions and Roll Calls: An Organizational Perspective." *American Political Science Review* 79:400-14.

Young, Iris. 1981. "Beyond the Unhappy Marriage: A Critique of the Dual Systems Theory." In *Women and Revolution: A Discussion of the Unhappy Marriage of Marxism and Feminism*, pp. 43-69. Ed. Lydia Sargent. Boston: South End.

Young, Louise M. 1971. "Hattie Ophelia Wyatt Caraway." In *Notable American Women, 1607-1950*, pp. 284-86. Ed. Edward T. James. Cambridge, Mass.: Harvard University Press.

Zinn, Howard. 1980. *A People's History of the United States*. New York: Harper & Row.

Zuckman, Jill. 1993. "As Family Leave Is Enacted, Some See End to Logjam." *Congressional Quarterly Weekly Report*, February 6, pp. 267-69.

About the Book and Author

The United States combines formal political equality with concentration of wealth and power in the hands of a few. Why, then, do the majority not use their votes to change this state of affairs? In this book, John Berg focuses on the U.S. Congress, arguing that the structure of the capitalist economy constrains the effectiveness of progressive political action.

Berg contends that neither pluralism nor institutionalism can provide a satisfying overall theory to explain congressional inaction in the face of inequality. He proposes instead a Marxist approach, holding that, as long as the capitalist organization of economic life continues, political struggle is confined within the limits posed by the need to maintain capitalist prosperity.

In separate chapters devoted to congressional representation of big and small business, organized labor, women, and African Americans, Berg shows how each group's interests are incorporated unequally into the internal structure of Congress. At one extreme, the needs of big business are treated as national crises requiring swift and united action; at the other, the representatives of African American interests have difficulty getting their proposals even heard.

The book concludes with a call for a politics of protest that uses congressional offices as levers for moving the public, while it avoids the false hope that inclusion in Congress can lead oppressed groups to the full integration into the institutions of power posited by pluralism.

John C. Berg is professor of government at Suffolk University. His political experience has ranged from work for Senator Gaylord Nelson (D-Wis.) in 1964 to a nine-month sentence in jail as the result of an antiwar demonstration in 1969. He is the editor of "What's Wrong with American Politics? (And What to Do about It)," a special edition of *New Political Science* published in the spring of 1994.

Index